Domestic Military Powers, Law and Human Rights

AF706875

This book examines the national and international law, human rights and civil liberties issues involved in governments calling out the armed forces to deal with civil unrest or terrorism.

The introduction of domestic military powers has become an international trend. Troops already have been seen on the streets in major Western democracies. These developments raise major political, constitutional and related problems. Examining the changes underway in eight comparable countries—the United States, Canada, Britain, France, Italy, Germany, Japan and Australia—this book provides a review and analysis of this trend, including its implications for legal and political rights.

The book will be of interest to the general public, as well as students, academics and policy-makers in the areas of human rights and civil liberties, constitutional law, criminal justice and security studies.

Dr Michael Head is Professor of Law at Western Sydney University, Australia. He is a well-known writer on civil liberties, war powers and emergency powers, and has written extensively in legal journals and the media on the military call-out provisions.

Domestic Military Powers, Law and Human Rights

Calling Out the Armed Forces

Michael Head

Routledge
Taylor & Francis Group
LONDON AND NEW YORK

First published 2020
by Routledge
2 Park Square, Milton Park, Abingdon, Oxon OX14 4RN

and by Routledge
52 Vanderbilt Avenue, New York, NY 10017

Routledge is an imprint of the Taylor & Francis Group, an informa business

First issued in paperback 2021

© 2020 Michael Head

The right of Michael Head to be identified as author of this work has been asserted by him in accordance with sections 77 and 78 of the Copyright, Designs and Patents Act 1988.

All rights reserved. No part of this book may be reprinted or reproduced or utilised in any form or by any electronic, mechanical, or other means, now known or hereafter invented, including photocopying and recording, or in any information storage or retrieval system, without permission in writing from the publishers.

Trademark notice: Product or corporate names may be trademarks or registered trademarks, and are used only for identification and explanation without intent to infringe.

British Library Cataloguing-in-Publication Data
A catalogue record for this book is available from the British Library

Library of Congress Cataloging-in-Publication Data
Names: Head, Michael, 1952- author.
Title: Domestic military powers, law and human rights : calling out the armed forces / Michael Head.
Description: Abingdon, Oxon ; New York, NY : Routledge, 2020. |
Series: International and comparative criminal justice |
Includes bibliographical references and index.
Identifiers: LCCN 2019036084 (print) | LCCN 2019036085 (ebook) |
ISBN 9780367343903 (hardback) | ISBN 9780429325489 (ebook)
Subjects: LCSH: War and emergency powers. | Civil-military relations. |
Armed Forces--Mobilization. | Human rights.
Classification: LCC K3344 .H429 2020 (print) | LCC K3344 (ebook) |
DDC 342/.0418--dc23
LC record available at https://lccn.loc.gov/2019036084
LC ebook record available at https://lccn.loc.gov/2019036085

ISBN: 978-0-367-34390-3 (hbk)
ISBN: 978-1-03-208321-6 (pbk)
ISBN: 978-0-429-32548-9 (ebk)

Typeset in Galliard
by Taylor & Francis Books

Contents

Preface vi
Key terms viii

1 Introduction: Causes for concern 1
2 A deepening international trend 5
3 The violent historical record 13
4 The United States: Sweeping aside protections against domestic military intervention 38
5 Canada: Advanced military planning 60
6 Britain: Preparing for disruption 80
7 France: Troops on the streets to combat social unrest 99
8 Germany and Italy: Post-war restraints eroded 110
9 Japan: Creeping militarisation 128
10 Australia: Legislating and expanding military powers 141
11 How can governments and military chiefs be held to account? 167
12 Wider legal, political and democratic implications: From 'terrorism' to 'subversion' 190

Bibliography 204
Index 220

Preface

A decade ago, my colleague Scott Mann and I produced the first-ever comprehensive book to examine the global trend toward the domestic mobilisation of the armed forces. Our warnings have proved prescient, both about the likelihood of greater use of troops against civilians and the exploitation of the 'war on terror' to lay the groundwork for deploying the military to deal with protests and other forms of dissent.

By 2020, troops will have been deployed on the streets of France, Britain and Belgium, as well as Italy. Moreover, the initial pretext of protecting the public from terrorists has given way to the suppression of economic and social discontent, as seen in the French government's dispatch of soldiers to deal with 'yellow vest' demonstrations. Across the Atlantic, an American president declared an 'emergency' to justify invoking purported executive powers to send troops to stop refugees crossing the US–Mexican border.

In the Preface to Domestic Deployment of the Armed Forces: Military Powers, Law and Human Rights (Head and Mann 2009), we wrote:

> As this book was being written, from late 2007 to early 2009, it became increasingly apparent that the world was confronting the worst economic breakdown since the last Great Depression of the 1930s. We believe that these conditions underscore the concerns raised in this volume. They make more likely the prospect that governments will use military force domestically in response to the economic, social and political tensions that will be generated by the financial crisis.

Far from dissipating, the impact of the global meltdown of 2008–9 has since deepened. Governments and central banks spent billions of dollars bailing out the banks, finance houses and major corporations, igniting yet another debt-fuelled share market bonanza. The income and wealth gap between the financial elites and the vast majority of the world's people grew wider. At the same time, the conflicts between the major capitalist powers intensified, particularly between the United States and its targeted rivals, notably China, Russia and the European Union.

Scott Mann and I explained in 2009:

> As young men, our concerns about the use of the armed forces against civilians arose from several experiences. They included the Indonesian coup of 1965–66,

> the Chilean coup of 1972–73, the Vietnam War, and the consignment of British soldiers to Northern Ireland in 1969. More recently, our concerns have been deepened by the global turn to militarism, both internationally and domestically, in the so-called 'war on terror' declared by the United States in 2001. As we explain, far too little public debate has been held on the historical, legal and constitutional implications of this political shift.

This new book builds on the work of our 2009 contribution. It still remains the case that too little attention has been given to this disturbing shift.

My thanks go to Western Sydney University and my colleagues in the law school for allowing me the time to research and write this volume. Such work is essential to a university's mission to inform society and generate debate. My students in Administrative Law have also contributed, through their interest and comments. I am again grateful to Routledge, particularly commissioning editor Alison Kirk, for supporting and encouraging publication of the new book.

As always, this book would not be possible without the love, assistance and support of Mary and our four adult children, Clay, Tom, Daniel and Kathleen.

Michael Head
Sydney
August 2019

Key terms

Domestic security A vague and expanding term, not generally officially defined, that refers to any perceived concern relating to public safety, designated infrastructure, vital economic interests or political stability.

Domestic violence An undefined official term, which does not refer to violence in the home, but to unspecified violence that justifies calling out the armed forces in the United States and Australia. The term is used in s 4 of article IV of the United States Constitution and s 119 of the Australian Constitution.

Emergency powers Extraordinary executive, prerogative or legislative powers to deal with perceived threats to the existing order, often triggering or closely related to powers to deploy troops domestically.

Martial law Regarded as the suspension of law altogether under conditions of emergency. Martial law declarations can authorise far-reaching military powers, even the right to summarily try and execute individuals, in order to put down civil unrest.

Military Aid to the Civil Authorities (MACA) A doctrine developed in Britain to encompass various domestic mobilisations of the armed forces, subdivided into three different categories—Military Aid to other Government Departments (MAGD), Military Aid to the Civil Power (MACP) and Military Aid to the Civil Community (MACC).

Military Aid to the Civil Community (MACC) The provision of military personnel, equipment and facilities to perform tasks that are the responsibility of civil authorities, but for which the civilian agencies may lack resources. This includes natural disasters, search and rescue operations, disarming explosives, other law enforcement assistance and ceremonial services, where the use of force is not necessarily anticipated.

Military Aid to the Civil Power (MACP)	The use of military combat resources to supplement or supplant law enforcement agencies, where the use of force, including lethal force, is anticipated and authorised, either explicitly or implicitly.
Military Aid to other Government Departments (MAGD)	The use of the armed forces to maintain services designated as essential, often in a strike-breaking role.
Posse comitatus	The posse comitatus principle originally provided for the authorities to organise civilian posses, not militia or regular armed forces, for both war and internal law enforcement. The doctrine arose in the Middle Ages, when the English king or his local representative, the sheriff, could conscript able-bodied free-men into a posse.
Posse Comitatus Act	A United States Act, first introduced in 1878, declaring it unlawful to employ any part of the federal armed forces as a posse comitatus, or otherwise, for law enforcement, except under such circumstances as may be expressly authorised by the Constitution or by act of Congress.
Reasonable and necessary force	Called-out armed forces members are generally regarded as having the legal authority to use potentially lethal force if they believe on reasonable grounds that the force is necessary to protect life, prevent serious injury, or (perhaps) protect designated property.
Rules of Engagement	Rules, usually highly classified, issued by the military to authorise and specify the levels of force authorised to be used by called-out members, both in general and in particular operations.
Subversion	A generally loosely defined term employed to identify political or social movements regarded as threats to the established order, whether violent or not.
Superior orders	A controversial defence that may be available to called-out military personnel who carry out otherwise criminal acts, under an order given by a superior, where the personnel had a legal obligation to obey the order.
Terrorism	A variously defined term usually couched in broad language that can cover political dissent. Under Australian law, a 'terrorist act' includes anything done 'with the intention of advancing a political, religious or ideological cause' and with the intention of 'coercing, or influencing by intimidation' any government (including a foreign government) or 'intimidating the public or a section of the public', if the act causes death, 'serious harm' to a person, 'serious damage to property', 'serious risk to the health or safety' of a section of the public or 'seriously

interferes with' an electronic, information, financial or transport system (Criminal Code 1995 (Cth) 100.1). The definition excludes 'advocacy, protest, dissent or industrial action', but only if the act is not intended to cause physical harm to a person or 'create a serious risk to the health or safety of the public or a section of the public'.

1 Introduction

Causes for concern

This book concerns a number of significant developments that have received inadequate official, academic and media attention, and are little known to the general public. Largely, in fact, governments and military commanders have kept their plans hidden from close scrutiny. The issues raised in 2009 in *Domestic Deployment of the Armed Forces: Military Powers, Law and Human Rights* (Head and Mann 2009) have grown more acute. Among the most important are the following:

- Large contingents of troops have been mobilised within some countries, such as the United States, Britain, France, Belgium and Italy, on various pretexts, from averting terrorist attacks (Britain, France, Belgium) to dealing with street crime (Italy) and preventing an 'invasion' of refugees (the United States). Governmental, executive and military powers initially adopted in the name of combatting terrorism have been used already to suppress social unrest, as in France, where the government deployed troops in the name of dealing with supposed violence by 'yellow vest' demonstrators protesting against austerity and social inequality.
- There is a global trend toward establishing greater executive or governmental powers to deploy the armed forces for domestic and political purposes. The international character of these processes points to underlying economic and political factors, which this book suggests are related to growing social inequality, rising domestic class tensions and worsening global economic and military conflicts.
- This trend includes Germany, Italy and Japan, where military or fascist dictatorships dominated before World War II. Re-militarisation is underway in both Germany and Japan, while in Italy governments have placed troops on the streets of major cities under the banner of combatting crime and 'illegal' immigration.
- In two leading countries, the United States and Canada, for the first time in history, separate military commands have been established, specifically tasked with preparing and conducting internal operations. In the United States, soldiers have been used against immigrants and refugees. In Canada, the military has been called in to support police operations.
- In Britain, new powers have been created to allow troops to be called out to deal with 'civil contingencies'. Thousands of troops have been deployed or placed on standby to deal with potential terrorist threats or political crises. In

Australia, military call-out powers have been expanded by legislation three times since 2000, adding to vague powers already in existence, with the attorney-general publicly referring to the need to deal with 'riots'.

- Powers have been adopted, in the name of fighting terrorism, to authorise the calling out of soldiers against civilians, yet the measures go far beyond terrorism. Troops can be deployed, including against protests and strikes, on vague and undefined grounds, referring to elastic terms such as 'security', 'emergency' and 'domestic violence'.
- Executive decisions can be made to call out the armed forces without effective parliamentary scrutiny, constitutional constraint or legal challenge. The powers are exercised by executive or military orders, with little prospect of reversal or reproach by legislatures, and courts have almost invariably refused to rule such orders, or other 'security'-related measures, unlawful.
- Once soldiers are deployed, they generally have sweeping powers, which may include authority to use lethal force, shoot down civilian aircraft, issue orders to civilians, detain and/or interrogate people, raid premises and seize documents.
- Recent years have witnessed increasing use of the armed forces in a wide range of domestic settings, from presidential inaugurations and parades to international political summits and major sporting events, as well as to repel asylum seekers and police civilian populations in occupied countries, such as Afghanistan and Iraq. These precedents have contributed to a militarisation of aspects of society, and sought to accustom people to the sight of troops on the streets.
- These developments are in addition to the considerable strengthening of the powers and resources of the police, para-military units, electronic surveillance and intelligence agencies, a process that has accelerated in the 'war on terrorism' since 2001. Increasingly, police have been armed with military-grade weapons and equipment.

These trends raise a number of critical issues, including the strengthening of the power of the state over citizens; the undermining of core democratic and legal rights; the erosion of civilian control over the military; and the growing role of what US President Dwight D. Eisenhower in 1961 called the 'military-industrial complex'.

Notably, these processes have been accompanied by expansions of military spending, reassertions of executive powers to launch military conflicts without parliamentary or congressional approval, and preparations for war between the major powers (Head and Boehringer 2019: 4–15). This book only assesses the 'peacetime' application of military call-out powers. Any major war, however, would have immense internal implications for civil rights, not least because the domestic powers of the military, as well as the police and intelligence services, would further expand, as happened in World War I and World War II.

This new volume may prove of particular interest to students, scholars and practitioners of law, as well as to military lawyers and experts. However, it is also directed at general members of the public, in the hope that it might inform and stimulate much-needed debate on these issues.

Economic turmoil, social inequality and militarism

In 2009, when *Domestic Deployment of the Armed Forces: Military Powers, Law and Human Rights* was published, the world had entered its deepest and most systemic economic breakdown since the Great Depression of the 1930s (International Labour Organization 2009: 6).

The impact of that global meltdown has since deepened. Governments and financial authorities have imposed its impact on the backs of the world working class and poor, in the form of less secure employment, stagnant and lower wages and austerity programmes. At the same time, governments and central banks have spent trillions of dollars bailing out the banks, finance houses and major corporations, igniting yet another debt-fuelled share market bonanza. Wealth has become more concentrated and the income and wealth gap between the financial elites and the vast majority of the world's people has grown wider.

A 2019 report by the British-based charity Oxfam International highlighted the accumulation of wealth at the heights of society. The report showed that during the previous year, the wealth of the world's billionaires increased by $900 billion, or 12 per cent, while 3.8 billion people—half the world's population—saw their wealth decline by 11 per cent. By 2018, just 26 people controlled as much wealth as the poorest 3.8 billion, compared with 43 people the year before (Oxfam 2019: 8–26). This inequality had accelerated since 2009, but it is a longer-term process. Workers' share of global income has fallen 'substantially' since the 1990s, with a systematic redistribution of wealth to both capital and the top income earners (International Labour Office 2019).

At the same time, the conflicts between the major capitalist powers have intensified, particularly between the United States and its targeted rivals, notably China, Iran, Russia and the European Union. US administrations have resorted to trade wars, technology bans, military interventions and threats to re-establish the global hegemony that Washington and Wall Street asserted after World War II. President Donald Trump's Fourth of July speech in 2019 was intended to be a demonstration of military power and greatness, and the unconquerable domination of American capitalism that, in Trump's closing words, 'will never fade, never fail, but will reign forever and ever and ever' (Kishore 2019).

Any resort to war to enforce, or contest, that supremacy would arouse popular opposition and inflame political and social discontent, increasing the likelihood of governments resorting to repressive measures, including military force.

During the Great Depression ushered in by the Wall Street crash of 1929, such tensions triggered social and political convulsions, as well as conflicts, trade wars and wars between rival national powers. In a number of major countries, notably Italy, Germany and Japan (as well as Spain), these developments led to the establishment or entrenchment of military-backed fascist or totalitarian regimes, and ultimately to World War II.

As in the 1930s, this economic and geo-strategic turmoil has generated not only serious social and class tensions, but also political discontent and challenges to the established order. Strikes and protests have begun to grow. In many countries, social democratic and conservative parties that ruled since World War II have suffered serious electoral collapses, while far-right and fascistic parties have exploited the disaffection.

For good reason, therefore, this volume reviews the pre-war rise of militarism and dictatorship in Germany, Italy and Japan and draws attention to disturbing signs that the post-World War II restrictions placed on the military in those countries are being eroded or overturned. At the same time, this book warns against any complacency that similar trends could not emerge in the Anglo-American countries, where significant shifts in the military's role and doctrine have occurred in the early years of the twentieth century. The history of these countries, outlined in Chapter 3, also reveals a marked tendency for the ruling establishment to resort to violent force, including the deployment of troops internally, in periods of fundamental challenge to the prevailing socio-economic order.

For all these reasons, it is necessary to be constantly on guard against the re-emergence of militarist tendencies. In the famous words of Thomas Jefferson, the principal author of the American Declaration of Independence, 'The price of freedom is eternal vigilance'.

2 A deepening international trend

During the first two decades of the twentieth century, significant shifts occurred in the domestic deployment of the military in Western-style parliamentary democracies in Europe, North America and Australasia. Three evolving trends emerged.

The *first* was the introduction of enhanced powers to call out the armed forces to deal with domestic disturbances, mostly, but not exclusively, under the banner of combatting terrorism. The *second* was the actual mobilisation of thousands of troops in civilian settings, starting with Italy, then France, Britain and the United States. The *third* was a shift in the most common rationale for such operations, from terrorism to broader perceived threats to the established order, such as 'street crime' and 'illegal migration' (Italy), 'violent' anti-government protests (France), potential Brexit chaos (Britain) and an 'invasion' of refugees (the United States).

For the first time since the upheavals that surrounded and followed World Wars I and II, people in such countries have been confronted by the sight of heavily armed soldiers patrolling the streets, guarding the borders or repelling refugees. Most ominously, French President Emmanuel Macron called out troops specifically to confront political protesters, that is, to join the police in combatting 'yellow vest' anti-austerity demonstrators. In a classic case of so-called 'mission creep', Operation Sentinelle, launched in 2015 with a public rationale of protecting society from terrorist attacks, morphed into the first use of French soldiers to deal with internal political unrest since the 1940s.

In Britain, the Conservative Party government revealed plans to call out thousands of troops, if necessary, to deal with potential chaos and upheaval in the event of a 'no deal' Brexit from the European Union. Across the Atlantic, the Trump administration deployed nearly 6,000 to the Mexican border, authorised to use 'lethal force' if needed to stop migrants reaching US soil (Van Auken 2018b).

These developments came alongside expanding powers handed to the police and intelligence agencies, and the growth of para-military police units. As *Domestic Deployment of the Armed Forces* warned in 2009, while the 'war on terror' provided the initial justification for the militarisation of domestic security measures, this process laid the basis for the wider use of the military amid intensifying socio-economic and geo-strategic tensions (Head and Mann 2009: 13–17).

Why is this of concern? What does it indicate about the state of society? There is a clear need for a review and analysis of this trend, including its implications for legal and political rights. Mobilising the military for internal use is normally associated with dictatorial regimes, not democratic ones. In the twentieth century, military methods of rule were most commonly associated with names such as Mussolini, Hitler, Franco, Suharto and Pinochet.

Calling out the armed forces and placing troops on the streets to deal with civil unrest is one of the most drastic and potentially life-threatening actions that a government or other authorities can take against members of society. Such recourse to the ultimate violent power of the state is likely to be a symptom of intense social antagonisms.

Unfortunately, modern history offers many examples of severe repression by governments that mobilise the military against the population. One need only recall the extermination of up to one million people in Indonesia in 1965–66 following the army coup led by General Suharto, the killing of thousands in Chile in 1972–73 after the coup of General Pinochet, and the murder of thousands by the Chinese regime after the Tiananmen Square uprising of 1989.

It has been commonly assumed that events of this horrific character cannot occur in Western democracies. However, soldiers now have been deployed internally and new measures have been introduced to facilitate the domestic mobilisation of troops. These developments suggest that official preparations are being made for possible clashes involving civilians and soldiers.

Eight comparable countries

This book examines the national and international law, human rights and civil liberties issues involved in Western governments calling out troops for domestic purposes. It probes the changes underway in eight comparable countries: the United States, Canada, Britain, France, Germany, Italy, Japan and Australia.

Why these countries? While divergent in various respects, they could be regarded as advanced industrial and capitalist states. They have been selected for several critical reasons. Four of them derive their political, constitutional and legal doctrines from the English heritage, which is often regarded as an exemplar of democratic traditions, having emerged out of the overturn of the previously autocratic foundations of the British monarchy. These four countries—the United States, Britain, Canada and Australia—are commonly held up as democratic models, contrasted with dictatorial or totalitarian regimes.

The other four countries chosen have post-World War II constitutional arrangements that enshrine measures said to provide safeguards against the return of the kinds of military-backed fascist or imperial regimes that took hold of each of these countries before the war. The people of France, Italy, Germany and Japan all experienced years of military repression and have strongly opposed any return to such methods of rule.

Yet in both sets of countries, there are disturbing indications of growing reliance by the ruling corporate and political establishments on the internal use of the armed forces.

No attempt has been made in this volume to examine wider global trends, including the resort to outright or thinly veiled military dictatorships in an array of former colonial or semi-colonial states, such as Egypt, Sudan, Pakistan, Burma and Fiji, and the prominent roles played by the armed forces in China, Russia and Vietnam. Instead, the focus is on asking how and to what degree the contemporary advanced democracies differ from such states when it comes to having the power to call out the troops to suppress internal unrest.

Numbers of ancillary questions arise. What parallels and differences can be detected in the developments in the two groups of selected countries since the turn of the century? Can an overall pattern be identified in either group or indeed between all the countries? If so, what are the causes?

There is reason for concern that in both groups of four countries the 'war on terror' has conditioned public opinion to accept the internal deployment of the armed forces, including for broader industrial and political purposes. The turn to militarism abroad, seen in the US-led invasions of Afghanistan and Iraq, has been accompanied by a tendency toward the militarisation of domestic life as well.

While not yet as dramatic as the events in France, Britain and the United States, the underlying trends have sped up in each of the other countries under review. In Canada, the formation of the Canada Command in 2006, primarily dedicated to internal operations, has been followed by advanced planning for the Canadian Forces to respond to threats deemed to constitute terrorism or danger to 'security'. In Australia, during 2018, for the third time since 2000, Australia's two major parties combined to push legislation through parliament that gave government ministers and/or the armed forces chief new or extended powers to mobilise the armed forces to deal with 'domestic violence'.

In Italy, where troops have been on the streets since 2008, when they were first mobilised, supposedly to crack down on crime, the visibility of the military mobilisation increased in 2017 when the government deployed 7,000 troops armed with submachine guns to patrol beaches, train stations and other locations in order to stop asylum seekers.

In Germany, a 'grand coalition' government of the conservative and social democratic parties embarked on a new stage in the remilitarisation of the country, both domestically and globally, with the adoption of a 2016 White Paper that asserted the right of the armed forces to intervene domestically in emergency situations. In Japan, deploying military troops domestically to suppress civil unrest was placed back on the political agenda in 2018 when a leading figure in the ruling Liberal Democratic Party proposed allowing the military to be used to put down public unrest.

Key issues

Little academic attention has been paid to these trends. Chapter by chapter, this volume examines the processes underway in each of these countries. It also provides an outline of the many constitutional and legal issues involved in calling out the armed forces, for example: (a) blurring the line between police and military functions; (b) giving soldiers 'shoot to kill' and other military-style powers on domestic soil; (c) challenging the separation of powers between the executive, legislature and judiciary; (d) overcoming federal-state-local divisions of responsibility; (e) affording legal immunities and 'lawful orders' defences to military personnel; and (f) overcoming the post-World War II 'pacifist' clauses.

This volume further examines the justifications offered for these developments, starting with the ongoing 'war on terror' declared by the US government and its allies in 2001. It initially provided the primary official rationale for the military call-out measures. Is that pretext credible? What exactly is the 'war on terror'? Are its features, including the military powers, temporary or do they have long-term implications?

Military call-out powers have been expanded in addition to substantial extensions in the size, sophistication and weaponry of police, para-military and intelligence agencies. These extensions began well before 2001, but also have accelerated since then. Thus, while a creeping militarisation of society and law enforcement has taken place, this process has been accompanied by the boosting and arming of the civilian state apparatus. The focus of this book is not those parallel police and intelligence developments, but none of its analysis should be read as an argument for supporting the continuing bolstering of the civilian arm of the state, as a supposed alternative to military intervention.

On the contrary, the simultaneous strengthening of the military and civilian 'domestic security' forces deepens the basic issues raised here. Why are all the state powers being intensified? Why are increasingly police-state measures being adopted, ultimately backed by the military option? It seems that despite the proliferation of heavily armed civilian policing agencies, backed by extensive surveillance forces and technologies, the powers-that-be are anticipating civil disorders or unrest that these agencies cannot control without calling in the armed forces. This dual expansion of the armed force available to the political establishment makes all the more necessary the task of probing the underlying politico-legal implications and socio-economic pressures.

The significance of these issues can be fully assessed only by reviewing the historical record, including the struggles that established the principles of military non-intervention in domestic affairs and civilian control over the armed forces. Among the historical experiences examined in this book are:

- The origins of the traditional taboo on domestic deployment, arguably dating back to the Magna Carta of 1215 and the seventeenth-century struggles against the absolutist monarchy in Britain.
- The early British experiences and the later troubles in Northern Ireland: from the Peterloo Massacre in 1819 and the Bristol and Featherstone riots to Northern Ireland, where between 1969 and 1993 the military killed 297 people, often in disputed circumstances.
- The aftermath of the American Revolution and Civil War: the roots of the 'traditional and strong resistance of Americans to any military intrusion into civilian affairs' (*Laird v Tatum*, 408 U.S. 1, 15).
- The bloody military violence unleashed in France during the nineteenth century, particularly in response to the 1848 revolution and the 1871 Paris Commune, and the use of troops during the major strikes of 1947–48.

- The lessons of pre-war and post-war Germany and Japan: the internal use of military forces by the Nazi and Japanese imperial regimes; the adoption of post-war constitutional protections.
- Australia's evolution from a military colony to civil society, including the use of martial law and other military powers to suppress convicts, Aborigines and workers, and the deployment of the military for industrial and political purposes in the twentieth century.

This volume then reviews the developments in each country in more detail and concludes by canvassing the underlying political and legal issues. What are the legal and democratic implications? How can the use of military powers be subjected to public scrutiny and legal restraints? What lies behind the global trend? What role is played by militarism, counter-terrorism, social polarisation and political instability? What are the reasons for concern, in terms of human rights, civil liberties, rule of law, civilian control of society?

The context: militarism and rising social tensions

The international character of the shift toward using the armed forces for domestic security makes it all the more important to critically examine the rationale and content of the measures. Moreover, the internal changes have been accompanied in each instance by expansions of the armed forces for external interventions, in the context of a turn to militarism by the United States and its allies, most notably in the Middle East.

Numbers of governments have used the threat of terrorism as a pretext to erode such vital principles as free speech, freedom of political association, prevention of arbitrary detention and the right to seek asylum. These measures have profound implications for civil liberties, as well as for the future of international covenants, such as the International Covenant on Civil and Political Rights. These global human rights instruments have proved largely irrelevant in curbing such powers.

Governments in many countries followed the lead of the Bush administration in the United States by declaring that the 11 September 2001 terrorist attacks in the United States required an indefinite 'war' against terrorism abroad, accompanied by curtailment of legal rights at home. Despite criticisms by civil liberties groups, governments introduced severe anti-terrorism measures, including detention without trial and proscription of organisations (for a comparison of the US and British legislation see Hancock 2002a: 2–8). Amnesty International condemned the Bush administration, for example, for breaching the International Covenant on Civil and Political Rights and other international protocols against arbitrary detention and inhuman treatment of prisoners (Amnesty International 2002).

While the 'war on terror' has provided the common justification for both the domestic and overseas militarisation of policy, there are reasons to conclude that the roots of the militarising trend lie deeper in growing socio-economic and geopolitical tensions. As mentioned in Chapter 1, and further examined in Chapter 12, we have once again entered a period of history that is marked by economic breakdown, social inequality and great power rivalries.

It should be noted that the justifications offered for greater military intervention in domestic affairs go well beyond terrorism. They include 'violent demonstrations', 'fighting crime', repelling or detaining asylum seekers and dealing with 'emergencies'. Emergency and emergency-type powers have been extended as well (Head 2016).

Countervailing arguments

Some scholars have argued that concerns about the elevated role of the military in society are exaggerated or even unwarranted because one must trust elected governments to use the military for legitimate purposes only. For example, Norman Laing, an Australian barrister with military experience, has suggested that calling out the Australian Defence Force (ADF) would not be 'the end of civilisation' because 'the ADF will only ever be deployed for a legitimate purpose' and 'one must have faith in those elected representatives to undertake such a responsibility' (Laing 2005: 521). Ironically, Laing's article began by recalling the protests against the Vietnam War and President Richard Nixon's invasion of Cambodia, which led to the use of the Ohio National Guard to shoot dead four innocent students at Kent State University in 1970 (Laing 2005: 507–508).

Laing said there was concern in 2000, when Australia's initial military call-out legislation was brought forward, that the ADF would be deployed onto Australian streets to disperse such protestors if they too caused a serious civil disturbance. However, he argued that this 'fear and paranoia' subsided over the following four years because: 'The current climate of terror has created an overriding and shifting attitude towards the ADF being called out' (Laing 2005: 509). This line of reasoning underscores the concern that Australian governments, with bipartisan support, have promoted and utilised 'the current climate of terror' to overcome public opposition to the deployment of the ADF on the streets.

Is it safe to simply say 'one must have faith' in elected governments? The opening years of the twenty-first century saw troops dispatched to invade a country and put down domestic resistance—in Iraq—on the basis of information supplied by intelligence agencies, security services and government leaders that was subsequently acknowledged to have been false. After the collapse of the falsifications used to justify the United States-led invasion—'weapons of mass destruction', 'nuclear stockpiles' and Saddam Hussein's supposed links to terrorism—one is entitled, perhaps even obliged, to approach all such government claims with considerable scepticism. Academic studies have concluded that the US and British governments engaged in deception and war propaganda to deceive their populations in order to try to overcome popular opposition to their military aggression (Head and Boehringer 2019: 46–63).

The 11 September 2001 outrages in New York and Washington were reprehensible but there is ample evidence that they provided the pretext for the implementation of plans prepared in certain Washington political circles much earlier—during the 1990s—for the conquest of Afghanistan and Iraq (Bacevich 2002). The Middle East and Central Asia, as is well known, contain the largest proven concentrations of oil and natural gas reserves in the world. For all their claims to be exporting democracy to the Middle East, Washington and its allies have for decades provided financial, diplomatic and military support to dictatorial regimes like the Saudi monarchy and the Gulf kingdoms (and previously the Shah of Iran), in the interests of dominating the resource-rich and strategically critical region (Shalom 1993: 63–88).

Domestically, there is no more reason to believe that the same US-allied governments are primarily motivated simply by the need to protect ordinary people from terrorism. On the face of it, none of the new terrorism or military powers were necessary to protect ordinary people against terrorism. In most jurisdictions, any conceivable terrorist activity, such as murder, bombing, hijacking, kidnapping and arson, was already a serious crime under existing law. Moreover, the police and intelligence services hardly needed new powers to detect terrorists. They already had powers to tap phones, install listening devices in offices and homes, intercept telecommunications, open people's mail, monitor on-line discussion, break into computer files and databases, seize computers and use personal tracking devices (for details see Head 2002b).

The official rationale for the anti-terrorism measures asserts that the 'war on terrorism' requires a 'new framework' for considering civil liberties and the rule of law. For instance, in 2004, Australian Attorney-General Philip Ruddock stated:

> The war on terror is like no other war in living memory. This is a war which may have no obvious conclusion, no armistice and no treaty. Victory in this war will not necessarily be measured by territory gained or regimes toppled. In this war victories will be measured by disasters averted and democracy strengthened. This war's victories will be measured by citizens feeling safe in their homes.
>
> (Ruddock 2004)

Ruddock loosely defined 'human security' as encompassing human rights, good governance, access to education and health care and opportunities for individuals to fulfil their potential. All these, the minister asserted, depended upon a secure environment. Thus, in the name of defending civil liberties and the rule of law, they are said to no longer have any independent or absolute existence. Instead, they have been subsumed under another concept, human security. Making 'citizens feel safe in their homes'—a highly political and subjective conception—became the chief criterion.

For powerful historical reasons, however, fundamental democratic rights should be regarded as absolute. They embody centuries of deep on-going political struggles. In Anglo-Saxon law, civil liberties—such as habeas corpus, the presumption of innocence, the requirement of proof beyond reasonable doubt for a criminal conviction, freedom of association and free speech—were substantially forged in the conflict against the absolutist monarchy, from the Magna Carta of 1215 and culminating in the English Civil War of the 1640s and the so-called Glorious Revolution of 1688. Among these fundamental rights is freedom from detention without trial, as the US Supreme Court, by a 6–3 majority, commented in June 2004, in ruling that Guantanamo Bay detainees, including two Australians, David Hicks and Mamdouh Habib, could seek writs of habeas corpus in US courts. The majority judgment, delivered by Justice Stevens, suggested that at stake were democratic conceptions dating back nearly 800 years to the Magna Carta:

> Executive imprisonment has been considered oppressive and lawless since John, at Runnymede, pledged that no free man should be imprisoned, dispossessed, outlawed, or exiled save by the judgment of his peers or by the law of the land. The judges of England developed the writ of habeas corpus largely to preserve these immunities from executive restraint. [*Rasul v Bush; Al Odah v United States* (2004) 542 U.S. (Cases no. 03–343, 03–334). Quoting Jackson J in *Shaughnessy* v. *United States ex rel. Mezei,* 345 U.S. 206, 218–219 (1953) (dissenting opinion)].

Likewise, as explored in Chapter 3, the right of citizens to live free of military intervention in society, especially in civilian political affairs, has been fought for through centuries of conflict against absolutism, dating back at least to 1215. Justice Douglas of the US Supreme Court referred to this historical record in the 1952 Youngstown case, when he stated 'our history and tradition rebel at the thought that the grant of military power carries with it authority over civilian affairs' [*Youngstown Sheet and Tube Co. v Sawyer*, 343 U.S. 579 at 632]. Today, it will be argued in this volume, it is necessary to go further and state unequivocally: Genuine democracy is impossible, and freedom of political opinion and communication a chimera, unless members of society are free from the fear of the mobilisation of the armed forces against dissent and discontent.

3 The violent historical record

Each of the countries reviewed in this book has a history of military repression, particularly directed against strikes and protests by workers. As will be reviewed in Chapter 5 and Chapters 7 to 9, Canada, France, Germany, Italy and Japan have such records. Formal legality, such as limitations on the French 'state of siege' doctrine, and protections of civil liberties inserted into the German Weimar constitution after World War I, proved no protection.

This chapter will focus in greater detail on three countries with a British background: the United Kingdom, the United States and Australia. In these countries there is a political and legal principle opposing the use of the military to suppress domestic unrest—an objection that dates back to the Magna Carta of 1215, and that was re-established or reinforced by the seventeenth-century struggles against the absolutist monarchy in England. Moreover, the principle is lodged in deeply felt public sentiment, based on accumulated historical experience.

According to a number of studies, King John's pledge in Chapter 39 of the 1215 charter that no free man would be taken, imprisoned or destroyed except by the 'law of the land' had been demanded at Runnymede specifically because the King had enforced his will by military means instead of civilian processes. Chapter 39 was invoked in 1327 against Edward II's resort to force by knights in arms (Engdahl 1985: 5).

Nevertheless, the Tudors and early Stuarts reasserted a royal prerogative to use 'martial law' against their subjects in times of supposed necessity, including to suspend or supersede the ordinary law, inflict summary punishments and suppress civil disorders by military force. These practices provoked parliament to draw up the 1628 *Petition of Right*, which declared them to be contrary to the law of the realm, and, in particular, the Magna Carta (Engdahl 1985: 6). The *Petition* demanded that Charles I remove the 'great companies of soldiers and mariners [who] have been dispersed into diverse counties of the realm ... against the laws and customs of this realm and to the great grievance and vexation of the people'. The *Petition* is regarded as making it unconstitutional for the Crown to impose martial law on civilians, at least by way of the old prerogative claim (Holdsworth 1902).

Charles I's continued claim to prerogative use of troops helped precipitate the English Revolution and civil war in 1642, which saw the King overthrown and executed, and the monarchy abolished until 1660 (Robertson 2005: 21–37). Ultimately, as a result of the 1688–89 settlement between the monarchy and the parliament, the *Bill of Rights* declared it illegal for the Crown to suspend laws, or raise or keep an army without parliamentary consent (Greer 1983: 580). More generally, after the 'Glorious Revolution' of 1688–89, military force was seen as a grave threat to civil government, and its subordination to civilian rule was established as a 'constitutional priority' (Greer 1983: 592). The *Riot Act 1714* called for civilian officials and posses (the posse comitatus) to disperse mobs and put down civil unrest, and authorised civilian personnel to use any force necessary to do so, but made no provision for the use of military force. A different act passed the same year authorised the use of militia, but only to deal with 'insurrection' or 'rebellion' as well as 'invasion' (Engdahl 1985: 6–7).

However, subsequent British history demonstrated a recurring resort to military force in periods in which the political establishment felt seriously threatened by any mass political or industrial movement.

British riots and strikes

During the late eighteenth and early nineteenth centuries, the emergence of protests fuelled by the conditions of the Industrial Revolution and the growth of the working class caused the British authorities to frequently resort to the military as riot controllers (Greer 1983: 581). Magistrates called for military assistance with increasing regularity, and in 1732 the Secretary at War informed the Attorney-General that such requests were always granted. The author Henry Fielding, who was principal magistrate at London's Bow Street from 1748 to 1754, described the *Riot Act* as 'the most necessary of all our laws for the preservation and protection of the people' because the English 'mob' had established itself as the Fourth Estate of the realm. The magistrate 'alone with the soldier barred the way of the riotous mob' (Babington 1990: 7, 11).

During the second half of the eighteenth century, soldiers killed hundreds of rioters as industrial disputes, anti-machinery protests and food riots spread. As a result, 'mistrust of the military when employed in assisting the civil authorities was endemic throughout the country' (Babington 1990: 12–18, 36). By the late eighteenth century, the use of military force had caused such popular discontent that the Secretary at War warned magistrates against too readily calling out troops: 'Frequent use of soldiers to suppress civil commotions has an evident tendency to introduce military government, than which there cannot be a more horrible Evil in a State' (Greer 1983: 592).

Nonetheless, in effect, successive governments, with the eventual acquiescence of parliament, relaxed the principle that the Secretary at War must approve any troop call out by a magistrate. As a result of the rising civil unrest, the courts elaborated a common law right and duty of magistrates to opt for military intervention. In a series of statements in his dual role as a judge and parliamentarian toward the end of the eighteenth century, Lord Mansfield resurrected the feudal posse comitatus doctrine, which had been effectively extinguished in the seventeenth century. Posse comitatus arose in the Middle Ages, when both law enforcement, including the suppression of riots, and the waging of war were conducted by the king or his local representative, the sheriff, conscripting able-bodied free-men into a posse (Greer 1983: 578–581). Lord Mansfield insisted that this disused power could be resumed by local magistrates and justices of the peace. The principle, however, was effectively transformed from one of mobilisation of civilian volunteers to one of military deployment—the original posse comitatus doctrine was premised upon civilian posses, not militia or regular armed forces.

In 1781, the chief London magistrate, Brackley Kennett, was charged with criminal breach of duty for refusing to read the *Riot Act* and order military intervention to put down the Gordon Riots. For several days, anti-Catholic protesters, after being turned away from parliament, had confronted authorities, burning down buildings (including Mansfield's house). Eventually, the King convened the Privy Council, which issued an order for the armed forces to act without waiting for magistrates. Some 15,000 troops moved into London and, as a result, an estimated 285 rioters were killed (Babington 1990: 21–31). For his reluctance to call in the troops, Kennett was convicted and fined 1,000 pounds. Lord Mansfield instructed the jury:

> The common law and several statutes have invested justices of the peace with great powers to quell riots, because, if not suppressed, they tend to endanger the constitution of the country; and as they may assemble all the King's subjects, it is clear they may call in the soldiers, who are subjects and may act as such; but this should be done with great caution
>
> (Greer 1983: 582)

Responding to those who denounced this doctrine as reminiscent of the 'martial law' prerogative claimed by the Tudors and Stuarts, Mansfield sought to distinguish between the use of troops in a military capacity and their roles as citizens, in the nature of the posse comitatus:

> The persons who assisted in the suppression of these tumults are to be considered mere private individuals acting as duty required … The King's extraordinary prerogative to proclaim martial law (whatever that may be) is clearly out of the question … The military have been called in—and very wisely called in—not as soldiers, but as civilians.
>
> (Engdahl 1985: 11)

Despite this distinction, which insisted that called-out soldiers were not above the law of the land, the Mansfield doctrine, as it became known, provided little protection for ordinary people against military violence, as the 285 deaths in London indicate.

From Peterloo to World War I

One of the most notorious mobilisations of the military against civilian protesters was the Peterloo Massacre of 1819. Cavalry troops charged into a crowd of 60,000 to 80,000 people gathered at St Peter's Field, Manchester for a public meeting, which had been declared illegal, to demand parliamentary representation. Shortly after the meeting began, local magistrates called on the military to arrest the speakers on the platform and to disperse the crowd. Soldiers on horses charged in with sabres drawn, killing 15 people and injuring 400–700, including women and children (Reid 1989).

Whereas the arrested speakers were charged with sedition, found guilty and jailed, a test case against four members of the armed forces ended in acquittal, because the court ruled that their actions had been justified to disperse an illegal gathering (Reid 1989: 204–205). In the meantime, nine days after the massacre, the Home Secretary, Lord Sidmouth, had conveyed to the magistrates the thanks of the Prince Regent for their action in 'preservation of the public peace' (Babington 1990: 46–58).

Citing a range of sources and authorities, one scholar noted the alacrity with which both the parliament and the judiciary were prepared to cast aside the constitutional principle against military intervention in the face of rising social unrest, which reached new heights during the Chartist movement for voting and other basic rights.

> [I]t is debatable whether the eventual acquiescence of Parliament in the 'Mansfield doctrine' constituted sufficient authorisation for the valid revival of the magistrates' common law duty. The judiciary, however, refused to consider the constitutional dimension and blithely built upon the *posse comitatus* principle without regard to its shaky foundations. Civil libertarian reservations about the increasing use of the army in riots seem to have been overwhelmed by the general establishment view that what was good for the maintenance of public order was desirable and, therefore, legal. The fear of disorder had by this stage largely replaced the spectre of military intervention in civil affairs as the *bete noir* of the status quo.
>
> (Greer 1983: 583)

Following the defeat of the 1831 parliamentary reform bill, riots broke out in Bristol, which soldiers dispersed by killing 12 people and wounding about 100 (Babington 1990: 75–84). These riots gave rise to the last English case in which calling out the troops was directly examined. In *R v Pinney* (1832) 5 Car & P 254; 170 ER 962, the mayor of Bristol and nine aldermen were prosecuted by the Attorney-General for breaching their common law duty to assemble a sufficient force to put down three days of riots, during which thousands of people, some allegedly armed with 'iron bars, iron crows, pickaxes, hammers, pieces of wood, and bludgeons' broke open a jail and forced the release of prisoners. A military major advised the mayor that it would be 'imprudent to put arms in the hands of young troops'. The jury found the defendants not guilty.

The law report of *R v Pinney* also records Tindal LCJ's *Charge to the Bristol Grand Jury* after the riots. Lord Tindal insisted that soldiers had a duty, as citizens, on their own authority, to do their utmost to 'put down riot and tumult'. Two officers who had refused to order the troops to fire without a magistrate's sanction were found guilty of neglect of duty, causing one to commit suicide. The third officer, who had fatally shot a boy during an incident, was acquitted of manslaughter. Lord Tindal instructed the Grand Jury that if the shot was 'discharged in the fair and honest execution of his duty, in endeavouring to disperse the mob', the killing was justified and amounted to accidental death only (170 ER 962, 969; Babington 1990: 84).

During this period, social tensions were so acute that it was widely recognised that summoning military personnel could inflame rather than subdue disturbances.

> Commentators were aware that the appearance of uniforms could provoke the crowd to further violence, especially since certain military units, for example the yeomanry, were identified with the propertied classes against whom the riots in this era were generally directed. The opposite could also, ironically, be the case. Other army units often identified with, and on occasion even joined, the rioters.
> (Greer 1983: 585)

These considerations, which were also bound up with the development of industrialised society and the emergence of a large working class, fed into the creation of a modern police force, dating from Sir Robert Peel's *Metropolitan Police Act 1829*. The establishment of police forces, first in London and then other centres, was initially met with great public hostility as well (Babington 1990: 59–84), Although the primacy of the police for enforcing public order gradually became established, the army continued to play a significant role, particularly in putting down protests demanding the right to vote. The rise of the Chartist movement led to the creation of police forces across the country, but armed militia were still called out frequently between 1834 and 1848 (Babington 1990: 100). In 1839, for instance, troops opened fire in Newport, Wales, killing at least 22 people (Babington 1990: 104–105).

As late as 1888, the Secretary of State for War listed 'the effective support of the civil power in all parts of the United Kingdom' as the principal duty of the British army. Another episode that illustrated the continuing power of magistrates to call out the troops without reference to the Home Office, was the Featherstone Colliery Riots of September 1893. Four people, including two bystanders, were killed when an infantry Captain ordered soldiers to fire on striking coal miners and their supporters after a local magistrate had read the proclamation from the *Riot Act 1714*. The 1893 *Report of the Select Committee on the Featherstone Riots* exonerated the Captain and his troops, saying 'The necessary prevention of such outrage on person and property justifies the guardians of the peace in the employment against a riotous crowd of even deadly weapons' (Whelan 1985: 272). However, the committee warned that 'officers and soldiers are under no special privileges and subject to no special responsibilities as regards this principle of the law'. The taking of life must be shown to be necessary and resort to military assistance must be the 'last expedient' of the civil authorities, but when such a call was made, 'to refuse such assistance is in law a misdemeanour' (Babington 1990: 122–132).

From the beginning of the twentieth century, the creation of larger police forces meant that troops were deployed less frequently to control riots. Nevertheless, military interventions continued, and so did fatalities. In mid-1906, a detachment of infantry was sent to patrol the Belfast docks to protect strikebreakers. After a mutiny in police ranks in sympathy with the strikers, soldiers patrolled city streets throughout the summer and opened fire on a pro-strike rally, killing two people and wounding at least five (Babington 1990: 133–134).

A parliamentary select committee in 1908 was told that during the previous 30 years, the military had been called out on 24 separate occasions in England and Wales (Babington 1990: 135; Jeffery 1985: 52). While insisting that the power to call out the troops must continue, the committee recommended that police forces should be 'so organised and administered as to obviate to the utmost possible extent any necessity for resorting to military aid' (Jeffery 1985: 53).

Even so, in 1910 troops were called out at Tonypandy, South Wales during a coal strike, and a miner was killed by a baton blow. Home Secretary Winston Churchill took personal charge of the operation, issuing an unprecedented order placing all the police and army forces under the command of an army general (Babington 1990: 137–140). The next year, troops were mobilised in Cardiff, London and Liverpool to help suppress strikes by seamen and dockers, and opened fire on striking workers at Liverpool, killing two. Two naval gunboats and a cruiser were sent to the Mersey and large contingents of soldiers took up positions in the city (Babington 1990: 140–141). During a rail strike later that year, the *Riot Act* was read a number of times, troops charged a crowd at Chesterfield with bayonets fixed and at Llanelli in Wales soldiers killed two men when a strike breakers' train was held up (Babington 1990: 141). After telling the House of Commons that an unprecedented challenge to government authority existed, Churchill sent out telegrams to police chief constables in all the affected areas informing them that the procedures for requesting military assistance via a magistrate had been suspended and that army commanders had a complete discretion to use their troops as they saw fit. Churchill came under criticism for instituting a type of martial law, yet the law officers contended that his measures were justified under the circumstances as the soldiers were merely exercising their rights and duties as ordinary citizens (Babington 1990: 142).

In 1912, Tom Mann and four other men were imprisoned for calling upon soldiers not to act against strikers. For publishing a pamphlet urging soldiers to 'refuse to murder your kindred' and 'help us win ... the world for workers', they were convicted of incitement to mutiny (Babington 1990: 142). Ireland remained another focus of military activity—in 1914, a detachment of soldiers fired on an unarmed crowd, killing three and wounding 32 people (Jeffery 1985: 53, 60).

Military strike breaking

Amid the social discontent after World War I and the 1917 Bolshevik-led socialist revolution in Russia, armed military units were called out when half the Liverpool police force went on strike in 1919. Four battalions and a troop of tanks were deployed, and two alleged rioters were shot, one fatally. At the height of the confrontation, the HMS Valiant steamed up the Mersey, carrying 8 × 15 inch guns (Bramall 1985: 79–80). At the subsequent inquest into the death, the coroner's jury returned a verdict of 'justifiable homicide' (Babington 1990: 146). According to Babington, the operation was a landmark because

> [T]his was the last occasion on which the Riot Act was ever read, before its repeal in 1967. It was also the last occasion to date on the British mainland on which soldiers either shot a rioter or charged a mob with fixed bayonets.
>
> (Babington 1990: 144)

During this period, soldiers were mobilised more often against industrial disputes, most notably in the British General Strike of 1926 (Laybourn 1993), although the decisions were made by the British government through the Home Office, not by local magistrates (Greer 1983: 586–587). There were intense debates within the British government and the military high command between 1919 and 1926 over whether to use regular troops, part-time Reserves, volunteer Territorial Army members and/or specially recruited Civil Guards or Constabularies against the strikes that erupted in the wake of World War I. Churchill, now the Secretary of State for War, led the charge for using troops, but there were no fundamental differences over using military force, if need be, to prevent any threat of social revolution. One historical account noted:

> The industrial scene was volatile. Grievances arising out of demobilization procedures, and the prospect of widespread unemployment for returning troops, not to mention—at least in the eyes of the government—the example of the Bolshevik Revolution, led to a situation in which the inevitable readjustments to the strains in society which the war had magnified but not initiated loomed as threatening challenges to the existing order.
>
> (Dennis 1981: 706)

Another historian underscored the impact of the October 1917 Soviet Revolution:

> Although talk of revolution had been in the air during the unrest of the pre-war years, the possibility and danger of actual revolution were vividly brought home to politicians and generals in Britain by the Russian Revolution and the violent unrest which swept across Europe at the end of the Great War. 'Our real danger now,' wrote the Chief of the Imperial Staff, 'is not the Boches but Bolshevism.'
>
> (Jeffery 1985: 54)

On occasions, troops were used in highly visible displays of strength, designed to intimidate striking workers and their supporters. In the 1919 Glasgow general strike, troops occupied the city centre and set up machine gun posts in the City Chambers. During strikes in 1920 and 1921, the army chief, Sir Henry Wilson, ostentatiously moved units, including tanks, into industrial areas. In the 1926 British general strike, when the government wished to open the strike-bound London docks, the military commander first marched a battalion of guards, 'with drums beating', through the East End to occupy the docks. Throughout the general strike, tanks and armoured cars drove into militant districts to 'impress' local residents (Jeffery 1985: 63). No fewer than 26 battalions were called out for civil duties during the nine-day strike, before it was ended by the Trades Union Congress. Soldiers patrolled railway lines, guarded buildings and installations, broke blockades, dispersed mass pickets and escorted food convoys, but were kept in the background as much as possible (Babington 1990: 149–150).

In the debates over using troops, the chief concerns in official and military circles were essentially tactical: whether sufficient soldiers could be deployed, given Britain's continuing interventions abroad; the possibility that any recourse to military violence could worsen popular discontent; and doubts about the reliability of troops under those circumstances. Given that many rank and file soldiers, if not officers, are drawn from the working class, this latter issue loomed large. Fear of 'revolutionary' unrest within the army in 1919 prompted the War Office to circulate a questionnaire to the commanding officers of all units in the United Kingdom to assess the political allegiances of their troops. Officers were asked to investigate whether the soldiers were affected by internal or external agitation, whether they would 'respond to orders for assistance to preserve the pubic peace' and whether they would 'assist in strike breaking'. In one incident in 1921, members of a naval reserve battalion declared that nearly all of them were trade union members and 'would lay down their arms if called upon to use them upon their fellow workmen' (Jeffery 1985: 60).

For these reasons, there was considerable discussion about forming para-military 'third forces', whether called 'citizen guards' or 'special constabularies' (Jeffery 1985: 55). In the end, the early collapses of the general strike in Glasgow in 1919, the railway strike later that year, and the 1926 general strike made the large-scale use of the armed forces unnecessary, but not before the War Office had taken the decision, in 1926, to use regular troops, and recruit 300,000 men to a generously paid para-military Civil Constabulary Reserve (Dennis 1981: 713–722).

Colonial massacres

There is a barbaric history of the use of martial law throughout the British Empire. On example is the 'Jamaica affair'. This concerned the suppression unleashed by Governor Edward John Eyre's proclamation of martial law in reaction to the Jamaica uprising of 1865 (Kostal 2005). Britain's former slaves and their descendants, while formally freed from bondage 32 years earlier, lived in dire poverty, exacerbated by a government plan to clear squatters from land that planters wanted to use for sugar production.

In October 1865, a protest outside the courthouse in Morant Bay, a town in Jamaica, turned violent (Kostal 2005: 95–98). Eyre declared martial law in the Morant Bay area and sent troops to suppress the insurrection. While the rebellion was effectively over in a few days, Eyre maintained martial law for a month during which time his forces killed 439 'blacks' (either shot on the spot or after a perfunctory court martial), flogged 600 men and women, and destroyed about 1,000 cottages and huts.

When Eyre returned to Britain in August 1866, his supporters held a banquet in his honour. Eyre defiantly asserted that his actions were not only constitutionally appropriate but politically necessary. The governor had a prerogative authority, he declared, located in the unwritten constitution, to proclaim martial law and put down unrest. In Jamaica that constitutional authority was confirmed by a local colonial statute. Nevertheless, Eyre ensured that an Act of Indemnity was passed to cover everything that he and his officials had done. A Royal Commission of Inquiry was sent to Jamaica, which issued a report critical of the duration of martial law and the measures adopted to enforce it. As expected, however, prosecutions within Jamaica of officials and military officers failed in the hands of British settler judges. The British government also refused to bring criminal proceedings.

Concerned about the sustainability of such methods of colonial rule, a Jamaica Committee, including leading liberals, such as John Stuart Mill (a supporter of colonialism), initiated private prosecutions of Eyre and two military officers but these failed too, essentially because of the judges' instructions to the juries. In his charge to a jury, Lord Chief Justice Cockburn said he not only 'accepted the fact of empire and the need to use force to preserve it' but also would not 'categorically condemn martial law' (Kostal 2005: 367, 483–484). Several Jamaicans sued Eyre in tort, and found the same judicial determination to shield the former governor. Justice Willes held that Eyre could not be sued for his conduct in Jamaica (*Phillips v Eyre* (1870) LR 6 QB 1, Exchequer Chamber).

Another example is the repeated imposition of martial law in Egypt, which was occupied by Britain from 1882. Significantly, the first declaration of martial law, in 1914, was bound up with Britain's formal assertion of sovereignty over Egypt. The British government proclaimed Egypt a 'protectorate' that year in the context of World War I and the British offensive against the Ottoman Empire, of which Egypt had been a province for four centuries (Reza 2007: 535). Thus British rule commenced with martial law, which was instrumental to the assertion of sovereignty itself.

During the war, the British poured masses of foreign troops into Egypt, conscripted over one and a half million Egyptians into the Labour Corps, and requisitioned buildings, crops, and animals for the use of the army (Vatikiotis 1992: 246). A British governor was placed in command of the Egyptian military and its actions were removed from the jurisdiction of the courts (Reza 2007: 535).

That imposition cannot be dismissed simply as a wartime measure, even if that were to be regarded as an exceptional circumstance. Martial law continued after World War I, directed against the 1919 uprising of Egyptian nationalism, and ended only temporarily after Britain declared the country nominally independent in 1922 (Reza 2007: 535). By mid-1919, about 800 Egyptians had been killed by Allied (mainly Australian) troops and twice that number had been wounded (Jankowski 2000: 112).

No one was held to account for the killings. Instead, the British government sent a commission of inquiry, known as the Milner Mission, to Egypt in December 1919 to determine the causes of the uprising, and to make a recommendation about the political future of the country. Lord Milner's report, published in February 1921, recommended that the protectorate status of Egypt be abandoned (Daly 1988: 249–250). In effect, although the independence movement was crushed, ongoing popular resistance forced the British to grant a modicum of independence to Egypt in 1922. The British kept control over the strategic and lucrative Suez Canal, however, and continued to dictate Egyptian policy through a proxy ruler (Vatikitotis 1992: 264).

India was the location for one of the worst civilian mass killings carried out by the British armed forces. In the massacre at Amritsar on 13 April 1919, the city's military commander, General Dyer, ordered his troops to fire without warning on a prohibited meeting of between 10,000 and 20,000 people, killing 379 and wounding more than 1,200. The incident inflamed anti-British sentiment across India, but Dyer was commended by his military superiors and treated lightly by the British government after the Army Council strongly opposed his dismissal. He was retired from active service, but not dismissed, let alone prosecuted (Jeffery 1985: 56–57).

From the 1940s to the 1970s

These experiences demonstrated the propensity of the British authorities to call out the armed forces against civilians if the establishment felt threatened, and the readiness of the courts to sanction such operations. This conclusion could be stated another way: serious discussion and preparations in ruling circles for domestic use of the military occurred at times when those in authority regarded the possibility of a social revolution or uprising as a real danger.

Surges of military operations, primarily against strikes, occurred in the late 1940s and early 1970s, also periods of considerable industrial and political turbulence. For Clement Attlee's post-war Labour government, strike breaking became 'second nature', with soldiers mobilised in 1945, 1947, 1948, 1949 and 1950 (Hennessy 1985: 98). Two decades later, troops were deployed as strike breakers in the Glasgow Fire Brigade strike of 1973, the Glasgow dustmen's strike of 1975 and the firefighters' strike of 1977–78, when some 20,000 military personnel were mobilised (Bramall 1985: 71). In 1972–73, the Heath government declared a state of emergency to combat a coal miners' strike and drew up a list of 16 key industries and the possibility of using military labour in the event of strikes (Hennessy 1985: 99–100).

During a 1974 miners' strike, which triggered the defeat of the Heath government, military exercises were conducted, involving Special Air Services (SAS) commandos, at London's Heathrow Airport. Tanks and heavily armed soldiers appeared around the airport. Although the exercises were conducted in the name of combatting threats of hijacking and other forms of terrorism, Field Marshal Lord Carver, the Chief of the Defence Staff, later admitted that 'fairly senior' officers had discussed plans for a military takeover in the midst of that political crisis (Guardian 1980). His comments appeared to be a reference to a 1974 series of articles in *The Times*, which reported that the main topic of conversation in officers' messes had been 'what would the British armed forces do if faced with a stalemate political situation, such as we may well have after the next election, with the extreme left pushing for power' (The Times 1974).

A decade later, following terrorist attacks in Europe, one of the largest ever security operations involving the military was mounted at Heathrow. Infantry and tanks patrolled the airport perimeter while officers of the Metropolitan Police D11 firearms unit were stationed inside terminals, armed with sub-machine guns (Babington 1990: 201). Meanwhile, in 1980, an SAS unit had stormed the Iranian embassy, ending a siege and killing five hostage-takers (Babington 1990: 205).

Throughout this period of upheaval from the late 1960s to the defeat of the 1984–85 miners' strike, the British military, drawing on its experiences in previous anti-colonial struggles and in Northern Ireland, developed a counter-insurgency manual, *Army Land Operations Manual, Volume III: Counter-Revolutionary Operations*, setting out procedures for when the British government called upon the army to aid police. The ideas in the manual corresponded closely to those of a high-ranking army officer, Sir Frank Kitson (McCulloch 2001: 176). Kitson's main thesis was that the army would have to be engaged in fighting 'subversion' and 'insurgency' in Britain. He defined subversion broadly to include 'the use of political and economic pressure, strikes, protest marches and propaganda' (Kitson 1971: 3). In his view, the military had to be prepared to intervene decisively to suppress opposition and uphold the existing order:

> If a genuine and serious grievance arose, such as might result from a significant drop in the standard of living, all those who now dissipate their protest over a wide variety of causes might concentrate their efforts and produce a situation which was beyond the power of the police to handle. Should this happen the army would be required to restore the position rapidly. Fumbling at this juncture might have grave consequences even to the extent of undermining confidence in the whole system of government.
>
> (Kitson 1971: 25)

Particularly from the 1970s onward, traditional civil policing methods also gave way to the use of heavily armed riot and para-military police units, such as the Special Patrol Group (SPG). In 1986, for example, the British government announced the purchase of 24 bullet-proof Land Rovers, 80 protected personnel carriers and 1,500 long truncheons for police use. Specialist units were trained to use sub-machine guns, CS gas and rubber bullets (Babington 1990: 197–202). Despite the establishment of these kinds of 'third forces' alongside the military and ordinary police, the twenty-first century has seen renewed moves to strengthen powers to call out the troops, suggesting that the powers-that-be are preparing for another period of intense and unpredictable disturbances (see Chapter 6).

Northern Ireland

Over the past four centuries, military aid to the civil power in the United Kingdom has been most frequently applied in Ireland. British rule was also maintained in more modern times through a para-military force, the Royal Irish Constabulary. During the Easter Uprising of 1916 and the 1919–21 civil war, the army's role was to suppress open insurrection and, later, guerrilla war. But the army also assumed riot control duties often enough for the Irish Command to issue a tactical instructions booklet, covering both potential and actual force. The methods to be used against potential force included military patrols to strike 'a terror in the locality, so as to prevent crime being perpetrated', while the tactics for actual violence included firing on crowds (Jeffery 1985: 61–63).

In the final three decades of the twentieth century, the British establishment had a major and ultimately unsuccessful experience with the deployment of the armed forces to Northern Ireland. That experience offers salutary lessons about the potential for military intervention to lead to heavy civilian casualties, and an intensification of violent civil conflict. Of course, Ireland was not a purely internal matter, given that the Irish people had been fighting British domination for four centuries. But following the partition of Ireland in 1921, the six counties of Northern Ireland, also known as Ulster, remained part of the United Kingdom. The subsequent conflicts in Ulster were bound up with the discrimination suffered by the generally working class Catholic minority (about one-third of the population), although their grievances were also centrally related to the demand for the reunification of an independent Ireland, a demand opposed by the generally better-off Protestant unionists and loyalists, who largely controlled the local police, the Royal Ulster Constabulary.

Street violence escalated in 1968–69 following the formation of the Northern Ireland Civil Rights Association, which campaigned against discrimination and for equal civil and democratic rights. After one night of rioting in August 1969, which left 10 civilians dead and 145 wounded, the British Labour government decided to send in the army. The government announced: 'The General Officer Commanding Northern Ireland has been instructed to take all necessary steps, acting impartially between citizen and citizen, to restore law and order. Troops will be withdrawn as soon as this is accomplished' (Hamill 1986: 7; Geraghty 1998: 22). Thirty years later, the troops were still there, though their duties had shifted from 'public order' to 'counter-terrorism'.

Three turning points arose that poisoned relations between the army and the Catholic minority, and provoked armed resistance, primarily led by the Irish Republican Army. The first came in July 1970, when the army imposed a three-day curfew in the Catholic suburb of Falls Road in Belfast, and conducted house-to-house searches (Hamill 1986: 34–40). The second event was the introduction of internment without trial in August 1971, with the initial detention of 346 Catholics (Hamill 1986: 56–70). The third was 'Bloody Sunday' in January 1972, when soldiers of the Parachute Regiment killed 13 unarmed civilians during a demonstration in Derry against internment (Bell 1993: 256–275).

The army quickly lost whatever early support it had among residents, yet the British government poured more troops into the province. From an initial deployment of 3,000 troops, the numbers peaked at 21,688 in July 1972, and were still at 12,000 when finally withdrawn in 1998 (Dewar 1997: 105). The mobilisation worsened the situation, at great cost to the population, with the number of civilians killed by the security forces growing from 10 in 1969 to 83 in 1972, before falling back to 10 in 1992 (Sutton 1994: 206). The total number of shootings (by all sides) in Northern Ireland grew from 73 in 1969 to 10,631 in 1972, and was still 348 in 1994 (CAIN Web Service).

The Northern Ireland exercise in 'military aid to the civil power' also led to the erosion of legal and democratic rights, not only in Northern Ireland but in Britain as well. Official secrecy was imposed on many crucial aspects of the operation, including the number of deaths attributable to the security forces, the number of such killings that resulted in criminal proceedings and the army's Rules of Engagement. Various measures were taken to shield soldiers from prosecution, providing de facto immunity. Investigative journalists who sought to obtain data and documents were threatened with prosecution under the *Official Secrets Act* (Geraghty 1998: chapters 7–8; Rasmussen 1999).

Finally, the Northern Ireland experience illustrates the difficulty of holding anyone, including members of the armed forces, legally accountable for the conduct of the military, even where deaths occur. Between 1970 and 1979, although the army killed 186 people in Northern Ireland, only 28 soldiers were prosecuted for offences involving shooting between 1972 and 1976, of whom 13 were convicted. One soldier was convicted of manslaughter, but his conviction was quashed on appeal (Rowe 1985: 201). After one soldier was acquitted of murder, the House of Lords was asked to provide an advisory opinion. The Law Lords said the 'reasonableness' of force was a question of fact for a jury. Lord Diplock stated that a jury ought to take into account that a soldier may have to make a split-second decision to open fire or not (*Reference under s 48A of the Criminal Appeal (Northern Ireland) Act 1968 (No. 1 of 1975)* [1976] 2 All ER 937). During the 1990s, one private was convicted of murder, where he fired a fatal shot into the back of a passing car (*R v Clegg* [1995] 1 AC 482), yet the British government released him on licence and he was ultimately acquitted of all offences after a series of re-trials (Guardian 2000).

Indemnities

One theme that runs through this troubled history is the readiness of British governments and authorities to exploit words such as 'emergency', 'essential' and 'security' to intervene militarily, or to act without clear legal authorisation and, if necessary, obtain retrospective indemnity. No less than seven Indemnity Acts were passed in Ireland between 1796 and 1800 to protect the authorities against legal liability for their unlawful acts (Lee 1984: 222). Whelan traced this trend and gave some examples, one of which was the British government's media announcement during the 1926 General Strike:

> All ranks of the Armed Forces of the Crown are hereby notified that any action which they may find is necessary to take in an honest endeavour to aid the Civil Power will receive, both now and afterwards, the full support of His Majesty's Government.
>
> (Whelan 1985: 289–290)

Another example was Attorney-General Sir Hartley Shawcross's advice during the 1949 docks strike about the doubtful legal enforceability of the emergency regulations:

> I do not think that matters … I have advised that this risk should be taken and that the Regulations should cover matters on which action is required without due regard to the niceties of the law. In an emergency the Government may have, in matters admitting of legal doubt, to act first and argue about the doubts later, if necessary obtaining an indemnification Act.
>
> (Whelan 1985: 289–290)

Shawcross's phrase, 'without due regard for the niceties of the law', illustrates the propensity and capacity of governments to dispense with the finer points of the 'rule of law' when confronted by serious political, social or industrial challenges to the established order.

Although the 1974 Heathrow operation was officially justified as a precaution against terrorism, the legal authority of the government to use the army was not clear (Lee 1984: 211). The editor of the *Criminal Law Review* proposed that resort be had to the royal prerogative to address the legal vacuum:

> If on a future occasion the legal powers of police and soldier prove inadequate, reliance may, in the last resort, have to be placed on the Royal Prerogative governing emergencies. That power, with its requirements of compensation, may be an acceptable means of filling in gaps in statutory and common law powers.
>
> (Lee 1984: 211–212)

Martial law

Notwithstanding the 1628 *Petition of Right*, British law has also been prepared to support recourse to the imposition of martial law, which is, in essence, the suspension of law altogether. Martial law declarations can pave the way for setting loose far-reaching military powers, including the right to summarily try and execute individuals, in order to put down civil unrest. After the final defeat of the absolute monarchy in 1688 and up until the nineteenth century, martial law was regarded as an emergency suspension of the rule of law, strictly confined to cases of necessity in times of war, not in times of peace when ordinary courts were open (Hale 2000: 26–27; Capua 1977). Yet, this view seemed to shift somewhat during the nineteenth century.

At the beginning of that century, Blackstone conceded that the rules regarding the power to declare martial law were unclear and capricious. Writing in 1809, he said martial law was 'built upon no settled principle, but is entirely arbitrary in its decisions'. Indeed, it was 'in truth no law but something rather than allowed as law, a temporary excrescence bred out of the distemper of the state' (Blackstone 2001: 413). Writing toward the end of the nineteenth century, however, Dicey asserted that the right to invoke martial law is 'a right inherent in government' (Dicey 2005: 543–545). According to *Halsbury's Laws of England*, martial law applies 'when a state of actual war, or of insurrection, riot, or rebellion amounting to war, exists' (Hailsham 1973: vol 8(2), para 821). Other authorities contend that a modified form of martial law can be declared in cases of internal insurrection or disorder that is beyond the power of the civil authorities to quell, applying the same test of necessity as applies to 'military aid to the civil power' (Wade and Phillips 1970: 409; Dicey 2005: 543).

Doubt exists as to the legal basis of martial law. It is said to be either an example of a common law right to employ force to repel force or, alternatively, a royal prerogative (Hailsham 1973: vol 8(2), para 821). Despite this fundamental uncertainty, the Privy Council in the 1902 *Marais* case on appeal from the Cape Colony extended the doctrine of martial law to apply even where the ordinary civilian courts were still sitting (*D F Marais v The General Officer Commanding the Lines of Communication and the Attorney-General of the Colony* [1902] AC 109). Martial law has been somewhat loosely described as 'the right to use force against force within the realm in order to suppress civil disorder' (Heuston 1964: 152). This formulation could justify dictatorial measures.

According to de Smith (a leading late-twentieth century authority on English constitutional and administrative law), if martial law arises, it is generally thought that the officer commanding the armed forces will become all-powerful and his actions 'non-justiciable and, for the time being, absolute, subject only to consultation (if this is feasible) with the civil power' (de Smith 1981: 511). 'Non-justiciable' means that the courts have no power to scrutinise the lawfulness of the actions taken.

Two Irish cases, *R v Allen* [1921] 2 IR 241 and *R v Strickland* [1921] 2 IR 317, maintain that the ordinary courts have jurisdiction to decide whether the state of disorder warranted martial law, but there is no precise and settled body of law for answering that question, which seems to depend on judging whether order could only be restored by handing over power to the military authorities. If the courts decide that martial law is warranted, then the military's actions will not be reviewable, at least not until the courts decide that the disorder has been pacified. Legal action could be brought against the military for manifestly unreasonable conduct and possibly for unnecessary use of force against people or property, but the law is unclear (de Smith 1981: 512). In de Smith's opinion, the legal uncertainty is academic in any case, because indemnity legislation would almost certainly be passed to exonerate those who acted in good faith to suppress an uprising (de Smith 1981: 514). Indeed, the British parliament passed such an Act of Indemnity to cover the 1920 declaration of martial law in areas of Ireland (Rowe 1985: 200).

From the American Revolution to Donald Trump

The British struggles against absolutism, followed by the American overthrow of British military rule, led the founders of the United States to regard domestic military intervention with profound repugnance. One Congressional Research Service report identified an 'Anglo-American tradition against military involvement in civilian affairs' (Doyle 2000: 1). The American experience began with the repeated use of British military troops to suppress disorders in the colonies, including the Boston massacre of 1770, when the army fired upon anti-colonial demonstrators, killing five (Engdahl 1971; Doyle 2000: 4). Engdahl, who examined this record in some detail, commented:

> The American colonists of the mid-eighteenth century were British subjects who considered themselves heirs to the liberties that had been won through the struggles of what was then relatively recent English history. Increasingly, however, they came to perceive the King of their time as hostile to the liberties thus claimed.
>
> (Engdahl 1985: 3)

The 1776 Declaration of Independence spelled out the anti-militarist stance of the United States in unequivocal terms. It condemned the King's use of armies to cause 'death, desolation and tyranny ... totally unworthy ... of a civilized nation' and specifically attacked the keeping of a standing army in peacetime (Hammond 1997). The Declaration denounced the King for 'protecting [British troops] by a mock trial, from punishment for any murders which they should commit on the inhabitants of these states' (clause 17) and for affecting to 'render the military independent of and superior to the civil power' (clause 14).

When the US Constitution was proposed in 1787, it met opposition on several grounds, but the most controversial was the provision for a standing army. In order to enforce the principle of civilian control, the Constitution restricted military appropriations to two years, designated the civilian President as the Commander in Chief and empowered the Congress to regulate the armed forces (Article 1, section 8, clauses 12 and 14; Article 2, section 2). At the same time, the Constitution forbad the States to maintain regular armed forces and its 'Guaranty Clause' provided only that the United States should protect the States against invasion and—upon the application of a State legislature or executive (when the legislature could not be convened)—'domestic violence' (Article IV, section 4).

Despite these protections, there was considerable agitation against the spectre of military law enforcement. As a result, the First Amendment guaranteed individual rights, the Fourth Amendment enshrined freedom from unreasonable search and seizure and the Fifth Amendment insisted that 'No person shall ... be deprived of life, liberty, or property without due process of law' (Engdahl 1985: 4–5). These provisions were regarded as bulwarks against military power. The founding fathers regarded the military's authoritarian nature as antithetical to democracy and potential threat to any democratic system of government (Hammond 1997: fn 42).

Following the experiences of the Civil War and the Reconstruction period, in which military methods, including martial law, were applied in the South, the Congress repudiated law enforcement by military means by adopting the *Posse Comitatus Act* of 1878, which declared:

> From and after the passage of this Act it shall not be lawful to employ any part of the Army of the United States as a posse comitatus, or otherwise, for the purpose of executing the laws, except in such cases and under such circumstances as such employment of said force may be expressly authorized by the Constitution or by act of Congress.

Thus, the Act not only ended the practice of using troops as a posse (pursuant to the British Mansfield doctrine); it prohibited all military involvement in domestic law enforcement, except with express Constitutional or Congressional authority. No room was left for calling out the troops via presidential or executive orders or regulations, unless they had explicit Constitutional or Congressional approval.

In two decisions in the 1970s, the US Supreme Court recalled these principles. In 1972, Chief Justice Burger invoked the 'traditional and strong resistance of Americans to any military intrusion into civilian affairs. That tradition has deep roots in our history' (*Laird v Tatum*, 408 U.S. 1, 15). Two years later, speaking on behalf of the court, Burger CJ observed that 'the decision to invoke military power has traditionally been viewed with suspicion and skepticism since it often involves the temporary suspension of some of our most cherished rights' (*Scheuer v Rhodes*, 416 U.S. 232, 246).

Nevertheless, US history displays a similar pattern to British history—when the ruling establishment fears serious social or industrial unrest it is quite prepared to defy or erode these principles and resort to military intervention, whether by the national armed forces or the National Guard. (The National Guard is not covered by the *Posse Comitatus Act*, because it is a state-based militia—see Hammond 1997.) By one estimate, federal troops were used for domestic operations, including riots and civil disorders, more than 200 times in the two centuries from 1795 to 1995 (Brinkerhoff 2002).

Military forces, usually state militia, were frequently called upon between 1875 and 1925, and again in the early 1970s, to break strikes, sometimes with deadly consequences. During the 1877 railroad strike, for example, 45,000 militiamen were mobilised in 11 states, and more than 100 strikers were killed and several hundred were wounded. In another instance, President Cleveland sent federal troops to 'preserve order' in Pullman, Illinois, in 1894 (Jacobs 1985: 130–131). In 1970, President Nixon declared a postal strike to be a national emergency, and dispatched 30,000 troops to replace strikers in New York, claiming that the strike threatened 'survival of a government based on law' (Hammond 1997; Jacobs 1985: 137). In 1981, President Reagan used troops to replace striking air traffic controllers, effectively crushing the PATCO union, and the military has also been utilised to break strikes by coal miners (Hammond 1997).

Political and social movements were also targeted. In 1932, during the Great Depression, thousands of World War I veterans gathered in Washington, D.C. to demand the government pay out the service certificate bonuses the veterans had received after the war. The veterans, known as the Bonus Army, set up an army-style camp in vacant lots and refused to leave even after a bill to pay out their bonuses was squashed in the Senate. A D.C. police effort to evict the veterans turned violent and two protestors were shot. After the failed police effort, President Herbert Hoover ordered the army, led by General Douglas MacArthur, to clear out the camps. Soldiers shot tear gas and torched the camp as veterans fled (Plesset 2018).

At the height of the urban riots of the 1960s, troops were sent into Detroit and other cities (Hammond 1997). During the anti-Vietnam War movement, four students were shot dead at Kent State University in 1970. Ohio Governor James A. Rhodes had sent National Guard troops to the campus at the request of the local mayor (Bills 1988; Caputo 2005). A month later, President Nixon established the President's Commission on Campus Unrest, known as the Scranton Commission, which he charged to study the dissent, disorder and violence breaking out on college and university campuses across the nation. The Commission issued its findings in a September 1970 report that concluded that the Ohio National Guard shootings were unjustified (President's Commission 1970). No one was held to account, however (see further Chapter 11).

Far from recoiling from military intervention, in 1972 the increasingly embattled Nixon administration promulgated a new set of regulations, 'Employment of Military Resources in the Event of Civil Disturbances', asserting legal authority for substantial military intrusions into domestic affairs, and reducing prior safeguards against misuse (Engdahl 1985: 2–3). The regulations purportedly derived their legality from federal statutes dealing with insurrections, unlawful obstructions and domestic violence (Title 10 U.S.C. ss 331, 332, 333), whose current form and revived use are discussed in Chapter 4. Further, the regulations asserted three additional sources of legal power. The first was a sweeping concept of an inherent executive emergency power to 'preserve public order'; the second was a purported executive power to protect federal property and functions; the third related to the Secret Service (Engdahl 1985: 19–31).

In 1973, at the Wounded Knee Indian village in South Dakota, the Nixon administration employed the military in a situation not even contemplated by those regulations. After several score supporters of the American Indian Movement, some armed, moved into the village, federal personnel cut off access, beginning a 71-day siege. No uniformed military personnel were visible, but the Directorate of Military Support was involved from the first day, a brigade of the 82nd Airborne was placed on alert, air force reconnaissance flights were conducted and, at one point, hundreds of troops were placed on six-hour alert, although ultimately not deployed (Engdahl 1985: 35–36). Courts rejected arguments that the operation breached the *Posse Comitatus Act*, on the basis that there had been no direct 'active' use of the army, only the 'passive' provision of military equipment and supplies (Hammond 1997). Some of the Indians, who were charged with interfering with federal officers, ultimately succeeded in having the charges dismissed because the *Posse Comitatus Act* had been violated by giving the military observers too much influence over civilian law enforcement decisions regarding negotiations, use of equipment and the policy on the use of force (Hammond 1997; Jacobs 1985: 222).

Also during the 1970s, evidence came to light of another aspect of military intervention into domestic politics—widespread military intelligence surveillance of civilians, notably political activists. Law suits failed to provide a judicial remedy. In *Laird v Tatum* (408 U.S. 1 (1972)), the case cited above, the US Supreme Court, while invoking a principle against 'military intrusion into civilian affairs', ruled that the plaintiffs, who suspected they had been placed under surveillance, lacked standing. The court found that they had not shown any direct injury and that mere knowledge of military investigative activity fell short of a 'chilling' of their First Amendment free speech rights. In what amounted to a 'Catch-22' situation, the judges refused to order the military to stop collecting information about civilians unless they could prove that they had been harmed by what the military was doing (Jacobs 1985: 223–226). The decision effectively gave a green light to the use of the armed forces to spy on citizens. It also illustrated the willingness of US courts to accept military interventions, even while formally adhering to an opposing principle.

In 1992, the first President Bush invoked provisions that permit the President to call out troops to suppress 'insurrections' or 'unlawful obstructions, combinations, or assemblages, or rebellion against the authority of the United States' that 'make it impracticable to enforce the laws of the United States in any State or

Territory'. About 4,000 soldiers and Marines were dispatched to Los Angeles at the request of California Governor Pete Wilson after the outbreak of riots sparked by the acquittal of four police officers who assaulted Rodney King. These troops were in addition to 10,465 national guardsmen and 1,717 federal law enforcement officers. A study of the deployment concluded that the heavily armed soldiers operated largely outside civilian control and that, although the troops killed no one, a 'bloodbath' could have easily resulted (Rasmussen 1999).

Federal troops have been mobilised many times for disaster relief, a practice that authorities argue does not violate the *Posse Comitatus Act*, because no civilian law enforcement is involved. However, such operations have the potential to spill over into law enforcement and also create a climate for military intervention into civilian areas. Previous operations have included soldiers patrolling urban areas, confronting looters and even providing election facilities, as happened after Hurricane Hugo in Florida in 1992, a quintessentially civilian political role (Hammond 1997).

Over the past three decades, the domestic use of troops against civilians has continued through the deployment of the military for the 'wars' on drugs and terrorism, and for immigration border patrols. The consequences of sending soldiers, trained to kill, to guard the Mexican border were tragically illustrated in 1997 when Marines killed an innocent 16-year-old boy, a local shepherd, near the border (Hammond 1997; Trebilcock 2000). Since 2001, far-reaching claims of presidential, executive or 'Commander in Chief' powers to call out the troops and authorise military surveillance have been pursued under the guise of combatting terrorism. These current developments are examined in Chapter 4.

Martial law in Australia

Although lacking America's revolutionary tradition, the Australian colonies of Britain also inherited a deep aversion to the domestic deployment of troops. Despite, or perhaps because of, their early history as subjects of military rule, the settlers developed antagonism to military intervention. After reviewing the archival records of a number of twentieth-century Australian episodes in which the issue of military action against civilians was raised, one study concluded:

> The distrust of the use of armed forces in domestic affairs is a long British tradition. The domestic use of armed forces in the early days of the penal settlement, the structure of the Australian population and its experience until the formation of the Federation, apparently, did nothing to weaken that tradition.
>
> (Beddie and Moss 1982: 72)

Martial law was invoked several times during the nineteenth century against convicts, Aborigines and workers (Lendrum 1977; Windeyer 1979). Governor King declared martial law in 1804 in New South Wales (NSW) to suppress an 'Irish insurrection'. Many participants in the revolt were tried by court-martial and a number were hanged (Lendrum 1977: 40). Another NSW Governor, Darling, rejected the urging of his Attorney-General to declare martial law in 1826 to use the military against

Aborigines who were resisting seizures of their lands. Darling was of the view, however, based on advice from the British Secretary of State Lord Bathurst, that he could use troops against Aboriginal people without such a declaration, as if they were 'open enemies' against whom war could be declared (Lendrum 1977: 42).

Two of the most barbaric declarations of martial law came in 1828 and 1830, when Governor Arthur of Tasmania mobilised troops to drive Aborigines from settled areas of that island state. Arthur twice invoked martial law even though Aboriginal retaliation against their dispossession had taken the form of isolated attacks, not a general war (Lendrum 1977: 41; Calder 2008: 127–150). In 1840, Governor Gawler of South Australia cited martial law, although not formally declared, as well as the war of law, as the legal justifications for the summary execution of two Aboriginal people rounded up by troops in the Coorong area, near the mouth of the Murray (Lendrum 1977: 29, 34). As late as 1867, British authorities sent regulations to the Australian colonies providing for declarations of martial law, although it seems that these regulations were not put into practice (Clark 2007: 17).

In his work, *Emergency Powers*, Lee 'hazards a guess' that the power to resort to martial law continues in Australia as a creature of the common law. Despite the uncertainty involved, Lee considers that, while legislation is generally preferable, the doctrine of martial law should not be buried 'for in the face of an extraordinary crisis it may come in useful … it may be better to rely on a "shadowy, uncertain, precarious something" than nothing at all' (Lee 1984: 224). This argument would seem to justify dispensing with the rule of law. The words quoted by Lee are taken from a nineteenth-century English judgment, where Cockburn CJ stated: 'Martial law when applied to the civilian is no law at all, but a shadowy, uncertain, precarious something, depending entirely on the conscience, or rather on the despotic and arbitrary will of those who administer it' (*R v Nelson and Brand* (1867) F Cockburn Sp Rep 86).

Strikes, unrest and political crises

Without resorting to martial law, in 1854, soldiers were used alongside police to mount an attack on the Eureka Stockade, which gold miners had erected to resist the efforts of the authorities to collect licence fees. About 30 miners and four soldiers were killed in the ensuing battle at Ballarat, and many more were injured (McCulloch 2001: 36). The great strike struggles of the 1890s saw troops mobilised against specific demonstrations and gatherings, with orders to shoot to kill strikers and their supporters. In one incident, Colonel Tom Price issued the following instruction to a volunteer unit during the extended Australian maritime strike of 1890:

> Men of the Mounted Rifles, one of your obligations imposes upon you the duty of resisting invasion by a foreign enemy, but you are also liable to be called upon to assist in preserving law and order in the colony … To do your work faintly would be a grave mistake. If it has to be done effectively you will each be supplied with 40 rounds of ammunition, leaden bullets, and if the

> order is given to fire, don't let me see any rifle pointed in the air; fire low and lay them out so that the duty will not have to be performed again.
>
> (McKinlay 1979: 377)

These experiences left bitter memories in the minds of ordinary working people. The Department of Defence web site's history of the Australian armed forces states:

> During the late 1880s and early 1890s, Australia's economy worsened, leading to reduced funding for the colonial armies and to the possibility of internal unrest. In 1890, during the Great Maritime Strike, the Victorian police expected rioting on a scale beyond their control. Six hundred troops including 200 from the Victorian Mounted Rifles were called out, and their presence in Victoria Barracks did much to dampen the threat. In the following year, the Queensland shearers withheld their labour when the pastoralists, refusing to recognise the Shearers' Union, began importing non-union labour from other colonies. The ensuing confrontation was deemed sufficiently serious to call out 1442 members of the Queensland Defence Force and send them to centres where the unionists were concentrated. By May 1891, the strike was virtually over, without the employers having conceded freedom of contract to the strikers. The troops received the thanks of the Queensland Parliament but earned the long held suspicion of several sections of the Australian community.
>
> (Department of Defence 2004)

The turmoil of the 1890s led to s 119 being inserted in the Constitution, to allow the military to be mobilised against 'domestic violence' when requested by a state government, at least where there was an 'uncontrollable situation' (Blackshield 1978: 6). In the early years of the twentieth century, Australian state governments requested military intervention on at least six occasions, to deal with such anticipated incidents as 'general strike riot and bloodshed', 'disturbances', wharf strike 'violence', 'labour troubles' and the 1923 Victorian police strike (Beddie and Moss 1982: 8–39). On each occasion, the Federal Government declined on the basis that the state police were capable of dealing with the threat (although troops were sent to guard federal buildings, including post offices, during the 1923 Victorian police strike) (Lee 1984: 201). Only one of those requests—by Queensland in 1912—was formally made under s 119. Perhaps as a result of the legal and political difficulties experienced in invoking s 119, the section has never been applied.

During the Brisbane general strike of 1912, Prime Minister Andrew Fisher rejected the Queensland government's request for troops, saying the situation could be controlled by police. Fisher also considered that the use of the military would have inflamed the discontent (Beddie and Moss 1982: 13–14). This decision is considered to have created a precedent for the proposition that s 119, which states that the Commonwealth 'shall' protect a State against domestic violence if the executive of the State applies for it, leaves the Federal government a discretion to send in the armed forces or not (Beddie and Moss 1982: 15–16). Federal Attorney-General Billy Hughes also argued, probably incorrectly, that the

Queensland application was defective because the request required a proclamation by the Governor of the State (Beddie and Moss 1982: 16–18).

Several of these episodes saw troops mobilised partially or assembled in substantial numbers without a formal call out. During the World War I conflicts over two defeated referenda to impose conscription in Tasmania from 1916 to 1917, following a request from the Premier, military units were placed on alert, arrangements were made with magistrates to call out troops and machine guns were requisitioned to be mounted on trucks (Beddie and Moss 1982: 21–23). In a 1923 Victorian police strike, the dispatch of army, air force and naval units to protect federal buildings (Melbourne was then the temporary national capital) was designed as a 'show of force'. The intimidating effect was reinforced by the presence of naval warships in Port Phillip Bay and the creation of a 'Special Constabulary Force' commanded by former general, Sir John Monash (Beddie and Moss 1982: 34–37). Moreover, the Melbourne operation established a precedent for the Federal government to deploy the armed forces domestically to protect its own interests (Beddie and Moss 1982: 37–38). During the 1928 waterfront dispute at Port Adelaide, the Defence Department issued ammunition and military equipment to the police, and special constables sworn into 'The Citizens' Defence Brigade' commanded by an army Lieutenant-Colonel were provided with rifles, ammunition and bayonets (Beddie and Moss 1982: 38–39).

Beyond the six formal requests for military intervention, plans existed for joint military-police operations against working people and political activists. In one recorded instance, in 1919 the army Chief of Staff held a meeting in Melbourne with senior NSW and Victorian police to discuss a cooperative response to any 'Bolshevik revolutionary action' launched under the cover of an industrial dispute. 'The Army was to provide military equipment, groups of picked men with machine guns and aeroplanes with bombs' (McCulloch 2001: 44).

Apart from establishing legal and political precedents for the informal use of the military to deal with civil unrest, these experiences illustrated how readily industrial disputes can ignite or intersect with broader popular unrest, with the potential to draw troops into armed conflicts with members of society in highly politically charged circumstances. The use of troops to break strikes does not require them to be formally called out—the argument being that their mobilisation does not involve the use of force—but such deployments may be 'highly controversial and may involve coercion, if not enforcement' (Beddie and Moss 1982: 78).

Troops were mobilised to break strikes on several occasions during the second half of the twentieth century, with Labor governments playing a leading role. In 1949, troops were initially mobilised to unload an Indian ship blacklisted by the unions, and then sent to work in open-cut coal mines. Troops carried weapons in their road and rail movements and to guard their camps, but worked unarmed, under police protection (Beddie and Moss 1982: 39ff). During the operation, soldiers threatened to break camp unless they were supplied with beer, and the Vice Chief of General Staff expressed fears of 'disturbances' involving the troops.

By sending in soldiers against the coal miners' strike of 1949, the Chifley Labor government set a precedent that the Menzies government extended to establish a plan for systematic military involvement in breaking strikes under the cover of maintaining 'essential services' and defeating 'communism'. The secret military plan, codenamed 'Operation Alien, continued from 1950 to 1955, even after the High Court ruled unconstitutional the government's use of the defence power to outlaw the Communist Party, and a subsequent referendum to ban the party was defeated.

Under the direct control of Prime Minister Menzies, 'Operation Alien' was launched shortly after the Communist Party Dissolution Act became law in October 1950. Its taskforce, which included high-ranking military officers, senior departmental officials and the assistant general manager of the Shell Company, adopted a model based on the handling of the 1926 British general strike (Louis 1992: 3–4). Ministerial authorisation was given for the army to be used in stevedoring in all states, coal mining and transport, even though legal experts offered conflicting opinions on the employment of troops in peacetime (Louis 1992: 6). Large numbers of troops were placed on standby for use on the waterfront and between mid-1951 and March 1952, soldiers loaded strike-bound ships at Williamstown, Geelong and Sydney (Louis 1992: 8–10).

In 1953, arrangements were made to send hundreds of troops to load ships at six ports affected by union action, although the sugar port of Bowen became the only one affected in the end (Louis 1992: 14). People in that town were 'awakened by the first of seven flights to land on the airfield at the outskirts of town' and 'feared that an air-borne invasion had occurred' (Louis 1992: 1). The deployment inflamed the situation, triggering wider protest strikes and the likelihood of national stoppages. Local businesses refused to supply the army, and work only resumed when the government agreed to withdraw the troops (Louis 1992: 2). By some interpretations, the Bowen intervention was a miscalculation (Beddie and Moss 1982: 50; White 2005: 449). The evidence suggests it was part of a wider scheme adopted by the Menzies government to provoke strikes by 'communist'-led unions, launch prosecutions and pursue its efforts to outlaw the Communist Party despite the defeat of the 1951 referendum (Louis 1992: 2–7). 'Operation Alien' was used once more in 1954, when troops loaded a ship with war material for the French government in Vietnam, and was not disbanded until late 1955 (Louis 1992: 18).

In 1970–71, the Gorton Government called out the Pacific Island Regiment (PIR), part of the Australian Defence Force (ADF), to suppress secessionist agitation in Papua New Guinea, then an Australian colony, administered under a United Nations Trusteeship. Since no state government request was involved, s 119 of the Constitution could not be invoked, and recourse to the defence power was problematic, since Papua New Guinea was not regarded as a foreign country. Moreover, the agitation that alarmed the government was a political movement seeking to end Australian rule. It seems that on legal advice, Defence Minister Fraser insisted on the issuing of a secret Order-in-Council, signed by the Governor-General, to authorise the call out, but its constitutionality remains questionable (Ward 1997: 13; Beddie and Moss 1982: 55). There were additional concerns in cabinet that military violence could bring UN condemnation and that the use of the PIR might provoke riots that the PIR could not control, requiring troops to be sent from Australia (Beddie and Moss 1982: 58). Detailed instructions were given to the territory's Administrator, including the requirement, spelled out in the Australian Military Regulations, that 'in the event of troops being ordered to fire the fire will be effective' (Beddie and Moss 1982: 60). He was given the power to issue intervention orders before seeking further Ministerial approval (Beddie and Moss 1982: 55). Ultimately, the troops were not actually used, but officials argued that the call-out decision, which was publicly broadcast, could also provide a powerful 'show of force' deterrent (Beddie and Moss 1982: 51–61).

The threat of military intervention was present during the constitutional crisis of 1975. Governor-General Sir John Kerr reportedly held his own meetings, as the titular Commander in Chief of the ADF, with senior defence officials before dismissing the Whitlam government (Coxsedge, Caldicutt and Harant 1982: 35, 96). On 6 November, five days before the dismissal, Kerr allegedly met with the secretary of the Defence Department, who afterward stated publicly that the government's suggestion of an investigation into the role of the US satellite communications bases at Pine Gap and Nurrungar in central Australia posed 'the greatest risk to the nation's security there has ever been' (Coxsedge, Caldicutt and Harant 1982: 35). Two days later another senior defence official briefed Kerr about CIA allegations against the Whitlam government, and a day later Kerr visited the Defence Signals Directorate for a briefing (Coxsedge, Caldicutt and Harant 1982: 96). A former Whitlam government cabinet minister alleged that Kerr secretly placed the armed forces on alert after the dismissal (Watching Brief 1986; Workers News 1976). Nevertheless, no troops were seen on the streets. Eventually, the widespread strikes and protests that greeted the dismissal subsided after Whitlam and Australian Council of Trade Unions (ACTU) president Bob Hawke appealed for workers to go back to work.

As will be reviewed in Chapter 10, the most dramatic military deployment occurred in 1978 when Prime Minister Malcolm Fraser and the New South Wales Premier Neville Wran called out nearly 2,000 soldiers in Sydney and the New South Wales Southern Highlands towns of Bowral and Mittagong after an explosion outside the Commonwealth Heads of Government Regional Meeting at the Sydney Hilton Hotel. To this day, the question of who was actually responsible for the bomb blast remains clouded in uncertainty and controversy. Following the collapse of two police prosecutions, there is no evidence that it was an act of terrorism (Head 2008). Nevertheless, the mass media and the federal and state governments immediately declared that the 'age of terrorism' had arrived in Australia. Two ensuing reports by Justice Hope (Hope 1977 and Hope 1979) and one by former London police chief Sir Robert Mark (Mark 1978) recommended a significant boost to the powers of the Australian Security Intelligence Organisation (ASIO), the establishment of the Office of National Assessments (ONA), the formation of the Australian Federal Police (AFP), wider domestic use of the army's Special Air Services (SAS), and the creation of 'anti-terrorist' and SWAT-style squads in state police forces.

Mark's report also revealed that Crisis Policy Centres had been set up to facilitate the provision of 'military aid to the civil power'. They were police-military 'nerve centres', run by the Protective Security Co-ordination Centre (PSCC), which included representatives of the Prime Minister's National Security Council, the ONA, ASIO and the Australian Secret Intelligence Service (ASIS, the external intelligence service), the military and the federal and state police (Mark 1978).

In 1983, the Hawke Government authorised RAAF flights over Tasmania to photograph work being conducted by the Tasmanian government in breach of Commonwealth regulations and in 1989, the same government authorised the dispatch of troops to combat protesters at the Nurrungar joint Australian-United States military satellite base. Both deployments generated political controversy and legal uncertainty, particularly with regard to the potential use of soldiers to confront demonstrators outside the Nurrungar base perimeter (Ward 1997: 14–18).

During the twenty-first century, the military has been deployed in civilian settings with unprecedented regularity, and often on a very large scale. Operation Gold for the 2000 Sydney Olympics was the second largest ADF operational deployment since the Vietnam War (after the INTERFET deployment to East Timor in 1999), while Operation Acolyte for the 2006 Melbourne Games was 'the largest ADF operation mounted in support of an Australian domestic event since 9/11' (Bergin and Smith 2006: 4, 6).

The Australian record, like that of Britain and the United States, indicates that it would be unwise to assume that the armed forces will not be used to put down civil or industrial unrest. Rather, a pattern emerges of governments calling in the military for support during periods of major upheaval.

4 The United States

Sweeping aside protections against domestic military intervention

President Donald Trump proclaimed a state of national emergency on the southern US border in February 2019. This marked a new stage in both the assertion of presidential executive power and the domestic use of troops against civilians. Trump declared the emergency specifically in order to mobilise the military to build a wall along the US–Mexico border, having already deployed troops to prevent refugees from entering the country. By doing so in defiance of Congressional votes not to allocate the full amount of money he sought to build a wall, Trump also usurped the constitutional prerogative of Congress to decide how public funds are to be spent. The president declared:

> I, DONALD J. TRUMP, by the authority vested in me by the Constitution and the laws of the United States of America, including sections 201 and 301 of the National Emergencies Act (50 U.S.C. 1601 *et seq.*), hereby declare that a national emergency exists at the southern border of the United States, and that section 12302 of title 10, United States Code, is invoked and made available, according to its terms, to the Secretaries of the military departments concerned, subject to the direction of the Secretary of Defense in the case of the Secretaries of the Army, Navy, and Air Force. To provide additional authority to the Department of Defense to support the Federal Government's response to the emergency at the southern border, I hereby declare that this emergency requires use of the Armed Forces and, in accordance with section 301 of the National Emergencies Act (50 U.S.C. 1631), that the construction authority provided in section 2808 of title 10, United States Code, is invoked and made available, according to its terms, to the Secretary of Defense and, at the discretion of the Secretary of Defense, to the Secretaries of the military departments.
>
> (Trump 2019)

The proclamation released by the White House confirmed that Trump was seeking to construct a border wall primarily by employing the resources of the US military and the Pentagon. Describing the situation at the border as one that 'threatens core national security interests' because it 'is a major entry point for criminals, gang members, and illicit narcotics', the proclamation stated: 'Because of the gravity of the current emergency situation, it is necessary for the Armed Forces to provide additional support to address the crisis' (Trump 2019).

As well as the *National Emergencies Act*, the proclamation invoked section 12302 of title 10, United States Code, part of a 1953 law that authorises the Secretary of Defense to mobilise up to one million military reservists for a period of up to 24 months. This section had been used to mobilise the reserves for deployment to Afghanistan and Iraq, having been invoked by President George W. Bush after the 9/11 attacks. In effect, President Trump was seeking to treat the US–Mexico border as a military battlefield, with immigrants and refugees cast as 'invaders' threatening the United States.

The president also invoked Section 2808 of title 10, which authorises the Pentagon to carry out construction activities in support of military operations. This was previously understood to refer to the building of barracks, fortifications, airstrips, roads, prisoner-of-war camps and other facilities required by the military during active combat operations. The wall along the US–Mexico border was to be treated as a similar military necessity.

The directive from Trump to Acting Secretary of Defense Patrick Shanahan authorised him to 'order as many units or members of the Ready Reserve to active duty as the Secretary … determines to be appropriate'. The secretaries of the departments of Defense, Interior and Homeland Security were additionally ordered to 'take all appropriate actions … to use or support the use of the authorities herein invoked, including, if necessary, the transfer and acceptance of jurisdiction over border lands' (Trump 2019). This was a broad grant of authority, effectively permitting a militarisation of the US–Mexico border.

This order amounted to a further erosion of the already corroded *Posse Comitatus Act* (PCA). The PCA bars the US military from engaging in law enforcement operations within the borders of the United States, without specific congressional authorisation, as discussed later in this chapter. To disguise the violation of the Act, President Trump's order described the military operation as a civilian one, 'to assist and support the activities of the Secretary of Homeland Security at the southern border'.

Despite the Trump administration's claims that the military was playing only a technical role, those units deployed include the 1st Battalion, 37th Field Artillery Regiment, the Marines' 1st Light Armored Reconnaissance Battalion, the 505th Military Intelligence Brigade, the 3rd Combat Aviation Brigade, the Weapons Company, 2nd Battalion and the 5th Marine Regiment. Moreover, Trump had often referred to immigration as an 'invasion' and in 2018 said soldiers would be able to 'shoot' immigrants at the border (World Socialist Web Site 2019).

More fundamentally, the presidential order defied the US Constitution. Article I, Section 9, Clause 7 of the Constitution reads, in part: 'No Money shall be drawn from the Treasury, but in Consequence of Appropriations made by Law.' This language has been understood previously to mean that the executive branch (which includes the Treasury) may spend money only as authorised by Congress.

A declaration of national emergency gives the president access to powers contained in at least 160 statutory provisions and dozens of Executive Orders, presidential directives and other regulations (Thronson 2013: 742–743; Head 2016:

175–179). According to a Congressional Research Service report, *National Emergency Powers*:

> These delegations or grants of power authorize the President to meet the problems of governing effectively in times of crisis. Under the powers delegated by such statutes, the President may seize property, organize and control the means of production, seize commodities, assign military forces abroad, institute martial law, seize and control all transportation and communication, regulate the operation of private enterprise, restrict travel, and, in a variety of ways, control the lives of United States citizens.
>
> (Congressional Research Service 2001: 1)

Congressional Democratic leaders called Trump's declaration of a national emergency 'unlawful'. A joint statement from House Speaker Nancy Pelosi and Senate Minority Leader Chuck Schumer declared: 'The President's actions clearly violate the Congress's exclusive power of the purse, which our Founders enshrined in the Constitution.'

Nevertheless, a month later, President Trump vetoed legislation passed by Congress to overturn the national emergency he had declared. Twelve Republican senators had joined all 47 Democrats to support a 'resolution of disapproval' that had been passed by the Democratic-controlled House of Representatives, but there was little likelihood of a two-thirds majority in either house to override the presidential veto.

Troops sent to confront refugees on the Mexican border

Before declaring the emergency, the Trump administration had, in November 2018, already deployed 5,900 soldiers to the border. Initially, that deployment was to end in January 2019, but was then extended until September 2019 (Taylor 2019). The troops were authorised to use 'lethal force' if necessary to stop migrants reaching US soil. The order, signed by the president's chief of staff, General John Kelly, granted the military the power to conduct 'a show or use of force (including lethal force, where necessary), crowd control, temporary detention, and cursory search' (Van Auken 2018b).

This followed a statement by President Trump that troops should answer any rocks thrown by migrants with gunfire (Van Auken 2018b). Asked by a journalist if soldiers would fire on refugees, Trump stated:

> It's the military. I hope there won't be that. Anybody throwing stones, rocks, like they did … to the Mexican police, where they badly hurt police and soldiers of Mexico … we will consider that a firearm, because there's not much difference where you get hit in the face with a rock.
>
> (Associated Press 2018)

This deployment violated not just the PCA, but also the right of refugees to claim asylum under the international Refugees Convention. That convention forbids punitive action against asylum seekers—people fleeing persecution. There was a real risk of troops opening fire on refugees, who had marched toward the border chanting: 'We are international workers, not criminals' (Van Auken 2018b).

President Trump's dispatch of troops to the US–Mexico border was not, however, completely unprecedented. It followed earlier similar, if less explicitly confrontational, operations authorised by the president's two immediate predecessors. President Barack Obama deployed 1,200 National Guard troops to the border in 2010, officially to help combat drug trafficking and the potential for spillover violence. Obama's deployment succeeded President George W. Bush's Operation Jump Start, which deployed 6,000 guards to surveil the southern border in 2006 (Plesset 2018).

To avoid accusations of breaching the PCA, President Bush had framed the operation as one to support the Border Patrol in controlling supposed illegal immigration and alleged related criminal activities. President Obama had followed suit in asserting that the PCA, which does not apply to the National Guard, permitted Guard troops to act in support of the Border Patrol, and state and local law enforcement officers (Longley 2019).

By deploying military units, and authorising them to use lethal force, President Trump went several steps further. Generally, US troops are authorised by rules of engagement to use force in self-defence. Some analysts warned that the president's order would not offer legal protection to soldiers who fired upon a migrant. Each domestic deployment of troops to any of the 50 states or US territories was governed overall by Chairman of the Joint Chiefs of Staff Instruction 3121.01B, 'Standing Rules of Engagement, Standing Rules for the Use of Force by U.S. Forces'. However each mission is said to be unique and the rules can be adjusted at a commander's request (Copp 2018).

The earlier erosion of the PCA is examined later in this chapter. It must be noted that Congress has facilitated this process. In 2005, the two houses enacted a joint resolution (H. CON. RES. 274). In part, the resolution stated:

> [B]y its express terms, the Posse Comitatus Act is not a complete barrier to the use of the Armed Forces for a range of domestic purposes, including law enforcement functions, when the use of the Armed Forces is authorized by Act of Congress or the President determines that the use of the Armed Forces is required to fulfill the President's obligations under the Constitution to respond promptly in time of war, insurrection, or other serious emergency. (Longley 2019)

Discarding the principles of 1776

Through the 1776 Revolution, the people of the United States took the lead in enunciating opposition to military interference in civil affairs. However, that principle has been subverted increasingly by successive administrations, both Republican and Democrat, and that process has intensified since 2001, amid the 'war on terror' and rising domestic social tensions.

In overthrowing British colonial rule, the American people inherited and defended a deeply felt hostility to the use of the armed forces to suppress discontent. Paragraph

14 of the Declaration of Independence charged the British king with affecting to 'render the Military independent of and superior to the Civil power'. A Congressional Research Service report published in 2000 on the PCA remarked: 'Americans have a tradition, born in England and developed in the early years of our nation, that rebels against military involvement in civilian affairs. It finds its most tangible expression in the nineteenth century Posse Comitatus Act' (Doyle 2000: 1).

As late as 1985, a legal expert could still write with some justification that 'To the conscience of the nation that fancies itself as the world's greatest democracy, the idea of military intrusion into the affairs of civil government is profoundly repugnant' (Engdahl 1985: 1). Even then, however, Engdahl warned that new foundations had been laid for military intervention within the United States during the Nixon administration of 1969–1974, when regulations were introduced to authorise the use of troops against civil disturbances. Despite such concerns being expressed in academic and civil liberties circles, those foundations have been revived and extended during the twenty-first century.

The principle of civilian supremacy over the military is enshrined in the US Constitution, which provides that the president is the Commander in Chief. But that provision has been interpreted in recent years to produce the opposite effect: the expansion of executive power and the concentration of political power in the hands of the president, resting on the military. Well-known examples have been the assertion of presidential authority to order the military incarceration of individuals, including US citizens, as 'enemy combatants' at Guantanamo Bay and elsewhere, secret renditions of people to be tortured in other countries, and military surveillance of domestic telecommunications without judicial warrants.

At the same time, the PCA has been eroded to the point that one US Army Reserve lawyer has described its effect in impeding the use of the military for 'homeland defense' as a 'myth' (Trebilcock 2000). Moreover, in 2002, the Pentagon established the Northern Command (NorthCom), giving the armed forces an unprecedented focus on domestic operations across the North American continent, and developed plans for military deployments during political crises. As part of NorthCom, in 2008, for the first time ever, an active duty regular Army combat unit was assigned to full-time use inside the United States (Cavallaro 2008).

Meanwhile, the military has played an increasingly visible role in domestic political events, including at presidential inaugurations. NorthCom forces were on high alert during President Barack Obama's 2009 inauguration, increasing air defences and deploying chemical attack experts and medical units. About 11,500 military personnel took part. About 4,000 National Guard members provided support to local law enforcement, boosting security on the National Mall and around Washington. There were 7,500 troops under federal control, including emergency medical teams and experts in chemical attacks (Barnes 2008).

There was a similar mobilisation for Donald Trump's 2017 inauguration, which was the subject of widespread protests. Some 5,000 National Guard troops were deployed, alongside as many as 28,000 police officers from across the country (Hermann 2017). There was also a disturbing and still officially unexplained military-related incident during Trump's swearing-in. Early in the president's address, ten military officers walked up and stood behind him so they would prominently appear in the camera shots beamed across the United States and the world. After 45 seconds, a Marine officer prompted the sailors and soldiers to leave (Connor 2017). It was an apparent attempt to provide a military backdrop to the president's speech.

Documents obtained months after the inauguration revealed plans had been made for a military parade during the event. Senior members of Trump's Presidential Inaugural Committee approached the Pentagon asking for a list and photographs of tanks, missile launchers and other military vehicles that could be deployed in the inaugural parade. The Pentagon at that time was reluctant to organise such a deployment, and Trump's aides dropped the proposal (Van Auken 2018a).

The *Washington Post* reported that Trump then asked Pentagon officials to draw up plans for a military parade down Washington's Pennsylvania Avenue later in the year (Van Auken 2018a). The planned parade, originally scheduled for Veterans Day 2018, was later postponed until 2019 because of public criticisms of the estimated $92 million price tag (Superville 2019).

President Trump's plans for such military displays led to his 2019 tribute to the armed forces in his Fourth of July address at the National Mall in Washington. Trump delivered his remarks from behind a wall of bulletproof glass, on a stage flanked on both sides by tanks and armoured vehicles. More than two-thirds of Trump's hour-long address consisted of homages to each of the five major branches of the American military, followed by flyovers of military aircraft from each. This included F-18, F-22 and F-35 fighter jets, nuclear-capable B-2 strategic bombers, and attack helicopters. Mixed in with them were Air Force One and Marine One, the personal transports of US presidents (Hall 2019).

Growing political use of armed forces

President Trump's Fourth of July display was unprecedented, but built upon a growing trend. In effect, the PCA has been eroded by the increasing use of military forces as security for essentially civilian events. 'National Security Events' covered by NorthCom have included sports events, State of the Union addresses, G-8 summits, Presidential inaugurations and funerals, and political conventions (Ehling 2008). During the 1996 Atlanta Olympics, more than 10,000 US troops were deployed, partially on the pretext of deterring terrorism. No questions were raised about infringement of the PCA, even though these troops would have been central to a law enforcement emergency if a terrorist attack had occurred (Trebilcock 2000).

For the Democratic convention, in addition to 1,500 heavily armed police officers, more than 1,000 National Guard troops were activated. Elements of the US Coast Guard were placed in charge of intelligence operations in designated areas, while the North American Aerospace Defense Command and the Northern Command also participated, in part to provide 'air cover'.

Such operations at party conventions not only amount to military intrusion into political affairs but also serve to help entrench the two-party monopoly of the political system.

Erosion of civilian control of the military

Beneath these developments is a tendency toward a reversal of the relationship between the military and civilian rule. In his 1961 farewell speech, President Dwight D. Eisenhower urged the American people to beware the potentially 'disastrous' political influence of the 'military-industrial complex'. He warned: 'This conjunction of an immense military establishment and a large arms industry is new in the American experience. The total influence—economic, political, even spiritual—is felt in every city, every Statehouse, every office of the Federal government' (Eisenhower 1961).

More than half a century on, that complex is far larger and more powerful than it was in Eisenhower's time. By 2020, the Pentagon would command an annual budget of more than three quarters of a trillion dollars (Seligman 2019). This would exceed the military budgets of nearly every other country combined, and the Pentagon operated more than 1,000 bases around the planet. It is a military that has engaged in repeated interventions over the past four decades, including in Grenada, Nicaragua, Haiti, Somalia, Libya, the former Yugoslavia, Afghanistan, Iraq and Syria, often to overturn governments. Its senior commanders have wielded de facto political power over entire populations in Afghanistan and Iraq (Van Auken 2007).

Likewise, the corporate side of the military-industrial complex has mushroomed, benefiting directly from military contracts and indirectly from the global assertion of American strategic and commercial interests. Led by Lockheed-Martin and Halliburton and the giant weapons and aerospace contractors, the 'complex' also includes the oil and energy conglomerates, the big construction, engineering and public utility companies and the biotechnology corporations. Other prominent firms are Boeing, Carlyle Group, General Atomics, General Electric and Northrop Grumman Corporation (Singer 2003; Chalmers 2004).

Those who have studied the American military establishment have issued warnings about its transformed role over the past period. One review by a military historian, Richard H. Kohn, concluded that 'in recent years civilian control of the military has weakened in the United States and is threatened today':

> The issue is not the nightmare of a coup d'etat but rather the evidence that the American military has grown in influence to the point of being able to impose its own perspective on many policies and decisions. What I have detected is no conspiracy but repeated efforts on the part of the armed forces to frustrate or evade civilian authority when that opposition seems likely to preclude outcomes the military dislikes.
>
> (Kohn 2002: 2)

Examples cited by Kohn included the public Joint Chiefs of Staff opposition to the Clinton administration's proposal to abolish the ban on open homosexual service, in which the chiefs floated rumours of their own and dozens of other resignations, encouraged their retired brethren to arouse congressional and public opposition, and then more or less openly negotiated a compromise with President Clinton, their Commander in Chief.

While the US Constitution contains explicit measures to ensure civilian power over the military, Kohn issued the following warning about the façade of civilian control:

> If one measures civilian control not by the superficial standard of who signs the papers and passes the laws but by the relative influence of the uniformed military and civilian policy makers in the two great areas of concern in military affairs—national security policy, and the use of force to protect the country and project power abroad—then civilian control has deteriorated significantly in the last generation.
>
> (Kohn 2002: 8–9)

Kohn argued that this development was unprecedented in American history. Five decades of warfare had created

> something entirely new in American history—a separate military community, led by the regular forces but including also the National Guard and reserves, veterans organizations, and the communities, labor sectors, industries, and pressure groups active in military affairs. More diverse than the 'military-industrial complex' of President Eisenhower's farewell address forty years ago, this 'military' has become a recognizable interest group. Also, it is larger, more bureaucratically active, more political, more partisan, more purposeful, and more influential than anything similar in American history.
>
> (Kohn 2002: 13)

In 2006, Kohn was joined by three other scholars to produce a discussion article, 'Coup d'état: Military Thinkers Discuss the Unthinkable', which was published in *Harper's Magazine* (Bacevich 2006). Andrew Bacevich, a professor of international relations and former career officer, commented:

> The question that arises is whether, in fact, we're not already experiencing what is in essence a creeping coup d'état. But it's not people in uniform who are seizing power. It's militarized civilians, who conceive of the world as such a dangerous place that military power has to predominate, that constitutional constraints on the military need to be loosened. The ideology of national security has become ever more woven into our politics. It has been especially apparent since 9/11, but more broadly it's been going on since the beginning of the Cold War.
>
> (Bacevich 2006)

Bacevich pointed out that the use of the US military against American citizens was not a hypothetical scenario, but had already taken place with the domestic spying operation mounted by the National Security Agency (NSA), which is part of the military.

It would be wrong to regard these developments purely as products of the Clinton and Bush administrations of 1993 to 2009. President Obama elevated three recently retired four-star officers to top government positions, an unparalleled representation of the military in a Democratic administration. There also were further signs of military readiness to defy civilian authority. General Raymond Odierno, the US commander in Iraq, held a press conference in early 2009 in which he dismissed Obama's campaign pledge to withdraw US combat troops within 16 months. Obama's pledge would still have left tens of thousands of 'non-combat' forces, but Odierno went further, announcing that the speed and level of combat troop withdrawals would be determined by the military according to its assessment of the security situation on the ground in Iraq (Grey 2009).

The Trump administration featured, at various stages, generals and ex-generals in top-ranking posts, including retired Marine General Jim Mattis as Defense Secretary. Retired Marine General John Kelly was named first to head the Homeland Security Department and then became White House Chief of Staff. Army General H.R. McMaster replaced Air Force General Mike Flynn as the National Security Advisor. Retired General Keith Kellogg was chief of staff of the National Security Council.

Undermining the Constitution

Both the Declaration of Independence and the Constitution embody a principle, based on the 'Anglo-American tradition', opposing domestic military mobilisation against the citizenry. The Declaration of Independence indicted the King for rendering 'the military independent of and superior to the civil power'.

The Constitution restricts military appropriations to two years, designates the president as the civilian Commander in Chief and empowers the Congress to regulate the armed forces (Article 1, section 8, clauses 12 and 14; Article 2, section 2). Its 'Guaranty Clause' provides that the military may only be used to protect a State against 'domestic violence' if requested by a State legislature or executive, when the legislature cannot be convened (Article IV, section 4).

It is also possible to see in the First, Second, Third, Fourth and Fifth Amendments—with their promises of individual rights, a civilian militia, freedom from the quartering of troops, freedom from unreasonable search and seizure and no deprivation of life, liberty, or property without due process—an underlying constitutional principle barring the use of a standing army to interfere in civilian affairs (Doyle 2000: 12).

There is some judicial support for this proposition. Members of the Supreme Court seemed to acknowledge a larger constitutional principle in both *Youngstown Sheet and Tube Co. v Sawyer*, 343 U.S. 579 (1952) and *Laird v Tatum*, 408 U.S, 1 (1972). In *Youngstown*, the court struck down an attempt, via a Presidential order, to use the armed forces to seize and operate the country's steel mills, which were threatened by a nationwide strike. The court held that the president's constitutional and statutory powers as president and Commander in Chief were not sufficient to support such an executive order, when Congress had specifically refused to grant such authority by statute. That decision still leaves open considerable scope for military intervention where Congress has not expressly taken an opposing stand (Doyle 2000: 15).

In *Laird v Tatum*, the Court commented that the 'philosophical underpinnings' of the Constitution explained 'our traditional insistence on limitations on military operations in peacetime' (408 U.S. at 15–16). Nevertheless, the court refused to order the military to stop collecting information about civilians. It held that a claim that First Amendment rights were chilled was non-justiciable unless citizens could show evidence of specific harm or the realistic threat of specific harm.

Likewise, in 2008 the Supreme Court refused to hear an appeal brought by the American Civil Liberties Union and other groups challenging the Bush administration's warrantless domestic wiretapping programme, conducted by the NSA, a military agency. The wiretapping programme began in 2001 but was first revealed to the public through a media leak in 2005. The programme, the full details of which are still not known, included domestic spying in breach of the Foreign Intelligence Surveillance Act (FISA). In 2006, a US District Court judge ruled that the programme violated the First and Fourth Amendments, the separation of powers and FISA.

When that ruling in *ACLU v NSA* was overturned on appeal, the challengers were caught in a 'Catch-22' situation. The government refused to identify the individuals targeted by the NSA programme, on the grounds that this information was secret. However, the appellate court upheld the government's argument that only those who could prove they had been specifically targeted by the programme could have standing to sue. The Supreme Court rejected a further appeal without comment.

The courts have long been reluctant to recognise the authority of military tribunals over civilians (Doyle 2000: 12). This view was upheld, albeit in a limited manner, in the Guantanamo Bay habeas corpus cases that challenged the constitutionality of the military commissions established to try 'enemy combatants'. In 2004, the Supreme Court, by a 6–3 majority, ruled that Guantanamo Bay detainees could seek writs of habeas corpus in US courts. The majority judgment, delivered by Stevens J, suggested that at stake were democratic conceptions dating back nearly 800 years to the Magna Carta of 1215 (*Rasul v Bush; Al Odah v United States*, 542 U.S. 466 (2004)).

Four years later, in *Boumediene v Bush*, 553 U.S. 723 (2008), the Supreme Court ruled 5–4 that Guantanamo detainees could immediately file habeas corpus petitions in US district courts challenging the legality of their confinement. Most had been held at the US naval base under brutal conditions, often enduring solitary confinement, water-boarding and other coercive techniques or torture, for more than six years, without having the merits of their cases reviewed by a court of law. However, the ruling did not question the executive branch's ability to declare someone an 'enemy combatant', a power the Supreme Court upheld four years earlier in *Hamdi v Rumsfeld*, 542 U.S. 507 (2004).

Later in 2008, a 5-to-4 decision by the US Court of Appeals for the 4th Circuit backed the Bush administration's contention that the president has such power. In

Al-Marri v. Pucciarelli (4th Cir. July 15, 2008), the court effectively overturned a decision reached by a three-judge panel of the same court in 2007, which compared the assumption of such sweeping powers to military rule and the oppression of the American colonies by King George III. The appellate ruling denied habeas corpus to Al-Marri, a legal resident of the United States before the White House declared him an enemy combatant in 2003 and ordered the military to detain him in a Navy brig in South Carolina. The government claimed that an Authorization to Use Military Force (AUMF) resolution passed by Congress in 2002 gave the president the power to carry out such detentions. Alternately, it asserted that the Commander in Chief has unchallengeable authority to imprison anyone without charges for the duration of a global war on terror.

Overall, the courts have failed to enunciate a wider constitutional principle against military intervention, even in the context of the *Posse Comitatus Act*, where the judges have generally avoided any examination of its possible constitutional underpinnings (Doyle 2000: 13–14). Thus, in *United States v Walden*, 490 F.2d 372 at 376, the court said 'we do not find it necessary to interpret relatively unexplored sections of the Constitution in order to determine whether there might be constitutional objection to the use of the military to enforce civilian laws'.

It therefore seems that military action must violate one of the explicit constitutional prohibitions or guarantees, such as habeas corpus, the right to jury trial, freedom of expression and freedom from unreasonable searches and seizures, before courts will object. This means that a president has substantial leeway, both as chief executive, charged with seeing that laws are faithfully executed, and as Commander in Chief, to mobilise the armed forces.

The Supreme Court has made it clear that the president does not require express Congressional or statutory authorisation to exercise such powers. If an emergency threatens the freedom of interstate commerce, transportations of the mails or some other federal government responsibility, he may call upon 'the army of the Nation, and all its militia … to brush away the obstructions' (*In re Debs*, 158 U.S. 364 at 381).

Such rulings have left the way open for increasingly aggressive assertions of presidential, executive and prerogative powers to use military personnel and resources against civilians, flying in the face of the clear intent of the Constitution. In effect, the role of Commander in Chief has been transformed from a guarantor of civilian supremacy over the military, to an instrument for utilising the armed forces against civil unrest and political dissent.

Constitutional presidential authority has been asserted to provide a broad basis for the mobilisation of military forces under the banner of homeland security. Particularly since 2001, the White House has asserted that the executive powers of the president and his position as Commander in Chief support wide-ranging exceptions to the *Posse Comitatus Act.* Defense Department regulations assert another 'constitutional' exception to the Act, founded on the 'inherent right of the U.S. Government … to ensure the preservation of public order and to carry out governmental operations … by force, if necessary'.

Stated so sweepingly, this 'federal functions exception' has the capacity to swallow the rule (Hammond 1997). Expanding federal authority over areas formerly reserved to the states, such as transportation, commerce, education and civil rights, has widened the scope of federal functions. During the 1960s, presidential authority provided the basis for sending troops to the South to enforce school de-segregation (Trebilcock 2000).

The guaranty clause and 'domestic violence'

The Constitution provides one explicit avenue for authorising domestic military intervention. Its language presents potential obstacles to presidential power to deploy the armed forces. The guaranty clause provides:

> The United States shall guarantee to every State in this Union a Republican Form of Government, and shall protect each of them against Invasion; and on Application of the Legislature, or of the Executive (when the Legislature cannot be convened) against domestic violence.

By distinguishing between invasion and domestic violence, the clause is clearly intended as a limitation on the president's executive power to send in federal troops. There must be a request by the state. Four obvious questions arise. First, what is domestic violence? It is not defined by the Constitution, nor has it been defined by legislation or judicial interpretation. Second, when can a state governor request military aid without waiting for the state legislature? Third, is the federal government obliged to accede to an application? Fourth, can a president send in federal troops without a state request?

'Domestic violence' is a vague term. Presidents have interpreted it to justify military interventions against 'an assemblage of rioters', 'mobs' and widespread violence (Bassiouni 1971: 372–373). Clearly these interpretations are broad enough to cover political protests and other forms of dissent that fall far short of armed violence. Only in one instance, in 1903, was a governor's request for troops denied because the disturbance did not amount to an 'insurrection'. In 1967, Attorney General Ramsey Clarke sent letters to all governors indicating that 'serious domestic violence' was needed, but the addition of the word 'serious' hardly clarified anything (Bassiouni 1971: 373).

The requirement for an application from the state legislature has been read as preventing a governor requesting troops while the legislature is in session. If the legislature is not sitting, however, presidents have not insisted on waiting for the legislators to gather to make a request. On their face, the words of the guaranty clause seem to limit unilateral action by a governor to where it is impossible to convene the legislature. In practice, most presidents have only required there to be difficulty in convening the legislature. On a few occasions, presidents have rejected requests because the language of the application was not unequivocally asking for intervention, as distinct from recommending it (Bassiouni 1971: 368–369).

Despite the Constitution's imperative phraseology—'shall protect'—the clause has generally been treated as leaving the president discretion to withhold aid. Pleas for troops have been rejected because a president thought the danger exaggerated or the state forces adequate to deal with the situation. The precedents indicate that a state must fully utilise all its forces, including its National Guard, before federal troops will be dispatched (Bassiouni 1971: 374–375).

Even though the guaranty clause specifically sets a state application as a pre-condition for deploying troops, it seems to have been accepted that this proviso only applies if there is no independent or concurrent federal interest in maintaining order. At least, legal opinion appears to allow for presidential executive or Commander in Chief powers to protect substantial federal interests, regardless of any state request (Bassiouni 1971: 375–376).

Stretching the guaranty clause

Aided by such legal opinions, the guaranty clause has become a vehicle for a wider expansion of presidential power. One of the greatest direct threats to civilian politics comes from the Civil Disturbance Statutes (10 U.S.C., sections 331–335), which allow the president to call up the armed forces and the National Guard (State militia) to suppress challenges to the political order, ranging from insurrections to 'domestic violence'. Section 331, covering insurrections against States, says:

> Whenever there is an insurrection in any State against its government, the President may, upon the request of its legislature or of its governor if the legislature cannot be convened, call into Federal service such of the militia of the other States, in the number requested by that State, and use such of the armed forces, as he considers necessary to suppress the insurrection.

Section 332 deals with various threats to federal authority, from unlawful combinations to rebellions:

> Whenever the President considers that unlawful obstructions, combinations, or assemblages, or rebellion against the authority of the United States, make it impracticable to enforce the laws of the United States in any State or Territory by the ordinary course of judicial proceedings, he may call into Federal service such of the militia of any State, and use such of the armed forces, as he considers necessary to enforce those laws or to suppress the rebellion.

Section 333 goes further to cover 'interference with State and Federal law':

> The President, by using the militia or the armed forces, or both, or by any other means, shall take such measures as he considers necessary to suppress, in a State, any insurrection, domestic violence, unlawful combination, or conspiracy, if it—

1 so hinders the execution of the laws of that State, and of the United States within the State, that any part or class of its people is deprived of a right, privilege, immunity, or protection named in the Constitution and secured by law, and the constituted authorities of that State are unable, fail, or refuse to protect that right, privilege, or immunity, or to give that protection; or
2 opposes or obstructs the execution of the laws of the United States or impedes the course of justice under those laws.

In any situation covered by clause (1), the State shall be considered to have denied the equal protection of the laws secured by the Constitution.

In 2006, the Bush administration succeeded in securing Congressional support for amendments that extended these powers. One amendment effectively widened the scope of section 333 from 'insurrection, domestic violence, unlawful combination, or conspiracy' to 'natural disaster, epidemic, or other serious public health emergency, terrorist attack or incident, or other condition' if the authorities of the State 'are incapable of maintaining public order'. In part, the Bush administration justified the change as a response to the monumental failings of the Hurricane Katrina relief operation in 2005. Expert commentators described the amendments as a diversion from the government's political embarrassment over the Katrina debacle, in which the military actually played a substantial part (Banks 2005).

In 2007, amendments were reversed. Democrat Senator Patrick Leahy opposed them, partly to defend States' rights and strengthen the role of the National Guard. He said the amendments 'make it easier for Presidents to declare martial law' and 'make it unnecessarily easy to assert federal authority over National Guard elements without the consent of governors'. President Bush initially vetoed the reversion to the original PCA, but later signed the reversal into law, in exchange for measures expanding the military budget, giving the National Guard higher status at the Pentagon, and a closer relationship with the Northern Command, and directing the Pentagon to work with the Guard in homeland defense planning (Leahy 2008). Thus, in the name of civil liberties, the Congress overturned the PCA changes, but bolstered the National Guard's substantial part in domestic military deployments. Moreover, the reversion still left the PCA in a severely eroded condition. In addition, President Bush attached a signing statement that he did not feel bound by the repeal (Goodman 2008).

The Bush administration's moves dovetailed with the National Security Presidential and Homeland Directive (NSPD 51, HSPD 20), promulgated in 2007. In the event of a 'catastrophic emergency', which the president can declare without congressional approval, NSPD 51 would institute virtual martial law under the authority of the White House and the Department of Homeland Security. It would suspend constitutional government under the provisions of Continuity in Government, leaving extraordinary powers in the hands of the president and vice-president. 'Catastrophic emergency' is loosely defined as 'any incident, regardless of location, that results in extraordinary levels of mass casualties, damage, or disruption severely affecting the US population, infrastructure, environment, economy, or government functions'. 'Continuity of Government' is defined as 'a coordinated effort within the Federal Government's executive branch to ensure that National Essential Functions continue to be performed during a Catastrophic Emergency'.

Eviscerating the *Posse Comitatus Act*

On its face, the *Posse Comitatus Act* stands as a strict prohibition against using the military for civilian law enforcement, complete with criminal penalties for violation. Its entire text, in its current form, states:

> Whoever, except in cases and under circumstances expressly authorized by the Constitution or Act of Congress, willfully uses any part of the Army or Air Force as a posse comitatus or otherwise to execute the laws shall be fined under this title or imprisoned for not more than two years, or both.
>
> (18 U.S.C. section 1385)

Congress has essentially left the PCA unchanged since 1878, and buttressed it with an additional proscription against the use of the armed forces to make arrests or conduct searches and seizures. Section 375 of 10 U.S.C. forbids the Secretary of Defense making regulations that permit direct participation by military personnel in 'a search, seizure, arrest, or other similar activity'.

It appears that no prosecution has ever been conducted for breach of the PCA, however. Moreover, the dearth of judicial interpretation has left its parameters 'substantially untested' (Hammond 1997). In addition, growing numbers of major and minor exceptions have been created, some by Congress and some by the courts. The cumulative result has been to blur the line between police, para-military and military intervention, undermine civilian control of the military and expose the population to the dangers of deadly force and de facto dictatorship. The following outline seeks to trace the erosion of the PCA to the point where 'reality bears little resemblance to the myth' and the PCA 'is more of a procedural formality than an actual impediment' to the domestic mobilisation of the armed forces (Trebilcock 2000).

In the first place, while the Act applies today to Army, Air Force, Navy and Marines, and their Reserve components, it does not cover the Coast Guard and the National Guard, at least as long as the National Guard is operating exclusively under the control of a state (Doyle 2000: 42–43). Only when federalised by presidential authority does the Guard become subject to the PCA. This exception gives the authorities access to 'huge military manpower resources' (Trebilcock 2000). The courts have also said that the PCA has no extra-territorial effect. It therefore does not prevent the military from conducting operations with law enforcement agencies abroad or mounting its own operations against civilians, including US citizens and residents, overseas (Hammond 1997).

Second, the courts have interpreted the PCA as only barring 'active', rather than 'passive' engagement in law enforcement. 'Execution of the laws' includes the arrest and detention of criminal suspects, search and seizure activities, restriction on civilian movement through the use of blockades or checkpoints, gathering evidence for use in court and the use of undercover personnel in civilian law enforcement. From the cases arising from the 1973 Wounded Knee confrontation, the courts have developed three tests:

1. whether military personnel have been in 'direct active use' in civilian law enforcement
2. whether the use of the military 'pervaded the activities' of the civilian officials
3. whether the military subjected 'citizens to the exercise of military power which was regulatory, prescriptive or compulsory in nature.

(Doyle 2000: 37)

Thus 'direct active' participation in making arrests has been deemed a violation of the PCA, but not taking a supporting role. Military personnel may be involved in planning law enforcement operations, as long as actual arrests of suspects and seizures of evidence are carried out by civilian personnel. Courts have held that providing supplies, equipment, training, facilities and certain types of intelligence information does not contravene the PCA (Trebilcock 2000; Hammond 1997). This semantic and artificial distinction ignores the reality that troops engaged in supposedly passive support roles can and will be called upon to use force against civilians if operations encounter resistance or other difficulties that threaten to exceed the capacities of the police or civilian authorities. Courts also have ruled that aerial photography and visual search and surveillance by the military do not breach the PCA.

Third, aspects of the language of the PCA can serve to narrow its scope. It is restricted to 'willful' misuse of the military. Although the few judicial interpretations of that requirement are somewhat conflicting, it seems that a court would not convict for anything less than deliberate disregard of the PCA, with the authorities acting with the knowledge that their conduct was unlawful (Doyle 2000: 35). This approach leaves considerable scope for government or military figures to argue that they acted innocently, thinking that their activities were within the boundaries set by the PCA. Courts have treated the phrase 'execute the laws' as confined to civilian laws, and allowed military personnel to perform military duties in a manner that assists civilian law enforcement—as long as the primary purpose of an activity is a military one. For example, a court permitted naval military police investigators to act as undercover informants in a civilian police drug operation near a naval base, for the purpose of minimising the flow of drugs into the base (Doyle 2000: 33).

Fourth, because the Act is a statutory creation, not a constitutional prohibition, it can and has been repeatedly circumvented by subsequent legislation. This has happened particularly since 1980, when the Reagan administration directed the Department of Defense to utilise naval and air assets for the 'war on drugs'. Congress subsequently approved this tasking, and extended it to immigration control, customs and tariff enforcement (Trebilcock 2000). By 1989, the military was designated the 'single lead agency' in the drugs war, a classic instance of mission creep. The Pentagon embraced new missions like drug interdiction as a means of boosting budget levels and improving public relations. In 1993, the Department of Defense budget included more than $1.4 billion for the drug-related missions (Hammond 1997).

The undermining of the PCA has been a bipartisan process. In 1995, for example, within one week of the bombing of a federal building in Oklahoma City, President Clinton proposed an exception to the PCA to allow military involvement in investigations related to 'weapons of mass destruction' (Hammond 1997).

The other most prominent Congressional exceptions to the PCA relate to: insurrections, espionage, terrorism and civil disturbances, natural disasters, nuclear materials, protection of national parks, investigation of crimes against the president or others in the line of succession, civil rights, fishery conservation, internationally protected persons and quarantine (Hammond 1997: fn 130; Doyle 2000: 20–23).

Another exception is the Uniform Code of Military Justice. The code gives the military the inherent right to maintain good order and discipline over its personnel through law enforcement, prosecution and punishment. As such, the code gives jurisdiction to the military to enforce both military and civilian laws against its own personnel (Trebilcock 2000: fn 5). These provisions may permit the military to protect its personnel from prosecution in civilian courts for alleged abuses of power committed during domestic operations.

After surveying the whittling away of the PCA, military reserve lawyer Trebilcock concluded:

> The erosion of the *Posse Comitatus Act* through Congressional legislation and executive policy has left a hollow shell in place of a law that formerly was a real limitation on the military's role in civilian law enforcement and security issues.
>
> (Trebilcock 2000)

The establishment of NorthCom

As part of a global reorganisation of the Pentagon, the creation of the Northern Command in 2002 set a new focus for the US military. Alongside the invasions of Afghanistan and later Iraq, for the first time a specific Pentagon command was established for domestic military intervention. NorthCom's stated mission was to defend the US 'homeland' and assist federal, state and local authorities.

Another step was taken in 2008, when for the first time a regular Army combat unit was deployed for full-time use inside the United States. The 4,000-strong First Brigade Combat Team of the Third Division was placed under the command of US Army North, the Army's component of NorthCom. The unit had spent nearly three out of the previous five years in Iraq, leading the assault on Baghdad in 2003 and carrying out house-to-house combat in the suppression of resistance in the city of Ramadi. It was the first brigade combat team to be sent to Iraq three times (Cavallaro 2008).

While active-duty units previously had been used in temporary assignments, such as the combat-equipped troops deployed to Los Angeles to suppress riots in 1992 and to New Orleans in the wake of the 2005 Hurricane Katrina, it was the first time that an Army combat unit had been given a dedicated assignment on US soil. The Pentagon's official announcements stressed the role of specialised units in a potential response to terrorist attacks, but the mission exceeds terrorism. *Army Times*, a specialist military publication, reported that 'they may be called upon to help with civil unrest and crowd control'. The article noted the connection and continuity between the unit's operations in Iraq and its domestic task:

> The 3rd Infantry Division's 1st Brigade Combat Team has spent 35 of the last 60 months in Iraq patrolling in full battle rattle, helping restore essential services and escorting supply convoys. Now they're training for the same mission—with a twist—at home.
>
> (Cavallaro 2008)

According to military officials quoted by *Army Times*, the deployment that began with the First Brigade Combat Team was to become permanent, with different units rotated into the assignment on an annual basis. *Army Times* reported that the 1st BCT would be kitted out with 'the first ever nonlethal package that the Army has fielded'. The publication reported, 'the package includes equipment to stand up a hasty road block; spike strips for slowing, stopping or controlling traffic; shields and batons; and, beanbag bullets'. Without explanation, the newspaper later retracted that portion of their report, stating that NorthCom said the weapons package was intended only for use in Iraq.

Army doctrine and rules of engagement for civil disturbance and 'riot control' planning have long recommended equipping troops with 'non-lethal weapons' for 'operations other than war'. The Center for Army Lessons Learned, located at Fort Leavenworth, Kansas, issued a primer on the subject, entitled *Civil Disturbances: Incorporating Non-Lethal Technology, Tactics, Techniques and Procedures*, in 2000 (Burghardt 2002).

In October 2008, the American Civil Liberties Union (ACLU) filed a Freedom of Information request for information from the government about the *Army Times* report. The ACLU said: 'This deployment jeopardizes the longstanding separation between civilian and military government, and the public has a right to know where and why the unit has been deployed' (ACLU 2008). The ACLU requested the Departments of Justice, Homeland Security and Defense to immediately make public all legal opinions, executive orders, presidential directives, memos, policy guidance, and other documents that authorize the deployment of military troops for domestic purposes.

Two months later, in December 2008, the *Washington Post* reported that the Pentagon had begun to implement plans to make 20,000 troops available to NorthCom on a full-time basis by 2011. The additional soldiers were to be assigned as they completed assignments in Iraq or Afghanistan. Bert B. Tussing, director of homeland defense and security issues at the US Army War College's

Center for Strategic Leadership, commented that the plan 'breaks the mold' by assigning an active-duty combat brigade to the Northern Command for the first time. Previously, the military required the command to rely on troops requested from other sources.

According to the *Post*, Deputy Defense Secretary Gordon England signed a directive in late 2007 providing $556 million over five years to fund the programme. Paul McHale, assistant defense secretary for homeland defense, said the use of 20,000 troops in a domestic deployment 'would have been extraordinary to the point of unbelievable' before the terrorist attacks of 11 September 2001, according to the text of a speech given to the Center for Strategic and International Studies, a Washington think tank, quoted by the *Post*. He described the new policy as 'a fundamental change in military culture'.

The Department of Defense Directive 3025.12, 'Military Assistance for Civil Disturbances (MACDIS)' provided for far-ranging use of the military against civil unrest:

> Ensure continuous planning by the DoD Components, both in the Department of Defense and in cooperation with civil government agencies for MACDIS operations that may be required during any time or condition of peace, war, or transition to war, *including any national security emergency*. ...
>
> The President is authorized by the Constitution and laws of the United States to employ the Armed Forces of the United States to suppress insurrections, rebellions, and domestic violence under various conditions and circumstances. Planning and preparedness by the Federal Government and the Department of Defense for civil disturbances are important due to the potential severity of the consequences of such events for the Nation and the population ... The President has additional powers and responsibilities under the Constitution of the United States to ensure that law and order are maintained.
>
> ('Military Assistance for Civil Disturbances [MACDIS]', Department of Defense Directive, No. 3025.12, February 4, 1994, 1, 3)

DoD 3025.12 also stated: 'Under reference (r), the terms "major disaster" and "emergency" are defined substantially by action of the President in declaring that extant circumstances and risks justify Presidential implementation of the legal powers in those statutes.' In other words, at least as far as the Pentagon is concerned, the 'circumstances' in which troops can be deployed are 'defined substantially' by the president.

Use of deadly force

If troops are called out, civilians appear to have few protections against the use of force, including lethal force. None of the statutory exceptions to the PCA define or limit the powers of military personnel. Instead, these critical issues are left in the hands of the Pentagon. DoD 3025.12 directed the Army Secretary to 'promulgate orders, rules, and regulations, as appropriate, to govern all MACDIS operations in which the use of force or deadly force is or can be authorized'. The secretary was also tasked with ensuring that all task force commanders 'promulgate supplemental rules of engagement and rules for the use of force'.

The Rules of Engagement for the 1992 Los Angeles riots deployment set three preconditions for the use of deadly force: (a) all other means have been exhausted; (b) there is no significantly increased risk of death or serious bodily harm to innocent persons; and (c) one or more of the following purposes exists: self-defense, prevention of a crime, defense of others, detention or prevention of escape of persons (Rasmussen 1999). These provisions left the way open for wide use of lethal force. A study of the operation, which noted that 'all other means have been exhausted', implied that non-lethal weapons were available to soldiers, but that was not the case. Few non-lethal riot and crowd control resources were distributed, nor did the soldiers, with the exception of some National Guard units, have any training in the use of non-lethal equipment. In one instance, on receiving a request to 'cover me', marines fired more than 200 bullets into a house with young children inside (Rasmussen 1999).

The study pointed out that decisions on the Rules of Engagement 'were left to all intents and purposes in the hands of the military' and the enforcement of those rules was 'at best haphazard'. Task force commanders devised the rules and Arming Orders, based on existing Department of Defense operational plans and regulations. There was no evidence that the relevant civilian authorities, the mayor and state governor, provided any input into the rules or how they were enforced. There was also substantial evidence that different units operated at different arming levels, and that this was widely known at the time (Rasmussen 1999).

Military plans and exercises

Since the formation of NorthCom in 2002, plans have been drafted and exercises conducted for large-scale internal troop deployments, usually under the banner of counter-terrorism preparedness.

According to a report published by the *Washington Post* in 2005, the Pentagon has developed plans for operations within the continental United States, in which terrorist attacks would be used as the justification for imposing virtual martial law on cities, regions or the entire country (Graham 2005). The article cited sources working at the NorthCom headquarters, located in Colorado Springs, Colorado.

While the plans are classified, they outlined 15 potential crisis scenarios, ranging from 'low-end', which the article described as 'relatively modest crowd-control missions', to 'high-end', after as many as three simultaneous catastrophic mass-casualty events, such as a nuclear, biological or chemical weapons attack. In each case, the military would deploy a quick-reaction force of as many as 3,000 troops per attack. More troops could be made available as needed.

The plans were due to be sent to the Defense Secretary for approval. Military lawyers had studied their legal implications, and canvassed the use of the National Guard, which is exempt from the PCA, to detain people. The plans also involved the military's intelligence agencies. The article described NorthCom's 'Combined

Intelligence and Fusion Center, which joins military analysts with law enforcement and counterintelligence specialists from such civilian agencies as the FBI, the CIA and the Secret Service' (Graham 2005).

Exercises have been conducted to test out domestic military capacities. One example is Exercise Vigilant Shield 2008, which was officially described as

> a Chairman of the Joint Chiefs of Staff-designated, North American Aerospace Defense Command (NORAD) and U.S. Northern Command (USNORTHCOM)-sponsored, and U.S. Joint Forces Command-supported Department of Defense exercise for homeland defense and defense support of civil authorities missions.

At various locations across the United States and the Territory of Guam, NORAD and NorthCom, along with the Pacific Command, the Department of Homeland Security and local, state and other federal responders exercised their 'response abilities against a variety of potential threats'. The purpose was said to be to

> provide local, state, tribal, interagency, Department of Defense, and non-governmental organizations and agencies involved in homeland security and homeland defense the opportunity to participate in a full range of exercise scenarios that will better prepare participants to prevent and respond to national crises.
>
> (NorthCom News 2007)

On occasions, residents of US cities have been confronted by armed troops conducting exercises in urban areas. In 2008, a company of Marines arrived in Toledo, Ohio, carrying M16 rifles and wearing camouflage uniforms to carry out foot patrols, drive military vehicles through city streets, and engage in mock gunfights and ambushes with blank ammunition. However, the mayor ordered the Marines to leave because the sight of armed soldiers patrolling city streets would 'frighten people' (Toledo Blade 2008).

During the 2008 Vibrant Response exercise at Fort Stewart, Georgia, three units of NorthCom's Consequence Management Response Force (CCMRF, pronounced 'sea-smurfs'), including two combat units from the 1st Brigade Combat Team, 3rd Army Division and the elite 82nd Combat Aviation Brigade, participated in mock drills designed to 'coordinate with local governments and interagency organizations such as the Federal Bureau of Investigation and the Federal Emergency Management Agency', according to a report on *U.S. Northern Command News* (NorthCom News 2008b).

Transformed role of the National Guard

Over the past few decades, two interlocking politico-legal processes have largely dismantled constitutional limits on presidential powers to mobilise the armed forces to suppress domestic unrest. One is the erosion of Congressional control over internal deployments, including regulations that permit the military, in some instances, to act without even presidential or other executive authorisation. The other is the overturning of state governors' authority over the increasingly federalised National Guard.

A little-analysed feature of the first development is the underlying transformation during the twentieth century of what the US Constitution intended to be state-controlled militias, with domestic responsibilities, into a major component of the federal armed forces, under presidential control. To satisfy opposition to military intervention, the architects of the Constitution proposed the state militias—the precursor to the National Guard—as the primary fighting force in domestic situations. The states would appoint the troops' commanders, thus ensuring militia loyalty to the state and providing a check against the federal government's ability to use a standing army to cut across state sovereignty (Gardina 2008: 1032). The Constitution gave Congress the authority to 'provide for calling forth the Militia to execute the Laws of the Union, suppress Insurrections and repel Invasions' (Article 1, section 8, clause 15).

After the US defeat in the Vietnam War in 1975, President Gerald Ford ended conscription, leading to the creation of a smaller military composed of active-duty forces and a large Reserve contingent. The Reserve forces are a combination of the state-based National Guard units and the Reserve units, mainly composed of retired active-duty personnel. This means, in effect, that the National Guard troops are no longer under the sole command of the states—as part of the Reserve forces, they are, by definition, a part of the federal armed forces (Gardina 2008: 1042–1043).

In 1986, Congress passed the Montgomery Amendment that largely barred state governors from withholding consent for the deployment of the National Guard, and this legislation was upheld by the Supreme Court in *Perpich v. Department of Defense* (496 U.S. 334 (1990)). Federal control over the National Guard effectively increased as a result of heavy reliance on the Reserves for the invasions of Afghanistan and Iraq in 2001 and 2003, and subsequent operations. By some estimates, in September 2005, more than one-third of the 135,000 troops in Iraq were National Guard members (Gardina 2008: 1054).

Conclusion

The 'war on terror' declared in September 2001 accelerated processes leading toward a greater mobilisation of the US military, both at home and abroad. Actions such as the overturning of the governments in Afghanistan and Iraq, not only gave the military direct experience against civilian populations but were accompanied by intensive preparations for domestic use of the armed forces, also in the name of combatting terrorism. For the first time in US history, an entire command, NorthCom, was established for internal use.

In the process, basic constitutional principles have been transgressed and the only specific legislative protection against military intervention, the *Posse Comitatus Act*, has been further eroded, both in law and practice. At the root of these developments has been a corrosive undermining of civilian supremacy, described by one former military officer as a creeping coup d'état. A resurgence of social and class tensions, as witnessed in Los Angeles in 1992, could see troops called out against civilians in a manner not experienced since the American Revolution itself.

5 Canada

Advanced military planning

Largely behind the backs of the Canadian population, a fundamental shift in the role of the Canadian military has taken place since 2001. The formation of the Canada Command in 2006, primarily dedicated to internal operations, has been followed by proposals for an enlarged domestic role, accompanied by advanced planning for the Canadian Forces to respond to threats deemed to constitute terrorism or danger to 'security'. As reviewed later in this chapter, one such proposal, a 2011 policy paper written by Chris Madsen, a professor at Canadian Forces College, the military's training institution, provided an insight into the preparations being made. It began by asserting:

> The military is principally a tool of the government in power, most particularly the prime minister and minister of national defence, to be organized and ready to provide armed violence if and when deemed necessary in the public interest and toward state ends.
>
> (Madsen 2011: 1)

The ease and apparent normalcy with which the military can be deployed domestically was illustrated in 2019, albeit in what seemed to be a purely civilian law enforcement operation. In a blaze of publicity, the Canadian Armed Forces was approved to join a manhunt for two murder suspects. Public Safety Minister Ralph Goodale tweeted that the Royal Canadian Mounted Police (RCMP) had asked for air support. 'In the criminal investigation of the two fugitives in northern MB [Manitoba], the RCMP have requested aircraft support from the Cdn Armed Forces. Prompt reply—YES,' he wrote.

The minister's media statement was similarly perfunctory, without any explanation of the precise legal mechanism by which the authorisation was issued:

> I received a request from RCMP Commissioner Brenda Lucki to provide assistance in the efforts to find the two suspects in these murders. On behalf of the Government of Canada, the Minister of National Defence, the Honourable Harjit Sajjan, and I have accepted the formal request for federal assistance, for a Canadian Armed Forces aircraft to aid in the search near Gillam, Manitoba.
>
> (Goodale 2019)

Although media headlines in Canada and internationally declared that the military had intervened in the manhunt, as if to favourably promote the operation, the formal authorisation seemed limited to one aircraft. Nor did this operation involve any of the military call-out measures, reviewed later in this chapter, to deal with civil unrest. Nevertheless, the episode demonstrated the blurring of the line between police and military roles, and the readiness of governments to mobilise the military for domestic purposes.

Reversing the pacifist image

Like their British and American brethren, Canadian people have long displayed antipathy to the use of the armed forces on home soil. One Canadian military historian notes: 'The application of military force by a democratic government within the confines of its own borders, and in some cases against its citizenry, has long been a controversial and politically sensitive topic' (Maloney 1997: 135).

In 1935, for example, when the Ontario government requisitioned the military to deal with a depression-era disturbance, the government was soundly defeated at the following year's election (Lerhe 2004: 9).

To some extent that underlying sentiment finds expression in law. The Constitution Act of 1867 established a military–civilian demarcation. While the armed forces ('militia, military and naval service and defence') were placed under the exclusive jurisdiction of the federal government by subsection 91(7), law enforcement and public safety were placed in the hands of the provinces.

Military operations against civilian populations, including French colonists and the Aboriginal peoples, featured heavily in the early history of Canada (Gillmor and Turgeon 2001). Moreover, troops were used regularly against striking workers in the early years of the twentieth century (Heron 1998; Fudge and Tucker 2004). By the late twentieth century, however, Canadian governments had established an international image of a less militarist society than its much more militarily powerful southern neighbour, the United States (Gillmor 2002).

Since the advent of the 'war on terror' in 2001, the US-led invasions of Afghanistan and Iraq, and with the growth of global economic, strategic and military tensions, this image has been repudiated. Prime Minister Stephen Harper summed up the shift in his message at the front of the 2008 Canada First Defence Strategy, where he wrote of 'rebuilding the Canadian Forces into a first-class, modern military', 'keeping our citizens safe and secure' and 'ensuring that Canada can return to the international stage as a credible and influential country' (Canada First 2008: 1).

In 2017, Prime Minister Justin Trudeau's government presented a new defence policy that called for $62 billion in additional military spending over two decades. That included a 73 per cent hike in military spending over a decade, rising to $32.7 billion in 2026–27. This would increase the defence budget to 1.4 per cent of GDP, still below the NATO target of 2 per cent (Jordan 2017).

Citing a new period of global instability, military rearmament by competing foreign powers and 'challenges on the home front', the 2008 national defence strategy committed Canada to a substantial expansion of the Canadian Forces

(CF), with the ambition of sustaining major operations simultaneously both abroad and internally. Notably, of the six core missions defined in the national defence strategy for the CF, three explicitly related to domestic security operations in civilian settings: supporting major international events such as the 2010 Vancouver Winter Olympics and the G-8 summit of the same year; responding to terrorist attacks; and supporting civilian authorities during crises.

The document projected a more active domestic role for the CF, asserting that 'Canadians rightly expect their military to be there for them in domestic crises'. Annual military spending was to be increased to more than $30 billion by 2025–26, treble the 1986–87 level, and the number of CF personnel from about 82,000 in 2000–1 to 100,000 by 2027–28 (Canada First 2008: 3, 7, 11, 14).

Steps have been taken to prepare to use these expanding forces internally. In 2008, the Canada Command and its US counterpart, the Northern Command, signed a Civil Assistance Plan that allowed the military of each nation to support the other during 'civil emergencies', including terrorist incidents and 'criminal activity'. According to Madsen: 'The contingency planning done by Canada Command contemplates the possibility of one or more significant terrorist incidents occurring inside the country and has exercised command arrangements accordingly' (Madsen 2011: 8). During the same period, thousands of Canadian troops were deployed to Afghanistan, while the elite Special Air Services-style Joint Task Force Two (JTF2), the main unit that would be deployed domestically in the event of a crisis, has been used in Iraq, Haiti and possibly other countries.

This turn to a more aggressive military posture internationally is likely to increase the possibility of domestic military intervention for a number of reasons. In part, such operations generate a political and military climate of opinion more favourable to greater utilisation of the armed forces. At the same time, public opposition to militarism, as witnessed by the large demonstrations across Canada and globally in 2002 and 2003 against the Iraq war, may well fuel political discontent that may ultimately be met with military might. The 'blooding' of soldiers in operations against civilians abroad may also make the political and military establishment more confident that the CF has the capacity, training and internal resolve needed to confront citizens at home.

Canada's entire civilian national security apparatus has been transformed since 2001. By 2008, the term 'national security' or a close equivalent, such as 'security of Canada' had appeared in more than 30 Canadian statutes, often creating new government powers or limiting government obligations (Forcese 2008: 6–7). The Department of Public Safety and Emergency Preparedness, established in 2005, which goes by the name Public Safety Canada, hosts the Government Operations Centre, an interdepartmental and interagency body tasked with coordinating responses to 'anything—real or perceived, imminent or actual, natural disaster or terrorist activity—that threatens the safety and security of Canadians or the integrity of Canada's critical infrastructure' (Forcese 2008: 77–78).

The 'domestic security' focus from 2006

A Defence Policy Statement, *A Role of Pride and Influence in the World*, issued in 2006, announced a shift in Canadian policy, which would mean making domestic security the primary focus of the Canadian Forces:

> Events such as the tragic attacks against our neighbours on September 11, 2001, demonstrate that Canada is also vulnerable to terrorism and threats emanating from failed and failing states around the world. To respond to these threats, the new policy statement sets out a plan to make Canadian security the first priority for the Canadian Forces. To better protect Canada and Canadians, the Canadian Forces will be reorganized to more effectively and quickly respond to domestic crises, as well as support other Government departments as required ...
>
> It will require the Canadian Forces to re-examine their approach to domestic operations. Most significantly, the Forces will now view Canada as a single operational area where the best available resources from our maritime, land, air and special operations forces can be brought to bear on a contingency, wherever it occurs. As such, the Canadian Forces will establish a single national operational command headquarters (Canada Command) to respond to domestic crises.
>
> (Canada Defence Policy Statement 2006)

Accordingly, in 2006, the Canadian Command was established to focus on domestic operations. Without any legislative authorisation, that shift was extended in 2008, when the commanders of the Canadian Command and the US Northern Command signed the Civil Assistance Plan (CAP). This could mean US troops being deployed against dissenting Canadians, and vice-versa. US Northern Command commander, Air Force General Gene Renuart, who signed the pact with his Canadian Command counterpart, Air Force Lieutenant-General Marc Dumais, described the document as 'a unique, bilateral military plan to align our respective national military plans to respond quickly to the other nation's requests for military support of civil authorities' (NorthCom News 2008a: 1).

Although the CAP was presented substantially under the banner of responding to natural disasters, its provisions are not confined to such emergencies. Among the examples cited in the plan were 'effects of a terrorist attack' and 'criminal activity'. Moreover, the use of violent force was envisaged: the plan referred to Rules of Engagement for use of force and stated that, without further oral or written direction, CF personnel were entitled to use force in self-defence, up to and including deadly force. The plan said it did not apply to support for law enforcement, which was to be included in the Canada-United States Combined Defense Plan (NorthCom News 2008a: 1, 2, 4).

Advanced military planning

Plans for the internal use of the CF are shrouded in secrecy, but a limited view was provided by Madsen, whose 2011 article, noted above, could be regarded as a semi-official outline, produced within the Canadian Forces College. In the course of advocating a greater domestic role for the CF, Madsen referred to aspects of the planning, as well as the assumptions of legal authority underpinning the operations. Madsen stated:

> The Canadian Forces possesses inherent capacity within Canada to deal with terrorist threats as part of broader government efforts to improve preparedness in the event of emergency or crisis … Canada's military maintains several dedicated units suited to activities and work connected with countering terrorism and mitigating its effects. The highly secretive Joint Task Force 2, whose formation pre-dates the terrorist attacks of 9/11, transferred the domestic counter-terrorism armed assault function from the Royal Canadian Mounted Police to the Department of National Defence.
>
> (Madsen 2011: 4–5)

Madsen pointed to procedures in place to authorise lethal military attacks:

> Although still a hypothetical scenario in Canada's case, the basic procedures and requirement for political approval prior to military action essentially stands the same today. Military pilots would be ordered to shoot down a civilian airliner under terrorist control in the last resort. Deployment of air, sea, and air defence forces during the Vancouver Olympics and Toronto G20 Summit during 2010 addressed the same contingency should terrorists strike.
>
> (Madsen 2011: 6)

The Canadian Forces College professor gave an example from 2010 of the already wider use of the military in a domestic civilian scenario, in the context of militarily intercepting refugee boats:

> The Canadian Force's tracking and interception of an unreporting ship carrying Tamil migrants and suspected terrorists toward the British Columbia coast represented yet another example of military forces used in a first responder capacity. Although representatives from the Royal Canadian Mounted Police and Canadian Border Services Agency were present to effect arrest and detention, a warship carried the intimidating firepower to ensure the vessel stopped and obeyed Canadian directions; indeed, the small boat boarding teams tasked to seize and secure the vessel were military from the warship.
>
> (Madsen 2011: 6)

Madsen emphasised the capacity of the CF to intervene quickly on home soil:

> At any one time, the vast majority of the 65,000 strong regular Canadian Forces are resident inside the country engaged in training, garrison, headquarters, and administrative duties. In keeping with section 33 of the National Defence Act, all regular force members 'are at all times liable to perform any lawful duty' when so ordered. In other words, they are subject to deployment

> as the government and chain of command sees fit for domestic purposes. In the event of a terrorist attack or serious national emergency, every available soldier and officer could be put on active service in formed units or individually as warranted. A further 27,000 personnel in the primary reserve are trained to certain levels of proficiency, whilst 11–15,000 former military and retired personnel are kept on the books in the supplementary reserve.
>
> (Madsen 2011: 7)

Madsen said 'contingency planning' by Canada Command contemplated the possibility of one or more 'significant terrorist incidents' occurring simultaneously inside the country. He stressed the power of the prime minister to deploy the armed forces, without any reference to cabinet ministers, let alone the parliament:

> Most particularly, one person, the prime minister, exercises under Canada's parliamentary system overwhelming power to commit military forces to operations, with or without the concurrence of ministers in cabinet and elected members of parliament from the ruling and opposition political parties ... The national command centre is at the disposal of the prime minister and the minister of national defence for real-time situational awareness and consultation with senior military leadership.
>
> (Madsen 2011: 8–90)

In canvassing the legal issues arising from domestic military operations, in particular the criminal and civil liability of CF personnel for killing or seriously injuring civilians, Madsen emphasised that protection could be provided by rules of engagement issued by the chief of defence staff:

> Should another Canadian be killed or seriously injured through military action, officers and soldiers could become liable to prosecution or civil remedies before the courts. To avoid such possibilities, troops deployed on domestic operations almost always work in formed units and groups under the command and orders of superior officers. Armed violence, when necessary, becomes a collective responsibility. Typically, issued rules of engagement govern when use of force may be used and under what conditions. For the purposes of domestic operations, rules of engagement are approved by the chief of defence staff and passed down through Canada Command to subordinate formations and units. In general, military planners and soldiers are expected to deploy the minimum force so authorized depending upon the situation, though specific rules of engagement may allow both deadly and nondeadly means.
>
> (Madsen 2011: 15–16)

Constitutional issues

Like the American Constitution, the Canadian constitutional instruments embody the principles of civil/military demarcation and civilian control over the military.

The Constitution Act 1867, s 91 (7) gave the federal legislature jurisdiction over 'Militia, Military and Naval Service, and Defence', thus reserving military matters to the national government. By contrast, ss 92 (14) and (15) placed law enforcement exclusively in the hands of the provinces. These provisions at least implicitly reserve to the provinces control over civilian law enforcement and limit the power of the federal government to intervene militarily. However, s 91 (27) allocated criminal law to the federal sphere, and the federal government has residual authority over matters not assigned exclusively to the provinces. The Supreme Court of Canada has interpreted the latter power as permitting the national parliament to legislate for national emergencies (Forcese 2008: 63).

Contradictory possibilities are thrown up by section 15 of the Constitution Act: 'The Command-in-Chief of the Land and Naval Militia, and of all Naval and Military Forces, of and in Canada, is hereby declared to continue and be vested in the Queen.' This provision today arguably vests command in civilian hands, via the vice-regal representative, the Governor-General, appointed by the federal government. However, the section also leaves open the possibility of the Governor-General exercising the old royal prerogative powers of the British monarchy to deploy the armed forces without the authority, or even against the wishes, of an elected government. (This possibility is discussed in Chapter 10, dealing with the similar situation in Australia.)

Canadian courts have also recognised the continued existence of the royal prerogative as a source of executive power, encompassing 'the powers and privileges accorded by the common law to the Crown'. Legislation can override or abrogate prerogative powers, but only if the statute makes this clear by explicit language or necessary implication. From some court rulings, doubt may still exist about whether a legislative scheme has replaced prerogative powers (Forcese 2008: 67–68).

Canada has two statements of basic rights, yet neither expressly prohibits or curtails the domestic mobilisation of the Canadian Forces to suppress political or social unrest. The *Canadian Charter of Rights and Freedoms* and the *Canadian Bill of Rights* do not allow for abridgement of rights during emergencies, but they do permit parliament to circumscribe at least some of the rights. Section 33 of the Charter allows the federal and provincial legislatures to exclude most Charter provisions by stating that a statute operates 'notwithstanding' the Charter. No parliament has utilised this power in an emergency situation, but it remains possible for this happen in a crisis (Forcese 2008: 35, 120–122).

Otherwise, section 1 of the *Charter* guarantees the rights and freedoms set out in it 'subject only to such reasonable limits prescribed by law as can be demonstrably justified in a free and democratic society'. This protection is far from absolute. In the event of a crisis involving military deployment, the issue of what are 'reasonable limits' may well arise. In *Operation Dismantle v. Canada Inc* ([1985] 1 S.C.R. 441), Wilson J. of the Supreme Court said the concept of 'right' used in the Charter had to 'take account of the fact that the self-contained political community which comprises the State is faced with at least the possibility, if not the reality, of external threats to both its collective well-being and to the individual well-being of its citizens' (at 489–490). While these remarks related to external threats, a similar claim could be made about internal threats.

Section 2 of the *Charter* recognises 'fundamental freedoms' of conscience and religion; thought, belief, opinion and expression; peaceful assembly; and association. Other sections set out certain democratic, mobility, equality and legal rights, some of which may limit military powers. For example, a person cannot be deprived of the 'right to life, liberty and security of the person' except 'in accordance with the principles of fundamental justice'. Everyone has the rights 'to be secure against unreasonable search or seizure' and 'not to be arbitrarily detained or imprisoned'.

These provisions can restrict violations of democratic rights, at least where the rules of procedural fairness have not been followed. In *Suresh v. Canada (Minister of Citizenship and Immigration)* ([2002] 1 S.C.R. 3, 2002 SCC 1), the Supreme Court ruled that deportation to face torture was generally unconstitutional and therefore Suresh was entitled to a fair hearing with procedural safeguards before being deported. However, the Canadian courts have generally treated military and national security considerations as overriding procedural fairness (for example, *Chiarelli v Canada (Minister of Justice)* [1992] 1 SCR 711). Moreover, the phrases 'reasonable limits', 'unreasonable' and 'arbitrarily' in the *Charter* leave considerable scope for military intervention, provided it is authorised by legislation, common law or judicially recognised prerogative powers. In a number of cases, the Supreme Court has suggested that the right to life, liberty and security of the person can be tempered or violated in times of war, national emergency or other security exigencies (Forcese 2008: 37).

Similar issues arise with the *Canadian Bill of Rights*, which declares 'human rights and fundamental freedoms' that include life, liberty, security of the person and enjoyment of property, except where deprived by due process of law. Other rights listed in section 1 of the *Bill* are equality before the law and the protection of the law; and the freedoms of religion, speech, assembly and association, and the press. However the protection of these rights and freedoms is far from guaranteed. Section 2 of the *Bill* merely specifies that federal statutes be construed and applied as not to abrogate, abridge or infringe any of the rights or freedoms, unless expressly provided otherwise by an Act of Parliament. Therefore, it remains possible for federal legislation to override these provisions, as happened with the *War Measures Act*, prior to its repeal by the *Emergencies Act* in 1988 (Forcese 2008: 119).

One scholar of Canadian national security law has concluded: 'In Canadian constitutional law, it seems clear that *Charter* protections may be tempered where national security threats are at issue' (Forcese 2008: 35). The same appears to apply to the *Bill of Rights*.

Overview of legal mechanisms

Notwithstanding the possible constitutional limits, a remarkable array of legal mechanisms exists for mobilising CF personnel and capacities, including intelligence resources, to deal with civil unrest.

- Part VI of the *National Defence Act* permits the Attorney General of a province to request 'military aid of the civil power' to suppress a 'riot or disturbance'. The request is made direct to the Chief of the Defence Staff—not the federal government—who is obliged by law to execute the request.

- Section 273.6 of the same Act allows the federal cabinet or Defence Minister to authorise the CF to 'perform any duty involving public service'. The section also empowers the cabinet or the minister to authorise CF assistance in any law enforcement matter, provided that it is considered to be in the national interest and cannot be effectively dealt with without CF assistance.
- The *Emergencies Act* confers extraordinary powers on the federal Cabinet, allowing it to govern by decree when it perceives the existence of 'threats to the security of Canada', including acts of serious political violence or activities aimed at overthrowing the system of government.
- The Solicitor General of Canada can, under the National Counter-Terrorism Plan and the Canadian Forces Armed Assistance Directions (CFAAD), call for armed assistance by the CF to respond to terrorist incidents or other disturbances affecting national security.
- The federal government can and does use the military in aid of its own responsibilities, such as guarding federal buildings and facilities.
- Various provisions allow for military assistance for disasters and emergencies.
- Assistance can be requested for the Royal Canadian Mounted Police (RCMP) in penitentiaries and customs enforcement.
- Under the 1996 Canadian Forces Assistance to Provincial Police Forces Directions (CFAPPFD), a Provincial Attorney General can request assistance through the Department of Public Safety and Emergency Preparedness Canada.
- The *Public Safety Act 2002* strengthened the powers of federal anti-terrorism and national security agencies, including the CF, to share critical information.
- As in Britain, martial law may be declared.

It should be noted that previous powers contained in the *War Measures Act* of 1914 were replaced in 1988 by the *Emergencies Act*. The *War Measures Act* conferred extreme powers on the federal government, allowing it to effectively rule by decree when it perceived the existence of 'war, invasion or insurrection, real or apprehended'. During both world wars, the Act was used to issue detailed regulations limiting the freedom of Canadians of foreign descent. The Act was invoked to authorise a military intervention in a domestic crisis in October and November 1970, when a state of 'apprehended insurrection' was declared to exist in Quebec and emergency regulations were proclaimed in response to two kidnappings by the separatist Front de Liberation du Quebec (FLQ).

Despite Canada's recent pacifist reputation, large-scale military interventions have occurred since the 1960s, including the FLQ crisis (1963–70), the 1976 Olympic Games, the Oka standoff (1990) and disaster relief in Manitoba (1997) (Maloney 1997: 135–152). Lesser mobilisations under the CFAPPFD occurred at Davis Inlet (1994), Gustafsen Lake (1995) and Ipperwash Provincial Park (1995) (Haslip 2002: 2). After reviewing these experiences, a Canadian military historian concluded that the mechanisms for military assistance to civilian authorities were 'extremely flexible' and ensured that 'the military is not overburdened with legalities' (Maloney 1997: 145).

The changes made in 2008 to the national defence strategy suggest that operations against civil unrest are likely to become more prevalent in the coming period. Significantly, an 'aid of the civil power' scenario on the CF's Defence Planning and Management web site is based the prospect of economic and social conflicts producing large-scale unrest and armed insurrections:

> Canada has been suffering through several years of drought and across the country water rationing has been enforced. Minor disputes over access to water have become more and more commonplace, pitting individual against individual and individual against industry. As water has grown more and more scarce, the groups involved in disputes have had time to become organized. The affected region has expanded to include the jurisdiction of two provinces. In at least one case a minor dispute has escalated creating large-scale unrest, including armed insurrections. The situation has reached a point where civilian authorities can no longer cope, and military assistance has been requested under Part XI of the National Defence Act.
>
> (Defence Planning and Management 2004)

The web site also refers to a restricted document entitled 'Crowd Confrontation Operations'.

CF's intelligence capacity has expanded in recent years, enhancing its collaboration with domestic intelligence agencies such as the RCMP and the Canadian Security Intelligence Service (CSIS). The Department of National Defence also hosts the Communications Security Establishment (CSE), the national cryptologic and signals intelligence agency, giving the military significant capacities to intercept and monitor telecommunications (Forcese 2008: 75).

National Defence Act

Potentially, the *National Defence Act* (NDA) provisions allow for considerable use of the armed forces to suppress domestic political unrest and dissent. The CF is liable to be called out whenever a 'riot or disturbance of the peace, beyond the powers of the civil authorities to suppress, prevent or deal with' occurs or is, in the opinion of a provincial attorney general, 'likely to occur' (NDA s 275). Considerable discretionary powers are placed in the hands of provincial attorneys general and the CF chief. Once an attorney general makes a written requisition, the Chief of the Defence Staff must call out out the armed forces, and cannot dispute any statement of fact contained in the requisition. Nor can a provincial government call into question the competence or authority of the attorney general's requisition (NDA s 280).

The Chief of the Defence Staff, in turn, has broad powers to call out such parts of the CF that he or she 'considers necessary for the purpose of suppressing or preventing' any riot or disturbance. These powers are exercised independently of the federal government, although they are 'subject to such directions as the [Defence]

Minister considers appropriate in the circumstances' (NDA s 278). Called out CF personnel automatically acquire all the powers of police officers, which include powers of arrest, search and seizure and use of lethal force, as well as whatever powers they hold as soldiers. They are deemed to have 'all of the powers and duties of constables' in addition to 'their powers and duties as officers and non-commissioned members'. However, they 'shall act only as a military body and are individually liable to obey the orders of their superior officers' (NDA s 282). The latter clause could be interpreted as legally requiring troops to obey superior orders, regardless of whether those orders are lawful.

No time limits are set for call outs, which can be scaled up or down at the discretion of the CF chief. The CF will remain on duty, in such strength as the Chief of the Defence Staff deems necessary, until the provincial attorney general notifies that the armed forces are no longer required (NDA s 283).

In addition, s 273.6 of the Act allows the federal cabinet or Defence Minister to authorise the CF to 'perform any duty involving public service'. The section also empowers the cabinet or the minister to authorise CF assistance in 'any law enforcement matter', provided that it is considered to be in the national interest and that it cannot be effectively dealt with without CF assistance. Moreover, the section provides a blanket authorisation for law enforcement assistance 'that is of a minor nature and limited to logistical, technical or administrative support'. Thus, s 273.6 is capable of supporting considerable military involvement in civilian affairs. It creates a wide executive discretion to mobilise the CF without public notice or even parliamentary oversight.

Emergencies Act

The *Emergencies Act* permits the Canadian government to rule by executive orders and regulations in any 'national emergency', which is defined broadly as 'an urgent and critical situation of a temporary nature' that 'seriously endangers the lives, health or safety of Canadians' or 'seriously threatens the ability of the Government of Canada to preserve the sovereignty, security and territorial integrity of Canada'. Four kinds of emergency are provided for: public welfare (natural disasters), public order (internal security), international (external threats to security or territorial integrity) and war (war or other armed conflict, real or imminent). Considerable scope exists for domestic military intervention under the other three headings, but 'public order emergencies' explicitly relate to suppressing certain types of political opposition.

A public order emergency, covered by Part II of the Act, is one that arises from 'threats to the security of Canada' as defined by the *Canadian Security Intelligence Service Act*. Section 2 of that statute refers to espionage, sabotage, foreign influenced activities, 'acts of serious political violence' for the purpose of achieving a 'political, religious or ideological objective' within Canada or a foreign state, and activities 'directed toward or intended ultimately to lead to the destruction or overthrow by violence' of the Canadian system of government. Although the definition exempts 'lawful advocacy, protest or dissent', unless linked to any of the proscribed activities, the section leaves open considerable scope for emergency rule directed against various forms of political dissent, particularly if they can be depicted as potentially violent.

Once a public order emergency has been declared, the Governor in Council (normally on behalf of the federal cabinet) can issue far-reaching orders, including banning public assemblies, stopping travel and seizing control of public services, and imposing summary convictions for up to six months of imprisonment. There are no unlimited search and seizure powers, previously available under the *War Measures Act*, for a public order emergency, but they remain for an international emergency. Emergency powers can last initially for 30 days and be continuously renewed. Ministers and other personnel exercising emergency powers 'in good faith' are protected from personal legal liability, although government liability and compensation remain. Parliamentary scrutiny is weak and belated: either House of Parliament can revoke an emergency declaration, but only after a delay of at least seven sitting days (*Emergencies Act* ss 3, 16–26, 47–48, 58–59).

The statute states that it does not confer on the government the power to detain, imprison or intern Canadian citizens or permanent residents 'on the basis of race, national or ethnic origin, colour, religion, sex, age or mental or physical disability' (*Emergencies Act* s 4). This proviso, however, does not preclude detention on political or ideological grounds, nor does it apply to non-citizens without permanent residency status.

How the Act can be used to trigger military mobilisations can be seen from natural disaster operations. The public welfare emergency provisions of the Act were activated to direct the CF to support provincial and local authorities in the Saguenay floods of 1996, the Manitoba floods of 1997 and the ice storm event of 1998. Because of the lack of adequate civilian emergency services, especially on a national scale, the CF is often depicted as the only agency capable of responding effectively to such calamities (for example, McCluskey 2004). In this way, public opinion is conditioned to accept, and even demand, military interventions.

One limitation on use of the Act, compared with its predecessor, the *War Measures Act*, is that under s 25(3), the Governor in Council cannot declare a public emergency unless requested by a province, or the emergency extends to more than one province. Thus, as with the *National Defence Act*, the power to invoke the emergency powers and call in the troops depends on provincial consent, at least until a wider emergency (beyond a single province) is said to exist. For that reason, there have been calls from within military and police circles for the Act to be amended (Lerhe 2004: 17).

Forcese states that it is doubtful whether the Act could be used, as the *War Measures Act* was in October 1970, to abridge fundamental civil liberties. He explains that the Act's preamble says that the 'special temporary measures' are subject to the *Charter*, the *Canadian Bill of Rights* and 'must have regard to the International Covenant on Civil and Political Rights, particularly with respect to those fundamental rights that are not to be limited or abridged even in a national emergency' (Forcese 2008: 124). However, such preambles are not legally binding and, as previously discussed, the *Charter* and the *Bill of Rights* provide no secure protection of basic rights in the context of an alleged national security emergency.

Forcese acknowledges that the 'fog of war' may cloud the ability of the public and the courts to challenge government actions taken under the banner of an emergency, particularly a political emergency. Forcese cites Ignatieff's warning that emergencies are most corrosive of democracy when they are proclaimed 'on grounds that involve bad faith, manipulation of evidence, exaggeration of risk, or the prospect of political advantage' (Forcese 2008: 116–117). An added difficulty noted by Ignatieff is that the executive invariably claims to hold secret and undisclosable information that justifies the emergency powers (Ignatieff 2004: 51). Referring to the 'war on terror', Ignatieff suggests that 'in a long twilight war, largely fought by secret means, the key issue is maintaining as much legal and legislative oversight as is compatible with the necessity for decisive action' (Ignatieff 2004: 39). However, Ignatieff's proposition leaves open considerable room for a government to argue that the need for 'decisive action' takes precedence over, or is not compatible with, civil liberties and legal scrutiny.

National Counter-Terrorism Plan

The Solicitor General of Canada, under the authority of the Government of Canada, is responsible for the National Counter-Terrorism Plan. The plan establishes lines of communication and policy to guide officials in resolving a terrorist incident. It also describes the authorities and responsibilities of federal departments and agencies in a counter-terrorism situation, and outlines the legislation, conventions and agreements to which Canada is a party. The procedures for employing a military unit in a counter-terrorism situation are also detailed in the National Counter-Terrorism Plan.

The Canadian Forces Armed Assistance Directions (CFAAD) establishes the procedures for the request and provision of armed assistance by the CF to the RCMP to resolve disturbances affecting the national interest. Provisions have also been made to ensure that CF resources can be expeditiously positioned close to the site of a disturbance while the situation is developing, and before any armed assistance is authorized. The CFAAD come into play on the basis of a request by either:

- The Commissioner of the RCMP submitting to the Chief of the Defence Staff for the positioning of a military force in anticipation of a request from the Solicitor General; or
- The Solicitor General of Canada submitting to the Minister of National Defence for the provision of such assistance by the CF to the RCMP, and for the purpose of assisting in suppressing, preventing or otherwise dealing with the disturbance.

CF members engaged in armed assistance activities would be given the status of police officers.

Since 1993, the Canadian Forces have provided the country's federal antiterrorist forces, replacing the RCMP in that function. Joint Task Force 2 (JTF2) is the CF unit responsible for federal counter-terrorist operations. Its mission is to provide

> a force capable of rendering armed assistance in the resolution of an issue or a potential issue that affects national security. While JTF2's primary role is counter-terrorism, its personnel can be employed in any type of military operations, which include, but are not limited to, surveillance, security advice and close personal protection.
>
> (Canadian Forces 2008)

While the unit has a primary focus on counter-terrorism, its roles have expanded over the years and it has likely assumed roles similar to that of the British Special Air Services (SAS) and the United States Delta Force.

The Canadian government has been secretive about releasing any information about the capabilities, organisation and operational missions of the unit. However, some information has appeared (Pugliese 2002). JTF2 states that the year 2001 was an important milestone in its history when the unit was committed to the US-led International Special Operations Forces coalition in Afghanistan. This deployment was the first time that JTF2 was acknowledged to have served in a major combat role outside Canada (Canadian Forces 2008).

Wider use appears to be being made of the JTF2. According to the Canadian Broadcasting Corporation, JTF2 was in Haiti at the time that Haitian president Jean-Bertrand Aristide was ousted from power. The unit protected the Canadian embassy and secured the airport. In 2006, the Pentagon and the British Foreign Office both commented on the instrumental role JTF2 played in rescuing a British and Canadian 'Christian Peacemaker Team' that was being held hostage in Iraq. There has been speculation in the Canadian media on possible JTF2 operational deployments elsewhere, including in conflicts involving native groups in Ontario, Quebec and British Columbia and other domestic security operations.

Military surveillance and intelligence

The CF and Department of National Defence (DND) have significant surveillance and intelligence capacities that can be used domestically. Defence Intelligence performs a variety of functions, including collecting and analysing material in support of CF's deployments, which may be internal. It also cooperates with the civilian security and police agencies, such as the Canadian Security Intelligence Service (CSIS) and the RCMP in the area of domestic intelligence. DND also hosts the Communications Security Establishment (CSE), a signals intelligence agency that has substantial electronic eavesdropping capacities.

In theory, both the CF's SIGINT Operations Centre (CF-SOC) and the CSE are constrained in intercepting purely domestic communications—that is, they are subject to the provisions of the *Criminal Code* and *CSIS Act* that affect the police and CSIS. However, the *National Defence Act* permits the Defence Minister to authorise interceptions of internal communications in order to obtain 'foreign intelligence', and four such authorisations were in place as of 2006. Even in official circles, doubts exist about whether such intercepts are compatible with the *Charter of Rights and Freedoms* (Forcese 2008: 75, 453–463). Former Chief Justice Lamer, in his 2005–6 report as CSE commissioner, complained that 'supporting documentation provided by CSE as part of requests for the Minister's authorization address the underlying foreign intelligence requirements only in general terms' (Forcese 2008: 457).

A brief history and six case studies

Following the acquisition of Canada in 1760, the British army garrison troops replied to requests for 'aid to civil power' in accordance with their military regulations. In 1868 Canadian laws concerning the police, illegal assembly and riots were enacted, and the *Militia Act* authorised calling out Canadian troops. British practice generally remained the model, although Regulations and Orders for the Canadian Militia replaced the British ones in 1870. In 1924 the power of calling out troops was moved from local authorities to provincial attorneys general.

From 1796 to 1870 British troops, occasionally helped by local militiamen, provided aid to the civil power roughly 100 times. Since then Canadian troops have helped maintain or restore public order 140 times and have helped repress penitentiary riots 20 times. Half the former occurred before 1900, usually because of absence, shortage or improper training of police.

During the years before and after World War I, soldiers were mobilised whenever strikes threatened the established order. In the words of two prominent labour historians: 'When strikes took the form of mass unrest involving unskilled workers, troops were deployed.' And during 1906, the use of military force 'spiked dramatically', when the troops were called out four times in 1906 to deal with mass strikes by unskilled workers (Fudge and Tucker 2004: 18, 49)

The most notable strike of this period was the Winnipeg general strike of 1919. The 21 June confrontation with the Mounties and soldiers, following earlier arrests and confiscation of documents, resulted in 30 casualties, including one death. However, the use of troops was not confined to Winnipeg; they were also mobilised during the subsequent Vancouver general strike, against Quebec textile workers in 1920, coal miners in St Johns and Halifax in 1922, Sydney steelworkers in 1923 and Nova Scotia miners in 1925 (Heron 1998: 35–36, 67–68, 113).

Since 1933, troops have not been involved in strikebreaking except under the *War Measures Act* (now the *Emergencies Act*) and all call outs except one have taken place in Ontario and Quebec, which are the only provinces not policed by the RCMP. Over half the penitentiary call outs have occurred since 1962, and in most cases the army did not have to use force. On five occasions, troops have been used against Aboriginal peoples, from the Red River Rebellion of 1870 to Oka in 1990 (Haslip 2002: 4).

During the late 1990s and the early years of the twenty-first century, with the development of substantial anti-globalisation and anti-capitalist demonstrations against summits of world leaders, the CF was mobilised regularly to assist police in preventing or suppressing protests at such gatherings. For the 2001 Summit of the Americas in Quebec City, some 1,200 CF personnel joined 6,700 police and hundreds of customs officers in the security operation, with another 3,000 soldiers on standby at nearby CF bases. Heavily armed police used tear gas, water cannon and rubber bullets, with CF troops maintaining a support role (Legras 2001). The 2002 G-8 summit in Alberta saw the largest homeland mobilisation of troops since the 1970 FLQ crisis. More than 6,000 CF personnel and 4,500 police were deployed to enforce a 6.5-kilometre no-go zone around the summit venue, while three anti-aircraft missile batteries were set up and CF-18 fighter jets policed a 150-kilometre no-fly zone (Adelaide 2002).

Six case studies underline the broad scope for military intervention against domestic unrest.

Quebec crisis 1963–1970

The Quebec crisis, which began in 1963, ultimately involved several simultaneous military operations, each relying on a different legal mechanism. The Front de Liberation du Quebec (FLQ) began a bombing campaign in 1963, with a view to galvanising support for separatism. At that point, the provincial government explored with regional army commanders the possibility of deploying troops. The army commander advised that military intervention would only spread FLQ activity beyond Montreal and that if troops were wanted, a formal request would have to be made for Aid of the Civil Power. No such request was made in 1963, but two were made in 1969 after a further spate of bombings and a substantial pro-FLQ protest in Montreal. On the first occasion in March, a mechanised infantry battalion was deployed to back up police, although its services were not required to disperse the protest. In October, during a civil service and police strike, a battalion was again mobilised on standby, while troops protected federal facilities and conducted mobile patrols (Maloney 1997: 138–139).

In 1970, after the FLQ kidnapped a Quebec minister, the provincial Premier asked Prime Minister Trudeau to invoke the *War Measures Act* and 'send in the army'. Trudeau, however, would only agree to a formal Aid of the Civil Power request under the *National Defence Act*. While the Premier apparently vacillated for several days, the army chief drew up a plan for intervention, codenamed Operation Essay, should the Quebec government request it. In the meantime, the federal government, through the office of the Solicitor General, requested military assistance for the RCMP to secure federal government buildings in Ottawa, provide armed escorts for federal officials and provide a quick reaction force. Codenamed Operation Ginger, this deployment involved 1,000 soldiers. Once the Quebec Attorney General formally requested military aid, some 9,000 troops were placed on alert or dispatched to about 150 sites designated for protection.

After a Cabinet debate, Trudeau then went further, invoking the emergency powers of the *War Measures Act*. Trudeau's view was that the *National Defence Act* provisions were too restrictive, because they did not cross provincial boundaries (Maloney 1997: 138–139).

Under the emergency regulations, the FLQ was declared an illegal organisation, normal liberties were suspended, and arrests and detentions were authorised without charge. Ultimately more than 12,000 troops were deployed in full battle order for a massive show of force to the citizens of Montreal. Airborne forces were brought in to conduct special operations, while soldiers conducted cordon and search operations jointly with Quebec provincial police. Over 450 people were detained in Québec, most of whom were eventually released without the laying of charges.

In all, ten shots were fired, all warnings, without casualties. It could easily have been worse. At one point, Trudeau directed the Vice Chief of Defence Staff to place 'tanks on all the bridges in Montreal and men all over the city to show these pipsqueaks who has the power'. When troops arrived in Ottawa without Rules of Engagement and sought advice from the RCMP on what to do when approached by unknown individuals, they were told 'shoot them, but let us know afterwards so we can clean up the situation' (Lerhe 2004: 10).

The 1970 crisis demonstrated the potential for political misuse of, or interference in, domestic military mobilisations. It also revealed the real danger of fatalities, as well as drastic infringements on civil liberties. In response to criticism, Trudeau later pledged to refine and limit the application of the Act. The Act had not been modified by the time his government was defeated in 1984, but in 1988, the *Emergencies Act* was passed to replace the *War Measures Act* (Lerhe 2004: 11).

1976 Olympic Games

For the 1976 Montreal Olympics, federal Cabinet decided that the legal way to mobilise military support was to have the Solicitor General formally ask the National Defence Minister to provide assistance to the civil authority. In other words, the action was envisaged as preventative, rather than active and involving Aid of the Civil Power. Nevertheless, preparations were made for armed intervention if judged necessary. CF tasks included VIP and site security at all Games venues, and armed response to any situation that developed. The training 'threat scenarios' included demonstrations as well as acts of terrorism. The military deployment, some 16,000 personnel, was deliberately large, designed to act as a visible deterrent. Soldiers carried small arms, but were not in full battle dress as they had been in 1970. Jets and helicopters enforced no-fly zones. However, there were no specific terrorist threats to the Games and no incidents eventuated (Maloney 1997: 140–141).

The 1990 Oka standoff

In 1990, the Quebec government requested aid of the civil power under the *National Defence Act* to dismantle barricades at Oka and Kanewake in Montreal erected by indigenous people, organised by the 'Mohawk warriors', who were protesting against a proposal to extend a golf course across a former burial ground. A small number of protestors, estimated at 50 to 70, were armed. More than 4,400 soldiers and 12 army battalions, including tanks, were deployed in another show of force. Operation Salon was assigned four tasks: remove barricades, restore freedom of movement, remove strong points and restore public order and security. The last task was particularly vague and open to broad interpretation.

Intensive operations ensued, including frequent night patrols, low-level helicopter flights, surveillance aircraft and well-aimed spotlight, some designed to unhinge the insurgents psychologically. Armoured personnel carriers were used to intimidate the indigenous activists into dismantling the barricades (Maloney 1997: 142–144).

Although, the mobilisation was requisitioned by the provincial government, in accordance with the Act, the federal Prime Minister signalled that the army would take over the barricades. This intervention cut across the legal procedure, whereby the Chief of Defence Staff (CDS) was meant to respond directly to the provincial Attorney General. During the operation, the CDS sat in on national Cabinet meetings, underscoring both the political involvement of the federal government and the close integration of the military high command into the civilian executive. Media releases were also placed under tight political control (Lerhe 2004: 11–12).

The 1997 Red River Flood and 1998 ice storm

Two military mobilisations of unprecedented magnitude occurred in 1997 and 1998 in response to natural disasters. A public welfare emergency was declared in 1997 to authorise the deployment of military personnel, and the Manitoba Premier also subsequently formally requested assistance to the civil authority. More than 8,500 soldiers, sailors and airmen participated. The floods were fought in battlefield style, complete with reconnaissance aircraft, ground units, satellite tracking, strategic airlift, military police controlling movements and armed units combatting looting (Maloney 1997: 144–145).

For the 1998 ice storm that struck a major portion of Quebec and southern Ontario, the federal government mobilised 12,000 troops, the largest such deployment in Canadian peacetime history. The operation revealed the deterioration of civilian emergency services and public utilities, such as Hydro-Quebec (Legras 1998).

The 1990s Somalia Affair

Although it was not a domestic deployment, during the mid-1990s, the Somalia Affair highlighted the propensity for military operations against civilians to lead to abuses, particularly when governments authorise aggressive conduct. The CF deployment to Somalia for a US-led mission—Operation Restore Hope—ostensibly for peacekeeping and humanitarian purposes, led to one local teenager, Shidane Arone, being tortured to death by Canadian soldiers, and two Somalis being shot in the back, one fatally. After grisly photos of Arone's torture were leaked to the media, causing public revulsion, the government felt compelled to conduct an official inquiry. Although the inquiry was later controversially cut short, evidence to the inquiry showed that Lieutenant-Colonel Matthieu authorised deadly force against unarmed Somalis inside the Airborne Regiment's compound, exceeding the Rules of Engagement (ROE). To justify his orders, Matthieu cited well-publicised comments of Foreign Affairs Minister Barbara McDougall who 'boasted that soldiers going to Somalia had been provided with ROE that permitted them to shoot first and ask questions later' (Lerhe 2004: 19, citing Canada 1997: 659–660).

G8/G7 summits in 2002 and 2018

Gatherings of world leaders have been used to accustom the public to internal military mobilisations, featuring 'no-go' security zones. In 2002, the G8 summit convened in Kananaskis County, Alberta, became the object of one of the largest domestic security operations in Canadian history. More than 6,000 CF personnel and 4,500 police were deployed in Kananaskis and the city of Calgary, about 100 kilometres from the summit site. A 6.5-kilometre no-go zone was established around Kananaskis Village and three anti-aircraft missile batteries set up, as a last line of defence should a plane evade the CF-18 fighters that enforced a 150-kilometre radius no-fly zone. The only road through Kananaskis County was blocked with security checkpoints (Adelaide 2002).

In preparation for the summit, the Chrétien government introduced legislation in 2001 to amend the *National Defence Act* to allow the Defence Minister to declare any area of land, water or air a 'military security zone'. In effect, the law would have provided another mechanism for domestic military intervention, and given the armed forces considerable powers over civilians. Such zones could have been declared in relation to, inter alia, 'property, a place or thing that the Canadian Forces have been directed to protect in order to fulfil a duty required by law'. The CF could 'prohibit, restrict or control access' to a zone, and 'forcibly remove' any person or vehicle found in the zone without authorisation (Bill C-42 (2001)). After considerable public outcry, the provision was withdrawn (Privacy Commissioner 2002).

In 2018, Prime Minister Justin Trudeau's government mounted another large police-military operation around the G7 summit in La Malbaie, a small municipality in Charlevoix County, 150 kilometres east of Quebec City. An Integrated Security Unit (ISU) was established, composed of 8,000 personnel from the CF, the RCMP, the Sûreté du Québec (the Quebec Provincial Police) and the municipal police of Quebec City.

Canadian authorities transformed the Manoir Richelieu into a fortress for the event. The hotel was at the heart of a security 'red zone' that was bounded by a 3.7-kilometre-long, 6-metre-high fence, sporting numerous surveillance cameras. The red zone was located within a 20-square-kilometre 'green zone', which included Route 362, the main road to La Malbaie, which was partially fenced off. A maritime and air exclusion zone, with a radius of 20 kilometres, was imposed by the CF, which requisitioned the nearby Charlevoix county airport (Girard 2018).

Conclusion

In line with the developments across the border in the United States, a major shift has occurred in Canada's military stance and capacity-building, for both overseas and domestic deployment, since 2001. Alongside the dispatch of thousands of troops to front-line fighting in Afghanistan, a dedicated Canadian Command has been established to make internal security a major function of the CF, matching and closely coordinating with the US Northern Command.

While the Canadian Constitution embodies a civil–military and federal–provincial demarcation, there are no explicit guarantees in the *Constitution Act*, the *Bill of Rights* or the *Charter of Rights and Freedoms* prohibiting or restricting the use of troops against domestic civilians. Moreover, a variety of legal avenues exist for mobilising the military internally.

Finally, there are good reasons for concern that any serious political disaffection or social unrest in the coming period will be met by military force, and indeed CF 'aid of the civil power' training scenarios suggest that preparations are being made precisely for such eventualities. Both the 1970 Quebec crisis and the 1990s Somalia affair reveal how easily such interventions could lead to civilian fatalities, as well as far-reaching violations of fundamental civil liberties.

6 Britain

Preparing for disruption

Despite the historical taboo, derived from the Magna Carta and the English Revolution, on using the military against civilians, the armed forces have been frequently mobilised to deal with civil and industrial unrest in the United Kingdom, particularly at times of heightened social and class tensions. Military interventions may well be associated by members of the public with dictatorships, not democracies, but as reviewed in Chapter 3 British history is replete with examples of troops being called out to put down riots, disturbances, protests and strikes.

Although this pattern appeared to recede after the early years of the twentieth century, with the rise of substantial and increasingly heavily armed police forces, the military option has been kept open, ready for use in times of crisis. Indeed, there is a view that the British military has an inherent and essential role in securing the state against internal political disaffection. One scholar of the subject has argued that 'It is a truism that the function of an army is to defend the state' and '[D]omestic security is an inescapable responsibility for any army. The "defence of the state" must include the capability to assist in the maintenance of public order and the suppression of internal unrest, insurrection or even revolution' (Jeffery 1985: 51).

During the twenty-first century, the militarisation of internal security forces developed at a rapid pace, first in the adoption of substantial new legal powers and then in initial displays of the use of these powers. As in other jurisdictions, the initial official explanation for these measures was the threat of terrorism, but the powers extend much further.

Brexit and Operation Yellowhammer

By 2018–19, the military call-out operations had gone so far as to prepare for unspecified economic and social disruption if Brexit negotiations with the European Union (EU) were to break down. After a Cabinet meeting in December 2018, Prime Minister Theresa May's official spokesman said ministers agreed that an emergency contingency plan was essential in case parliament rejected her proposed deal with her European counterparts for Britain's exit from the EU.

The announcement came in the context of a severe crisis of May's government and deep splits more broadly within the financial elite and political establishment over Brexit. Following the narrow 2016 referendum vote to leave the EU, the government originally committed the UK to exit the EU on 29 March 2019, but that deadline proved impossible to meet.

In announcing the emergency plan, Defence Secretary Gavin Williamson told the House of Commons that 3,500 troops would be ready to support the government in case of a 'no-deal' Brexit. 'We've as yet not had any formal request from any government department but what we are doing is putting contingency plans in place,' Williamson told the Commons. 'What we will do is have 3,500 service personnel held at readiness—including regulars and reserves—in order to support any government department on any contingencies they may need' (Britton 2018).

The Ministry of Defence later confirmed the troops would be put on alert in addition to 5,000 already on standby to deal with potential terror attacks (Watts 2018). This pointed to a broader plan for military mobilisations, beyond the pretext of protecting the public from terrorism.

According to a little-publicised official report, 10,000 military personnel had been available on standby since 2015 to assist the civil authorities for 'significant terrorist incidents at short notice'. The government had announced that shift in its *National Security Strategy and Strategic Defence and Security Review*, released in November 2015. These personnel were 'supported by a wide range of niche military experts and equipment, such as bomb disposal specialists' (UK government 2015: para 4.98).

By early 2019, it was reported that far larger numbers of troops would be prepared for deployment in the event of a crisis over Brexit. Junior Defence Minister Tobias Elwood was cited as saying 50,000 soldiers had to be readied for deployment on Britain's streets in the event of a 'no-deal' Brexit. The *Times* reported: 'Ministers at a no-deal Brexit planning meeting on Thursday [3 January] were told that 30,000 regular troops and 20,000 reserves must be ready to help manage the consequences' (Coates 2019).

Elwood was reported as warning that the troops had to be in place 'in case of civil unrest, to assist at Britain's airports and to ensure fuel and medical supplies'. This indicates plans to suppress industrial action and other forms of opposition. The source reported that Elwood 'suggested that fellow ministers should remember what happened in the fuel blockade in 2000 [when troops were used to protect fuel deliveries] and plan for that kind of thing on a mass scale' (Coates 2019).

Such a mobilisation would be extraordinary in size. Fifty thousand soldiers would be close to half the then size of the British Army, which stood at 81,500 regulars and just over 27,000 reservists. It was more than the force sent by the British government to Iraq in 2003 as part of the US-led invasion.

In March 2019, as the Brexit deadline loomed, the government announced that extraordinary powers would be introduced through its 'Operation Yellowhammer' 'command and control' contingency plans for a 'no-deal' exit from the EU. The government's COBRA committee, which is convened under conditions of national emergency, would be empowered to deal with all no-deal preparations, including having troops on standby. The military dimension of the crisis management operation—dubbed Operation Redfold—would operate from a bunker underneath the main Ministry of Defence building in London's Whitehall (Stevens 2019; BBC 2019).

The operation would allow sweeping powers embodied in the *Civil Contingencies Act 2004* to be activated. In January, the *Times* had revealed that scenarios for martial law were being considered and that 'curfews, bans on travel, confiscation of property [and] deployment of the armed forces to quell rioting are among the measures available to ministers' (Stevens 2019).

Troops on the streets: Operation Temperer

Eighteen months before the Brexit crisis, almost 1,000 troops were mobilised on British streets in May 2017 in a public show of military force, purportedly in response to a Manchester bomb attack. That mobilisation partially revealed what had been, until then, semi-secret plans for large-scale domestic deployments. Significantly, no attempt was made by the government to explain the exact legal basis for this dramatic deployment, pointing to an assumption of unchallengeable power to mobilise the military within the country.

British people were suddenly confronted by the sight of heavily armed soldiers at prominent locations in London, the capital, and other sensitive sites. *The Telegraph* reported:

> Soldiers, armed with SA80 rifles, from the Parachute Regiment, Royal Artillery and foot guards regiments could be seen in London. Small numbers of Royal Marines and RAF police are also deployed. As troops took up position at London tourist locations, visitors said the sight of soldiers in camouflage, carrying rifles was reassuring.
>
> (Farmer 2017)

Despite *The Telegraph's* insistence that the appearance of troops was 'reassuring' for visitors, it marked a substantial shift in British society and government policy. It was the first public manifestation of an underlying turn toward the elevation of the military into a frontline role in dealing with officially perceived threats to domestic order or stability.

According to the same media report, the Army said no date had been set to pull troops back to barracks after soldiers took on guarding duties at high-profile buildings, including Parliament, the Prime Minister's office at Downing Street, the royal Buckingham Palace, embassies and the Sellafield nuclear facility on the country's northwest coast.

The website *Warfare.Today* identified the military deployment as involving units from the Foot Guards, the 2nd Battalion, the Parachute Regiment (2 PARA) and the Royal Artillery, with additional assistance expected from the Royal Marines, the RAF Regiment and the RAF police (Warfare.Today 2017).

Prime Minister May's government announced that a total of 3,800 troops were available after the government triggered a previously little-known Operation

Temperer contingency plan. The government simultaneously raised the official terrorism threat level to its highest level for the first time in a decade (Farmer 2017).

The Scottish Government confirmed military personnel would guard 12 sites north of the border, including nuclear installations. West Yorkshire police also confirmed it had requested troops (Farmer 2017).

It was widely reported that this was the first time that Operation Temperer had been put into effect. The previous time uniformed British soldiers had been deployed in the UK was in 2003 when then Prime Minister Tony Blair authorised the deployment of 450 soldiers to Heathrow Airport.

However, Operation Temperer had been partly activated following a 2016 terrorist attack in Brussels, according to media reports. Special Forces units had been deployed covertly and armed response units put on high readiness.

Operation Temperer had been formulated secretly in 2015 in response to the perceived threat level following the January 2015 Île-de-France terrorist shootings, including the attack on the offices of Charlie Hebdo in Paris, that left 17 dead and 22 wounded. The British plan would follow the example of the French government, which sent 10,000 troops onto the streets of Paris and elsewhere around the country after those attacks. The UK version reportedly provided for up to 5,100 service personnel from all three services to be deployed to 'augment armed police officers engaged in protective security duties' at key sites across the country (Rayner 2017).

According to government sources cited by *The Telegraph*, Operation Temperer would be triggered only following a meeting of COBRA, a cabinet committee chaired by the Home Secretary (Gosden 2015). That places extraordinary and legally ill-defined power in the hands of a small number of political, intelligence, police and military officials.

Moreover, the plan was intended to be kept secret, but was disclosed in July 2015 after accidentally being uploaded to the National Police Chiefs Council website. Police spokespersons described the blueprint as routine contingency planning, but Baroness Jones, a member of London's Police and Crime Committee, told *The Telegraph* it would be 'unprecedented on mainland Britain' (Gosden 2015).

The plan was also said to be contentious with the Army leadership, due to concerns about it causing overstretch, morale problems and difficulties with deciding when to end operations. Prime Minister David Cameron had reportedly put the British Army on standby after the Charlie Hebdo attack but in the end accepted the arguments against deployment. The issue was discussed at meetings of COBRA, 'the government crisis group which brings ministers together with senior military and security staff' (MacAskill 2015).

Operation Temperer was activated again on 15 September 2017 when the government once more raised its terrorist threat level to critical in the aftermath of a bombing at London's Parsons Green Underground station, with military personnel replacing police officers on armed guarding duties.

An underlying shift

As explored in Chapter 3 on the troubled historical record, the British armed forces previously have been mobilised domestically against civilians, most notably in Northern Ireland when 21,000 troops were deployed to back the Royal Ulster Constabulary in Operation Banner, with bloody results. More recently, in 2003, Prime Minister Tony Blair's Labour government deployed 450 troops to Heathrow and other London locations during a terrorist alert (MacAskill 2015).

However, domestic military activities have intensified. According to a 2017 House of Commons Library Briefing Paper, 'Military Aid to the Civil Authorities' (MACA) occurred more than 80 times in 2016–17. This meant that military deployments of various kinds were occurring, on average, almost twice a week. The numbers came from the Ministry of Defence's Annual Report and Accounts, accompanied by examples of activities, including explosive ordnance disposal and support to counter-terrorism operations (Brooke-Holland 2017: 3).

No breakdown was provided as to which categories of MACA were activated. In the past MACA has been subdivided into three different categories—Military Aid to other Government Departments (MAGD), Military Aid to the Civil Power (MACP) and Military Aid to the Civil Community (MACC) (Brooke-Holland 2017: 1). Generally, only MACP operations have involved the use of potentially lethal force.

A House of Commons Library Briefing Paper asked the question: 'What is the legal basis?' The answer was sketchy:

> The legal authority to use Service personnel in operations under Military Aid to the Civil Authorities (MACA) is governed by the Civil Contingencies Act 2004 and the Emergency Powers Act 1964 (Section 2). In addition, service personnel can deploy under the Royal Prerogative for military tasks.
>
> (Brooke-Holland 2017: 2)

These powers are explored later in this chapter. The briefing paper said MACA 'had long been identified as one of the standing home tasks of the armed forces'. As evidence, it said:

> This was stated in the 2010 Strategic Defence and Security Review (Cm 7953) and again in the 2015 National Security Strategy and Strategic Defence and Security Review (Cm 9161). The 2015 SDSR set the armed forces eight missions, the first of which is: defend and contribute to the security resilience of the UK and Overseas Territories. This explicitly includes supporting the UK civil authorities in strengthening resilience. A policy review of MACA was published by the Government in February 2016 and in 2017 a new edition of Joint Doctrine Publication 02 UK Operations: the Defence Contribution to Resilience and Security, was published incorporating the main elements of the policy review. One of the key developments is greater involvement of Defence in planning for rather than simply responding to civil contingencies.
>
> (Brooke-Holland 2017: 2)

This outline suggests that, even if 'long identified' as a military task, a marked shift has been taking place in preparations for wider use of the military for 'security resilience', which would also mean suppressing civil unrest. The briefing paper stated:

> Defence is no longer considered a 'last resort option', the Vice Chief of the Defence Staff has said; rather 'defence should be ready and configured to play an early role in providing civil resilience. This was formalised in the 2015 Strategic Defence and Security Review which announced military planners are to be placed in key government departments to give the military a 'wider and more formal role in supporting national resilience contingency planning'.
>
> (Brooke-Holland 2017: 3)

A 2018 report on the Ministry of Defence's 'Modernising Defence Programme' further underlined the ongoing development of the military's domestic role. It stated:

> Defence is working ever more closely with our intelligence agencies and the National Crime Agency to deter and disrupt hostile state activity, and to deal with threats posed by organised crime. At home and overseas, we support the Home Office in delivering the Government's counterterrorism strategy, CONTEST. We provide specialist manpower to help deal with domestic contingencies, from flooding and severe weather to chemical weapons attacks.
>
> (Ministry of Defence 2018: 18)

Among the 25 tasks that 'Defence fulfils to help deliver the National Security Objectives' were three with explicit domestic aspects:

- Contribute to the resilience of the UK by supporting civil contingency operations and the protection of Defence's critical national infrastructure and cyber space
- Hold forces at readiness to support and conduct counter terrorism operations in the UK
- Contribute to the resilience of the UK by supporting the protection of non-Defence critical national infrastructure and cyber space.

(Ministry of Defence 2018: 19)

Military parades, featuring soldiers in full battle gear who had returned from overseas deployments, such as in Afghanistan and Iraq, also became a feature of life during the st century. In September 2018, for instance, several hundred soldiers from The Black Watch, 3rd Battalion of The Royal Regiment of Scotland marched through the streets of Inverness. The battalion had recently returned from a six-month tour in Iraq. In a series of homecoming parades, the battalion marched over four successive days through towns and cities in Black Watch's traditional recruiting areas, including Forfar, Dunfermline and Perth (Scripps 2018).

In a graphic display of firepower, soldiers on the marches wore body armour and carried assault rifles with bayonets attached. Some wore camouflage and carried sniper rifles. The soldiers marched alongside several large armoured vehicles equipped with manned, high-calibre machine guns.

Many of these demonstrations across the UK have been held in connection with the awarding of the 'freedom' of a city, town or borough to a particular regiment. These awards give the military units the right to 'march with drums beating, bands playing, colours flying and bayonets fixed' through the streets of the town. By 2018, roughly 640 such 'freedoms' had been awarded—at least 280 of which had been given since 2008 (Scripps 2018).

The British people were being inured to the regular presence of the armed forces on the streets. These displays served to glorify the military after years of widespread anti-war sentiment, especially since the widely opposed and rapidly discredited US-led invasion of Iraq in 2003. The parades and ceremonies were designed to create bonds between local populations and 'their' regiments.

A manufactured political climate

There are several indicators, including the political climate created by the 'war on terrorism' and the introduction of far-reaching emergency powers in the *Civil Contingencies Act 2004*, that preparations are being made for greater recourse to military operations to 'maintain public order' and 'suppress internal unrest'. The British government has been an active participant in US-led military interventions since 2001, sending the second largest contingents of troops to both Afghanistan and Iraq. British soldiers have been in the frontlines of house-to-house combat and patrolling of urban populations in both countries. Alongside this turn to military aggression have come moves to facilitate a greater military presence and role domestically.

In late 2008, the British government decided, in response to an official report (Report of Inquiry 2008), to launch a campaign to boost public recognition and support for the military. Among the proposals was an annual day to recognise and celebrate the work of the Armed Forces community. Another plan was that military servicemen and women be ordered to wear their uniforms in public as often as they could to help raise the profile of the armed forces. While officers would stop short of ordering personnel to wear uniform in public, they would be told to do so 'in all appropriate circumstances' including travelling to and from work on public transport, and at formal and semi-formal public events (Hickley 2008).

It seems that the report and recommendations arose from concerns expressed in media and official circles about public sentiment toward the military, largely because of the catastrophic wars in Afghanistan and Iraq, and about discrimination against members of the Armed Services. There also appeared to be a broader purpose of bolstering the military in the eyes of the public. The package of measures came 'amid growing concerns that many people in Britain know very little about the armed forces—despite their courage and sacrifice in recent wars—and often do not treat them with the respect they deserve' (Hickley 2008).

During 2007, a White Paper on constitutional reform was published that included a proposal to require parliamentary approval for military deployments abroad (Ministry of Justice 2007). Arguably, this particular proposition was a move to legitimise and legalise war-making decisions because of the controversies surrounding the decisions to join the wars in Afghanistan and Iraq. These engagements had been launched, without any parliamentary vote, let alone public plebiscite, under the royal prerogative, said to be personally exercisable by the Prime Minister. One of the prime movers behind the proposal, Conservative Party shadow minister William Hague, wrote in the *Guardian* on 15 May, 2007: 'The decision to go to war requires democratic legitimacy—so we must strengthen parliament's ability to challenge the executive on this matter' (Hague 2007).

The proposed parliamentary resolution was quite limited, with exceptions for 'emergencies' and 'national security' concerns, as well as for all Special Forces-led operations. These exceptions would cover many recent British military interventions, in which the Special Forces have been given the leading role. At the same time, the White Paper on constitutional reform made no specific mention of reducing or defining the scope of the royal prerogative power to deploy the armed forces domestically. That is, there was a contrast between the recommendations regarding external and internal use of the armed forces. The broader uncodified and vague conventions surrounding the prerogative powers were to be reviewed at some time in the future (Ministry of Justice 2007: 62).

Bitter experiences

Even before the post-9/11 period, the twentieth century had seen military mobilisations during industrial and political crises. The *Emergency Powers Act 1920* gave the United Kingdom government power to declare an emergency by proclamation in certain circumstances. These provisions were invoked 12 times during industrial and political unrest, notably during the 1926 general strike and the 1970–74 period of discontent that eventually led to the defeat of the Heath government (Walker and Broderick 2006: 39).

After the 1926 general strike, Military Aid to Civil Power (MACP) provisions were invoked formally only once during the twentieth century, during the 1980 siege of the Iranian Embassy in London. However, guards battalions were put on alert, though not used, during the 'Hunger Marches' of the 1930s Great Depression. Plainclothes units of the Special Air Services (SAS) and Royal Military Police undertook patrols within England against the Irish Republican Army (IRA) in the 1970s. In 1974, there were four highly publicised but unexplained joint police/military 'exercises' at London's Heathrow Airport shortly before the Heath government resigned (Jeffery 1985: 65).

As reviewed in Chapter 3, the latter part of the twentieth century was indelibly stained by a protracted and disastrous attempt to utilise military force to end civil conflict and resistance to British rule in Northern Ireland. Two decades of army deployment against alleged 'terrorist' opponents of British control produced numerous instances in which civilians were killed by troops. By 1998, more than

3,000 people, civilians as well as soldiers, police and prison officers, had lost their lives over 26 years. The toll included the infamous 'Bloody Sunday' events of 30 January 1972. During a disturbance in Londonderry following a civil rights march, shots were fired by the British Army. Thirteen people were killed and another 13 were wounded, one of whom subsequently died (Bloody Sunday Inquiry).

Despite these bloody experiences in Ireland, 2004 saw the adoption of legislation that potentially expands the scope for domestic military intervention, in the name of responding to emergencies. The *Civil Contingencies Act 2004* effectively replaced the Emergency Powers and Civil Defence legislation (Walker and Broderick 2006: 63–80, 153–188). It empowered 'Her Majesty' by an Order in Council (in ordinary times, this means the senior cabinet ministers) to issue sweeping emergency regulations in any event that 'threatens serious damage to human welfare' or 'serious damage to the environment' or 'war or terrorism, which threatens serious damage to the security of the United Kingdom' (s 19). These regulations can, inter alia, 'enable the Defence Council to authorise the deployment of Her Majesty's armed forces' and 'make provision (which may include conferring powers in relation to property) for facilitating any deployment of Her Majesty's armed forces' (s 22(3)(l) and (m)). The meaning and significance of these provisions are considered below.

Legal mechanisms for intervention

Current government and military policy assumes that considerable powers exist to mobilise armed troops internally to deal with a variety of threats to 'public safety' or 'order'. The 2005 Ministry of Defence document, *Operations in the UK, The Defence Contribution to Resilience*, set out policy guidelines for MACP. It stated:

> Based under common law, MACP is the provision of military assistance (armed if appropriate) to the Civil Power in its maintenance of law, order and public safety, using specialist capabilities or equipment, in situations beyond the capability of the Civil Power.
>
> (Ministry of Defence 2005: 4-1)

According to the guidelines, the legal basis for instructing Armed Forces personnel to provide MACP in the UK can be one, or a combination, of the following:

- Section 2 of the *Emergency Powers Act 1964* (plus the *Emergency Powers (Amendment) Act (Northern Ireland) 1964*) enables the Defence Council to issue instructions to undertake 'work of urgent national importance';
- Part 2 of the *Civil Contingencies Act 2004* empowers the Queen or a Senior Minister, in particular circumstances, to issue emergency regulations which can in turn enable the Defence Council to deploy the Armed Forces;
- A common law tenet indicates that citizens should provide reasonable support to the police if requested to do so. All members of the Armed Forces have a duty to provide the support normally expected of the ordinary citizen. The

same common law tenet enables a Defence Minister to direct the Armed Forces, on a case by case basis, to provide specialist support to the police.

- Queen's Regulations place an additional duty on military commanders to act on their own responsibility without a request by a civil agency where 'in exceptional circumstances, a grave and sudden emergency has arisen, which in the opinion of the Commander demands his immediate intervention to protect life or property'.

Thus, the guidelines assume or assert that alongside specific statutory provisions, there are potentially far-reaching common law and prerogative or executive powers to justify armed interventions. These can be invoked to deal with 'a varying range of criminal and malicious activities'. The request procedures envisage MACP operations for criminal investigations and major events (Ministry of Defence 2005: 4-2, 4B-2).

Significantly, the document sets out a long list of authorities considered to be a 'Civil Power' that can ask for military aid. A Civil Power is loosely defined as a 'civil authority that has constitutional or statutory responsibility for the maintenance of law and order'. The Civil Power is said to include not just government ministers and police forces but also the security and intelligence services, the Government Communications Headquarters (GCHQ), customs, coastguard and serious crimes agencies, and maritime, rail and air accident investigation branches.

The Ministry of Defence suggests that the *Emergency Powers Act* and the *Civil Contingencies Act* 'provide a stronger basis for' MACP activity than the common law. It insists that the common law imposes a duty on every citizen, including service personnel, to assist in the enforcement of law and order when requested, where it is reasonable to do so, and that this requirement forms the 'main basis for the MACP mechanism'. However, the guidelines state that this duty is 'difficult to formulate and cannot be relied upon in all circumstances to provide a legal basis for a response, especially if commanders use it without Defence Council authorisation' (Ministry of Defence 2005: 4-2).

Civil Contingencies Act

Under the *Civil Contingencies Act*, emergency powers can be triggered whenever the governing authorities, namely Her Majesty in Council, are 'satisfied' that an emergency has occurred, is occurring or is about to occur. The regulations can suspend, modify or override any other Act of Parliament, with the sole exception of the *Human Rights Act* (Walker and Broderick 2006: 44–45). Even statutes regarded as essential to civil liberties and basic constitutional rights, such as the *Magna Carta 1297*, the *Bill of Rights 1688*, the *Parliament Acts 1911–49* and the *Representation of the People Act 1983*, can be swept aside (Walker and Broderick 2006: 192). Regulations can last for up to 30 days, and can be renewed. They must be laid before parliament 'as soon as is reasonably practicable' and shall lapse after seven days unless both houses of parliament approve them, but in the meantime their effect is immediate. Moreover, even these limited provisions would mean little if parliament could not or did not meet.

Section 19 of the Act defines 'emergency' as follows:

1 In this Part 'emergency' means—

a an event or situation which threatens serious damage to human welfare in the United Kingdom or in a Part or region,
b an event or situation which threatens serious damage to the environment of the United Kingdom or of a Part or region, or
c war, or terrorism, which threatens serious damage to the security of the United Kingdom.

2 For the purposes of subsection (1)(a) an event or situation threatens damage to human welfare only if it involves, causes or may cause—

a loss of human life,
b human illness or injury,
c homelessness,
d damage to property,
e disruption of a supply of money, food, water, energy or fuel,
f disruption of a system of communication,
g disruption of facilities for transport, or
h disruption of services relating to health.

This definition covers a very wide range of circumstances, far beyond any perceived threat to human life. Moreover, sub-sections (4) and (5) permit the Secretary of State to rule whether an event or situation poses a threat to human welfare, and to amend the Act itself, subject to subsequent parliamentary approval. These sub-sections stated:

1 The Secretary of State may by order amend subsection (2) so as to provide that in so far as an event or situation involves or causes disruption of a specified supply, system, facility or service—

a it is to be treated as threatening damage to human welfare, or
b it is no longer to be treated as threatening damage to human welfare.

2 An order under subsection (4)—

a may make consequential amendment of this Part, and
b may not be made unless a draft has been laid before, and approved by resolution of, each House of Parliament.

Although the Blair government presented the Act as one concerned primarily with responding to disasters, the 2003 Queen's Speech specifically referred to terrorism, and the proposal was also driven by concerns about civil unrest, including the eruption of fuel price protests and pickets outside oil refineries in 2000 (Walker and Broderick 2006: xiii, 47). The definitions of emergency are extensive, considerably wider than the previous provisions under the 1920 Act and allow for politically 'interventionist stances' toward potential crises (Walker and

Broderick 2006: 63–76). Possible threats to 'human welfare' extend to 'damage to property' and disruption to supplies, communications or transport. No criteria are provided for the key tests of 'serious damage to human welfare' and 'war or terrorism, which threatens serious damage to the security of the United Kingdom'. 'Serious' is not defined, nor is 'security'. Ministers are given powers to specify that certain situations or events are emergencies.

Once an emergency has been declared, the authorities can assume 'almost boundless power' (Walker and Broderick 2006: 161). They can, among other things, prohibit assemblies, ban movement, create offences, deploy the armed forces and confer emergency powers on any individual. There are no specific powers of arrest or detention without trial, but the Act's sponsors refused to rule out such detention, which the courts have in the past been prepared to accept, even in peacetime 'civil emergencies' (see *Attorney-General of St Christopher, Nevis and Anguilla v Reynolds* [1980] AC 637).

The scope of emergency regulations is spelt out in s 22:

1 Emergency regulations may make any provision which the person making the regulations is satisfied is appropriate for the purpose of preventing, controlling or mitigating an aspect or effect of the emergency in respect of which the regulations are made.

2 In particular, emergency regulations may make any provision which the person making the regulations is satisfied is appropriate for the purpose of—

   a protecting human life, health or safety,
   b treating human illness or injury,
   c protecting or restoring property,
   d protecting or restoring a supply of money, food, water, energy or fuel,
   e protecting or restoring a system of communication,
   f protecting or restoring facilities for transport,
   g protecting or restoring the provision of services relating to health,
   h protecting or restoring the activities of banks or other financial institutions,
   i preventing, containing or reducing the contamination of land, water or air,

      i preventing, reducing or mitigating the effects of disruption or destruction of plant life or animal life,
      ii protecting or restoring activities of Parliament, of the Scottish Parliament, of the Northern Ireland Assembly or of the National Assembly for Wales, or
      iii protecting or restoring the performance of public functions.

3 Emergency regulations may make provision of any kind that could be made by Act of Parliament or by the exercise of the Royal Prerogative; in particular, regulations may—

   a confer a function on a Minister of the Crown, on the Scottish Ministers, on the National Assembly for Wales, on a Northern Ireland department, on a coordinator appointed under section 24 or on any other specified person (and a function conferred may, in particular, be—

- i a power, or duty, to exercise a discretion;
- ii a power to give directions or orders, whether written or oral);

- b provide for or enable the requisition or confiscation of property (with or without compensation);
- c provide for or enable the destruction of property, animal life or plant life (with or without compensation);
- d prohibit, or enable the prohibition of, movement to or from a specified place;
- e require, or enable the requirement of, movement to or from a specified place;
- f prohibit, or enable the prohibition of, assemblies of specified kinds, at specified places or at specified times;
- g prohibit, or enable the prohibition of, travel at specified times;
- h prohibit, or enable the prohibition of, other specified activities;
- i create an offence of—

  - i failing to comply with a provision of the regulations;
  - ii failing to comply with a direction or order given or made under the regulations;
  - iii obstructing a person in the performance of a function under or by virtue of the regulations;

- j disapply or modify an enactment or a provision made under or by virtue of an enactment;
- k require a person or body to act in performance of a function (whether the function is conferred by the regulations or otherwise and whether or not the regulations also make provision for remuneration or compensation);
- l enable the Defence Council to authorise the deployment of Her Majesty's armed forces;
- m make provision (which may include conferring powers in relation to property) for facilitating any deployment of Her Majesty's armed forces;
- n confer jurisdiction on a court or tribunal (which may include a tribunal established by the regulations);
- o make provision which has effect in relation to, or to anything done in—

  - i an area of the territorial sea,
  - ii an area within British fishery limits, or
  - iii an area of the continental shelf;

- p make provision which applies generally or only in specified circumstances or for a specified purpose;
- q make different provision for different circumstances or purposes.

These provisions mean there are virtually no restrictions on the powers that a government can assume, and enforce via the armed forces. However, emergency regulations cannot require a person to perform military service or prohibit any activity in connection with a strike or other industrial action (s 23(3)).

In a briefing on the legislation, Liberty (the National Council for Civil Liberties) called it 'the most powerful piece of peacetime legislation ever proposed in the UK' and warned that 'it seeks to grant the Government unprecedented powers to make emergency regulations which are unavailable under existing laws'. Liberty expressed concern that 'it is times of emergency that citizens' fundamental rights are at greatest risk' (Liberty 2004: para 4). Liberty also noted that the present government had shown an increased willingness to declare an emergency, citing the declaration of a 'technical' emergency following the September 2001 attacks in the United States. This declaration enabled the government to derogate from article 5 of the *European Convention on Human Rights*, thereby permitting indefinite detention without trial under the *Anti-Terrorism Crime and Security Act 2001* (Liberty 2004: para 5).

These views are not isolated. One detailed study of the Act described it as 'the most powerful and extensive peacetime legislation ever enacted', containing within it 'the tools for dismantling civil society', with 'the potential to inflict terrible damage on the constitution of the United Kingdom' (Walker and Broderick 2006: 188, 214). The authors also drew attention to the slim likelihood of any effective parliamentary or judicial review of actions taken under emergency powers. In effect, the legislation provides the framework for extra-constitutional and dictatorial forms of rule, backed by military force.

During the debate on the *Civil Contingencies Bill*, cabinet rejected without argument calls to clarify by statute the military's role. The government also dismissed a recommendation by a House of Commons Select Committee to define the prerogative power to engage in armed conflict. The government argued that a case-by-case approach was needed, and that the government was already sufficiently accountable to parliament (Walker and Broderick 2006: 44–45). The end result is that ill-defined and extensive prerogative and common law powers to call out the armed forces continue to exist, augmented by the 2004 legislation.

Vague common law and executive powers

The Ministry of Defence's reference to the common law duty to provide military aid being 'difficult to formulate' points to the uncertain scope and character of this power and the associated legal rights and liabilities of called-out service personnel. As noted in Chapter 3, the last judicial guidance on this subject was provided in 1832 in *R v Pinney* ((1832) 170 ER 962). The mayor of Bristol and nine aldermen were unsuccessfully prosecuted by the Attorney-General for breaching their common law duty to assemble a sufficient force to put down three days of riots. A military major had advised the mayor that it would be 'imprudent to put arms in the hands of young troops'. But in the related case, *Charge to the Bristol Grand Jury*, Lord Tindal insisted that soldiers had a duty, as citizens, on their own authority, to do their utmost to 'put down riot and tumult'. Two officers who had refused to order the troops to fire without a magistrate's sanction were found guilty of neglect of duty, causing one to commit suicide (Babington 1990: 84).

There has been some parliamentary endorsement of the common law duty. The 1893 *Report of the Select Committee on the Featherstone Riots* said resort to military assistance must be the 'last expedient' of the civil authorities, but when such a call was made, 'to refuse such assistance is in law a misdemeanour' (Babington 1990: 122–132).

Apart from the Queen's Regulations, *Operations in the UK* makes no mention of the prerogative powers of the Crown. The relationship between these and the asserted common law tenet remains unclear. The royal prerogative powers are vast in scope—they are said to cover any situation not otherwise dealt with by statute—and effectively unreviewable by the courts (*Burmah Oil Co. Ltd. v Lord Advocate* [1965] AC 101; Whelan 1985: 287).

In *Chandler v Director of Public Prosecutions* ([1964] AC 763, 800), Lord Hodson stated: 'The Crown has, and this is not disputed, the right as head of State to decide in peace and war the disposition of its armed forces.' In *Burmah Oil Co Ltd v Lord Advocate* ([1965] AC 75, 100), Lord Reid said: 'There is no doubt that control of the armed forces has been left to the prerogative ... subject to the power of Parliament to withhold supply and refuse to continue legislation essential for the maintenance of a standing army.'

It is remarkable that, some three centuries after the struggle for parliamentary and civilian supremacy over the British monarchy—and in a political system that professes to be democratic—the power of the government to call out the military is said to rest on vestiges of regal authority. In the words of two scholars, the prerogative power to control disorder 'is a dangerous mystery unwarranted in a democratic society' (Whelan 1985: 287).

Nevertheless, these murky powers provided the basis not only for the deployment of troops to Northern Ireland but more 'commonplace' uses of troops to dispose of explosives or in operations against terrorism. For example, there were 957 calls for explosives disposal in 2001, and 431 in 2002, as well as between 30 and 40 requests per year to assist police in anti-terrorism operations (Walker and Broderick 2006: 248). Thus, it appears that a wider internal use of the armed forces became routine in the 'war on terror', even before the *Civil Contingencies Act*, and without substantial public scrutiny or debate.

Another category of military intervention exists, Military Aid to the Civil Community (MACC), which generally covers unarmed assistance in weather or environmental disasters and major accidents, but can extend to shooting down a hijacked civilian aircraft. The Quick Reaction Alert (Interceptor) Force can open fire on such planes with Ministerial approval (House of Commons Defence Committee 2001–2: para 45).

Yet another kind of intervention, Military Aid to Other Government Departments (MAGD) comprises maintenance of essential services, often in a strikebreaking role, relying on s 2 of the *Emergency Powers Act*. Between 1984 and 2003, MAGD was invoked 15 times, including against the 1984–85 mineworkers' strike, ambulance and firefighters' stoppages, and fuel pickets in 2000. Soldiers have also set up temporary prisons at times of overcrowding and industrial disputes (Walker and Broderick 2006: 248–249). These operations, while unarmed, contain the potential to spark conflicts with strikers and others that could involve the arming of troops if the police proved unable to contain the situation.

Ordinarily, the Defence Council, which consists of military leaders as well as government ministers and officials, exercises the prerogative powers on behalf of the Crown. The council is based in the Ministry of Defence and is normally chaired by the Secretary of State for Defence. In cases of MACP, a military commander would contact the Ministry of Defence (Counter Terrorism and UK Operations) to seek formal approval from the Minister. Police agreement would be required, but with the advent of the *Civil Contingencies Act*, it has been suggested that, as well as police, regional and emergency coordinators could request military assistance under MACA arrangements (Walker and Broderick 2006: 249–250). However, where military unit commanders receive police or emergency services requests and consider that a 'grave and sudden' emergency demands 'immediate intervention to protect life and property', they are authorised by the *Queen's Regulations for the Army* to respond on their own authority. They must subsequently seek ministerial approval. For MAGD operations, a Defence Council Order must be signed by two members of the council, including a minister (Walker and Broderick 2006: 250).

All these powers and arrangements operate above and beyond the *Civil Contingencies Act*. That is, they can be instigated without any formal declaration of a state of emergency under the Act (Walker and Broderick 2006: 251). Taken as a whole, considerable legal powers are said to exist to authorise calling out the troops to deal with a wide variety of alleged threats to society, including civil unrest, industrial action and acts of terrorism, and these measures have been augmented by the 'almost boundless power' that can be asserted under the 2004 Act.

Legal powers and lethal force

Called-out military personnel have been given no specific statutory powers, but the Ministry of Defence guidelines assert substantial common law powers, including to use lethal force and make arrests. The Ministry states that soldiers must act within the law and have no special legal powers beyond those of the ordinary citizen. Nevertheless, they 'may use reasonable force to prevent crime, including in self-defence'.

Although service personnel 'should not normally' make arrests, 'in certain circumstances there may be no other option'. The Ministry's policy is that soldiers can arrest people even to prevent a breach of the peace, which is defined as an occasion where a person causes harm or appears likely to cause harm to persons or property, or acts in a manner likely to provoke violence to others (except in Scotland, where arrest powers are slightly less). The guidelines state that force is lawful if the immediate object is to prevent crime (including public order offences), arrest offenders, self-defence or the defence of others (Ministry of Defence 2005: 4-3, 4A-1).

Military law provides that troops must obey lawful commands. Secret rules of engagement will be approved by Ministers (Ministry of Defence 2005: 4A-2).

These may purport to authorise or even require the application of lethal force, as they did in Northern Ireland.

Both the common law and parliament have condoned deadly force to deal with disturbances. After the Bristol riots that followed the defeat of the 1831 parliamentary reform bill, an officer who had fatally shot a boy during an incident was acquitted of manslaughter. Lord Tindal instructed the Grand Jury that if the shot was 'discharged in the fair and honest execution of his duty, in endeavouring to disperse the mob', the killing was justified and amounted to accidental death only (Babington 1990: 84).

When four people were killed after soldiers fired on striking miners, the 1893 *Report of the Select Committee on the Featherstone Riots* exonerated the commanding officer and his troops, saying 'The necessary prevention of such outrage on person and property justifies the guardians of the peace in the employment against a riotous crowd of even deadly weapons' (Whelan 1985: 272). The committee simply warned that 'officers and soldiers are under no special privileges and subject to no special responsibilities as regards this principle of the law'. The taking of life had to be shown to be necessary (Babington 1990: 122–132).

Secret preparations

The 2005 *Operations in the UK* document reported that the military had 'pre-prepared contingency plans for the use of Service personnel in specific MACP situations', but did not elaborate. Instead, it disclosed an intention to keep MACP preparations and operations hidden from the public as much as possible. The Ministry of Defence emphasised that planning for MACP is likely to be 'highly sensitive'. Due to 'legal and operational security restrictions', 'most MACP support receives no publicity' and 'under no circumstances should any comment be made about UK Special Forces involvement' (Ministry of Defence 2005: 4-4, 4-5).

Once called out, service personnel were instructed not to discuss their work with, or answer questions from, members of the press or the public. Even the possibility of arresting prying journalists is raised. 'Except in a situation where arrest under the Official Secrets Act would be permissible, it is not possible to prevent photographers or television cameramen from recording, but Service personnel should not be drawn into conversation' (Ministry of Defence 2005: 4A-3).

Likewise, the document called for measures to hide from the public any preparations to use lethal force. 'If the potential use of firearms is considered necessary, usually as a last resort in civil disturbances, a force so armed should be kept in reserve and out of sight of those involved in the disturbance.' The Rules of Engagement covering the use of force are also kept secret (Ministry of Defence 2005: 4A-2).

A 2002 Ministry of Defence White Paper signalled an intention to enhance the military's capacity for domestic deployment by establishing Reserve Reaction Forces of, on average, 500 Reserves for each region (a total of 6,000) (The Strategic Review 2002: Ch. 5). The Reserves can be mobilised under the *Reserve*

Forces Act 1996, s 52, which allows a call out where 'it appears to Her [Majesty] that national danger is imminent or that a great emergency has arisen'. In a 2003 paper, the Ministry of Defence reported that 14 Civil Contingencies Reaction Forces were being established, though the numbers were later depleted by operations in Iraq (Walker and Broderick 2006: 246).

London Olympics 2012

The 2012 London Olympics involved a substantial military deployment, alongside an unprecedented police mobilisation. By late 2008, the security budget for the Olympics had risen to £1.5 billion. In addition to thousands of police and security guards, the operation featured military troops, helicopters and jets. According to one newspaper report:

> The Army is to be drafted in to help protect athletes and hundreds of thousands of spectators from an atrocity … Military helicopters will patrol overhead, and jets will be on standby to intercept any suspect private plane heading for the main Olympic stadium in Stratford, east London … The security operation is expected to be largest in peacetime Britain … Unmanned military planes, as used to monitor the Taliban in Afghanistan, could be deployed to monitor suspected terrorist aircraft.
>
> (Merrick 2008)

According to a BBC report, an extensive closed circuit television (CCTV) network monitored people in London, combining 10,000 Metropolitan Police Service cameras with thousands of traffic and congestion cameras. The overall network of up to half a million cameras, the largest in the world, was controlled from a bomb-proof bunker operated jointly by the military, police and intelligence services (Morgan 2008).

RAF Reaper drones were also used for surveillance and intelligence-gathering during the Games, the first time that unmanned aircraft have been allowed to fly over the heavily populated capital. The drones have infra-red sensors, ground-scanning radars, electronic eavesdropping equipment and high-definition cameras, providing for intensive spying and bugging directed against civilians. In addition, manned fighter aircraft were stationed at several bases near London to enforce an air exclusion zone and intercept aircraft, with powers to shoot down civilian aircraft regarded as a threat (The Herald 2008).

The RAF's association with the London Olympics was given a high public profile when the Red Arrows, the RAF Aerobatic Team, performed a fly-past at the 2008 handover ceremony in London at the conclusion of the Beijing Olympics. The military's engagement with the Games was enhanced by the British Olympic Association's selection of the Aldershot Garrison, often described as the home of the British Army, to host the British Olympics team's pre-games preparation and processing camp.

Conclusion

As in the United States and Canada, Britain's involvement in US-led militarism abroad has been accompanied by enhanced military call-out powers at home. Unlike in Australia (see Chapter 10), British governments have thus far not introduced specific legislation authorising call outs and creating express powers for soldiers. However, the *Civil Contingencies Act* has created substantial military deployment powers and unprecedented framework for extra-constitutional and dictatorial forms of rule.

Moreover, Ministry of Defence policies are based on vague and sweeping common law, executive and prerogative powers that purportedly can authorise the use of troops against a wide range of challenges to 'public order'. Secretive preparations have been made for Military Aid to Civil Power.

Throughout British history, troops have been mobilised against civilians in periods of acute political and social conflict, and it appears that the powers-that-be are preparing for further such convulsions.

7 France

Troops on the streets to combat social unrest

An historical turning point was reached when troops were deployed on the streets to deal with social and political unrest in France during 2019. It was the first time since the late 1940s, during the post-World War II period of immense political and industrial upheaval, that the French military had been mobilised to deal with civil disobedience.

President Emmanuel Macron called out soldiers against 'yellow vest' protesters who demonstrated against austerity measures and social inequality. This operation was said to be an extension of Operation Sentinelle, which was launched in 2015, yet that operation's public rationale was combatting terrorist threats. Although the government denied that soldiers would be directly involved in confronting civilian demonstrators, but would provide security around key sites, clashes between army units and protesters were clearly envisaged by the authorities if military force were deemed necessary.

The 'yellow vest' deployment

In March 2019, French government spokesman Benjamin Griveaux announced that President Macron would mobilise army units during weekend protests, which had been held every week since late 2018. Starting as a protest against increased fuel taxes, the 'yellow vest' demonstrations had become a substantial movement against Macron and his government, demanding that the president resign.

The official reason given by Macron's government for this deployment was dubious. The government claimed that after the looting of stores on Paris's Champs-Elysees during a 'yellow vest' march, only troops would have sufficient numbers to guard buildings and free up riot police to crack down on allegedly violent protesters. Doubts remained, however, about whether 'yellow vest' participants were responsible for the looting (Lantier 2019a).

The governor of the Paris military district told France Info that soldiers had been authorised to fire on the 'yellow vests'. Asked by a journalist whether soldiers were capable of carrying out law enforcement duties, General Bruno Le Ray replied:

> Our orders are sufficiently clear that we do not need to be worried at all. The soldiers' rules of engagement will be fixed very rigorously ... They will have

> different means for action faced with all types of threats. That can go as far as opening fire … if their life is threatened or the life of those people they are defending.
>
> (Lantier 2019b; Willsher 2019)

Le Ray added that soldiers would have the same rules of engagement for shooting protesters as those for gunning down terrorism suspects, effectively equating protesters against inequality with terrorists. Police and military powers introduced under the banner of the 'war on terror' were to be used against political and social unrest.

Opposition politicians expressed concerns that any shooting of civilians by troops would inflame the discontent (Mallett 2019). President Macron later downplayed the significance of sending the army against the 'yellow vests', saying the army was 'in no way responsible for maintaining order and public order'. He mocked criticisms of his resort to the army as a 'false debate' fuelled by 'those who play at scaring themselves and others' (Lantier 2019b; Willsher 2019).

Despite the president's public reassurances, some soldiers told the media of their concerns, which included the prospect of firing assault rifles against demonstrators. One anonymously told France Info:

> We have no business interfering in this 'yellow vest' business. We do not have the necessary equipment, we just have truncheons and little pepper spray bottles like what girls have in their purses. After that, the next thing we have is our assault rifles. … So, if we go up against too many protesters, unfortunately we will probably see fatalities.
>
> (Lantier 2019b; Willsher 2019)

Another soldier said:

> It is absurd, it's arbitrary. We are not prepared for this. In technical terms, we fight military enemies. And the enemy cannot be the entire population, that is not possible. That is the situation they are trying to put soldiers in today.
>
> (Lantier 2019b; Willsher 2019)

Some military experts verified these concerns. 'The last time the state requisitioned the army for policing operations was in 1947–1948,' Élie Tenenbaum, a defence researcher, told France 24. In 1947, a series of strikes had taken an 'insurrectional' turn, according to the then Interior Minister, who deployed the army to help the police. Although the situation was different in 2019, 'it is not uninteresting to wonder what could happen if rioters attacked public buildings, as Sentinelle troops are not equipped to respond to this type of threat', Tenenbaum said. Instead of riot shields or intermediate weapons, they were armed with lethal weapons (Mazoue 2019).

Interior Minister Christophe Castaner made a stark reference to the historical issues involved in mobilising troops to suppress domestic opposition. He invoked the mantle of World War I-era Prime Minister Georges Clemenceau. Referring to the policing of the 'yellow vest' demonstrations, he proclaimed: 'Your model is Georges Clemenceau. His hand never trembled when the task was to fight for France, and nor must yours' (Bonnet 2019). Castaner was recalling Clemenceau's record as interior minister. After the Courrières mining disaster in 1906, Clemenceau brought in troops to crush the strikes that erupted in the coal mines (Bonnet 2019).

In late 2018, President Macron also deployed military forces to Réunion to attack 'yellow vest' protesters blockading the island, a French overseas department in the Indian Ocean.

To justify sending squads of gendarmerie military police and national police, Macron tried to discredit the 'yellow vest' demonstrators, who were protesting his fuel tax increases, citing acts of vandalism allegedly carried out in and around the movement. He warned the state would 'brook no negotiations', adding: 'What is happening at La Réunion is very serious. We have engaged the necessary means and we will continue to do so: our military will be deployed starting tomorrow to re-establish order' (Torres 2018).

Macron did not say which military units would go to repress the Réunion population. But a squad of gendarmerie from Troyes and another from Maisons-Alfort were to join the four squads already on the ground. Police unions also announced the upcoming arrival of 28 officers of the Anti-Criminal Brigade and a departmental intervention force (Torres 2018).

Amid these developments, the French national intelligence and counter-terrorism organisation's five-year public strategy document, released in 2019, identified 'subversive movements' and the threat of 'insurrectional violence' in the population as a key threat to the existing order (Morrow 2019).

The National Intelligence Strategy published by the National Intelligence Coordination for the Fight Against Terrorism was personally approved by President Emmanuel Macron. It signalled a shift from the organisation's first five-year 'road map', published in 2014. The 2014 version had identified its five areas of operations as terrorism, espionage and economic interference, the proliferation of weapons of mass destruction, cyber attacks and organised crime. The 2019 report established a new category: 'Anticipation of crises and the risk of major ruptures'. Under the headline 'Violent subversion', it stated:

> The growing strength of movements and networks of a subversive character constitutes a factor of crisis that is all the more preoccupying because they are aimed at weakening, and even destroying, the foundations of our democracy and the republican institutions through insurrectional violence.
>
> (Morrow 2019)

By 'subversive' movements, the document meant not only 'violent actions against people or goods', but 'also the collection of traditional demands that these movements employ in order to infiltrate and radicalise them'. According to this definition, 'traditional demands'—such as against layoffs and welfare cuts, for higher wages, improved living standards, against war and for social equality—were not legitimate political demands. They were 'employed' by 'subversive' forces.

Operation Sentinelle

France became a prominent testing ground for the large-scale deployment of troops from 2015 onward. On the pretext of responding to terrorist attacks, the Socialist Party government of President François Hollande declared a state of emergency, invoking article 18 of the Constitution. The government mobilised more than 100,000 security personnel throughout the country, including regular police, gendarmes, para-military riot police and 10,000 soldiers.

Operation Sentinelle, in which combat troops patrolled streets and guarded key sites—from places of worship to art galleries, and nursery schools to Métro stations—was the army's first wide-scale peacetime military operation on mainland France. It became impossible to walk the streets of any major city without running into troops decked out in camouflage or officers dressed in black, toting automatic rifles. The *Guardian* reported: 'The constant presence of camouflage uniforms everywhere from quiet neighbourhood streets to Métro carriages, patrolling past schools at home-time or milling through markets, has transformed the cityscape' (Chrisafis 2016).

Likewise, the government in neighbouring Belgium responded to alleged Islamic State-inspired attacks to place 1,800 heavily armed combat troops on the cobbled streets of Brussels. By 2017, the numbers were down to 7,000 and 1,200 respectively, still a significant proportion of the deployable army personnel in each nation.

In August of that year, French Interior Minister Gerard Collomb announced that Operation Sentinelle would continue in a modified form. Speaking to BFM TV, he said:

> We are going to redefine the mission in order to make it more mobile. That means we might not just have 7,000 soldiers deployed … at fixed positions, but maybe 3,500 at specific posts and 3,500 deployed in a more flexible way.
> (France 24 2017)

Thus, the 'emergency' mobilisation commenced by the Hollande's government was continued, initially indefinitely, under Hollande's successor, Emmanuel Macron.

The modification of the deployment reflected concerns at the impact of the protracted operation on the morale and effectiveness of the troops involved. They faced lengthy stints of duty against civilians, and became targets for attacks. They were often housed in temporary and poor accommodation, plagued with leaks, lack of heating and extreme hardship (Chrisafis 2016).

These conditions produced at least one suicide. The 26-year-old soldier committed suicide with his weapon, a Famas assault rifle, according to a military source, in his accommodation at the Ministry of Defence (Euler 2017).

Already by 2016, according to media reports, ex-generals and other military analysts voiced fears that the indefinite character of the operation, involving a significant proportion of the army, was compromising the battle readiness of the French armed forces. The *Guardian* reported:

> Political commentators and ex-military figures have started to query whether deploying soldiers in what one rightwing senator called a mere security guard role is an efficient use of a highly trained—and now highly stretched—army … The French army, along with the British, is one of the biggest forces in Europe—it is deployed across the world, in operations ranging from Mali and the Sahel to Iraq, championed by Hollande, the Socialist who has been labelled 'war chief' for his decision to intervene abroad. And yet Sentinelle is so vast that it is currently the biggest military operation in volume of any French operation anywhere in the world. Of all the French soldiers currently on military operations, half of them are deployed on streets at home.
>
> (Chrisafis 2016)

General Vincent Desportes, a former director of France's War college and then a professor at Sciences Po, told the *Guardian* that even before Operation Sentinelle the army had been over-deployed, warning that troops could now face burnout. He said because of the high demand for patrols on home soil, 'soldiers are not having rest time and are losing the collective training and *savoir-faire*'. He felt the benefit was negligible because soldiers simply standing guard were not being used to their best ability and Operation Sentinelle's chief role was just as a political 'anti-anxiety' measure (Chrisafis 2016).

By 2017, it was obvious that the ubiquitous presence of troops on the streets was, if anything, exacerbating the danger of terrorism rather than reducing it. In October of that year, France 24 reported:

> Six soldiers were injured on Wednesday after a suspect rammed his car into a group of soldiers, the latest in a series of attacks targeting French security services. The attack has renewed questions over the efficiency of Opération Sentinelle's anti-terror patrols, which have often become the targets of attacks themselves. 'It is essentially just posturing that has zero operational impact,' Jean-Charles Brisard of the Center for the Analysis of told *France 24*. 'Sentinelle has never stopped, prevented or hindered any terrorist attack in France since its creation in 2015.'
>
> (France 24 2017)

In reality, the political 'posturing' served to obscure two underlying truths. First, the terrorist attacks in Paris and across Europe were an outcome of the wars in the Middle East waged by the United States and its European allies, and were carried out by individuals well known to the intelligence agencies. Second, the creation of this terrorist threat was exploited by successive governments to provide a justification for military measures whose target was not primarily terrorists but the mounting social and political discontent among workers and broad layers of the population.

In November 2017, nearly two years after its imposition, the state of emergency formally expired. It was by far the longest time that democratic rights had been suspended in France since the state of emergency was created by law and then imposed in 1955, amid the Algerian war for independence against France.

During the state of emergency, there were over 4,300 extrajudicial searches and seizures, and more than 750 people were placed under house arrest. Just under 1,000 legal cases were opened, 75 security zones were set up, and 41 people were still under house arrest. However, the state of emergency led to only 20 counter-terrorism investigations (Lantier and Ira 2017).

Previous domestic uses of troops

As noted by Interior Minister Castaner and the commentators cited above, 2019 was not the first time that army units had been mobilised to suppress unrest that was seen as a threat to the ruling establishment. But it was the first such large-scale deployment in 70 years, indicating the seriousness with which the French government regarded the danger presented by the 'yellow vest' discontent.

The result of the last major intervention of the army against workers on French soil, in the major strikes of 1947–48 after World War II and the fall of European fascism, was a massacre. As 350,000 miners went on strike, the army occupied the mines with an authorisation to fire on the strikers. The resulting clashes led to six dead, thousands of wounded, and the firing of 3,000 miners, a decision legally recognised as discriminatory in 2011 (Lantier 2019b).

This occurred during an acute political crisis. The Communist Party, which then commanded broad support in the working class, had just left the ruling coalition with the Gaullists and Socialists, having initially opposed the strike movement. Interior minister Jules Moch, a Socialist, mobilised 60,000 CRS riot police and soldiers to force the 15,000 strikers back to work (Bonnet 2019).

During the 1954–62 war for Algerian independence, the army was used to torture and kill Algerians rising up against French colonialism, barely more than a decade after these same methods were used in France itself by the Nazis and the Nazi-collaborationist Vichy regime. The Algerian operation left over 300,000 dead (Lantier 2019b).

In 2013, after former Socialist Party presidential candidate Ségolène Royal called for sending the army to Marseille, history professor Jean-Marc Berlière reviewed the history of the French army's use for police operations in an interview in *Le Monde* (Torres 2019).

In the nineteenth century, Berlière explained, the army's repeated murder of workers, including women and children, during strikes and May Day rallies provoked enormous class anger:

> Massacres like those that periodically took place—at Fourmies, Narbonne, and so on—seriously hurt its image, which was already badly damaged by suspicion of social and political collusion due to its engagement during strikes on the side of the employers.
>
> (Torres 2019)

After the October 1917 Revolution in Russia during World War I, which saw mass mutinies in the French army, the government decided it could no longer trust the army for domestic policing. 'After the victory and the sacrifices of the 1914–1918 war, it was no longer possible to use the victorious army for internal operations,' Berlière said. Asked whether the French army was active after World War I in domestic policing inside the borders of current-day France, he added: 'Basically, no. The political risk was too great: what would be the attitude of the conscripts?' (Torres 2019).

A history of military repression

France's modern history of military deployment to suppress civil unrest, particularly working-class uprisings, goes back further, to the nineteenth century. It is a violent record, featuring the slaughter of thousands of people. Following the defeat of Napoleon Bonaparte in 1815 and the restoration of a monarchy, brutal repression recurred throughout the century. One study of 'domestic state violence' in France identified five waves of repression—1816–18, 1832, 1834, 1848, 1851–52 and 1871. These waves exceeded the violence displayed during frequent food riots, strikes and outbreaks of resistance to conscription (Brown 1999: 616).

The 'state of siege', a doctrine developed during the *ancien regime*, before the 1789 French Revolution, was adapted for use by the emerging capitalist class, or bourgeoisie, against the growing and rising proletariat, or working class. Among the documented military massacres were those committed at Paris and Lyon in April 1834, when soldiers inflicted heavy casualties putting down revolts. At Lyon, troops outnumbered insurrectionaries almost ten to one, used cannons to flatten barricades and houses, and killed more than 300 people in six days. An even more notorious massacre occurred in Paris that same month (Brown 1999: 617).

Far greater military atrocities were committed during the 1848 revolution. It was part of a wave of popular democratic revolutions across Europe, in which, for the first time, leading roles were played by the embryonic industrial working class.

Following the February 1848 mass overthrow of the Orleans monarchy of Louis Philippe, who abdicated and fled to Britain, an elected government proclaimed the Second Republic. But reflecting the interests of the most powerful business layers, this government increasingly dismantled the social concessions, such as the employment workshops, that had initially been made to the workers and poor who mounted the revolution.

On 23 June 1848, the working class of Paris rose in protest over the closure of the National Workshops. On that day, 170,000 people came out into the streets to erect barricades. The government appointed General Cavaignac to lead the military forces to put down the uprising.

Cavaignac first withdrew his soldiers from Paris to allow the insurgents to deploy their barricades, and then returned with overwhelming force to crush the uprising. From 24 to 26 June, there were battles in the streets of the working class districts of Paris. An estimated 5,000 insurgents were killed at the barricades; 15,000 were arrested, and 4,000 deported (Séguin 1990: 108–109). However, even with a force of 120,000 to 125,000 soldiers, Cavaignac still required two days to complete the suppression of the uprising. Fearful of a renewed rebellion, the government continued a state of siege until 12 October (Rudé 2005: 164–179).

Moreover, this bloodshed was accompanied by summary executions and imposition of military justice. Setting aside an earlier Tribunal de Cassation ruling that the use of military courts to try civilian insurgents was unconstitutional, four military commissions decided the fate of over 11,000 prisoners, 255 of whom were handed over to military courts as leaders or instigators of insurrection. Political deportations were also ordered, with 3,357 people sentenced to transportation (Brown 1999: 617–618). One historian concluded: 'The savagery of the fighting, the summary executions during combat, and the use of military justice afterwards, testify to deep-seated fears of working-class insurgency' (Brown 1999: 618).

After the working class rose up, frightened by this new social force, which threatened their property and privileges, the capitalist and middle-class leaders preferred to reconcile themselves with feudal reaction. The Constitution of the short-lived Second Republic in France was written on the back of a bloody military onslaught against the workers of Paris (Marx 1969a: 34–35). Formal legal protections were soon cast aside. In the words of two scholars:

> Following the imposition of a state of siege on Paris between June 24 and October 12, 1848, and the introduction of article 106 of the Constitution of the Second Republic—providing that a law would be promulgated for the regulation of the institution of state of siege—a law was passed on August 9, 1849, which sought to regulate such issue as the declaration, termination, and the effect of a state of siege. However, the law of 1849 was thereafter used to impose indiscriminately and arbitrarily a state of siege regime for extended periods of time and on a wide scale.
>
> (Gross and Ni Aolain 2006: 27)

By the time of his December 1851 coup, Louis Napoleon had dissolved the National Assembly without having the constitutional right to do so, and became the sole ruler of France. When opposition erupted, even greater repression ensued. In Paris, the authorities cynically allowed the armed resistance to develop openly in order to provide a pretext for crushing it more fully. According to one study: 'Widespread insurrection provoked the formation of flying columns authorized to shoot fugitives and summarily execute armed rebels. Thirty-two departments were put under a state of siege which again activated exceptional military justice' (Brown 1999: 618).

Significantly, as is characteristic of military repression, the mobilisation of troops was accompanied by the evisceration of basic legal and democratic rights. The violent operations on the streets were sanctioned and enforced by military tribunals that paid no regard for legality. One historian commented:

> The sheer numbers involved … the kangaroo court procedures (defence attorneys were never present at a hearing, no witnesses were heard, and the defendant himself was physically absent from the 'court' room), the total disregard for civil or criminal law in determining guilt or innocence … and the severity of the sentences imposed—all indicate—that the new wave of repression was an extremist measure.
>
> (Brown 1999: 618–619)

This lawlessness was assisted by the failure of civilian judges to resist this mockery of judicial procedure. It typified what one study labelled 'liberal authoritarianism', in which ruling elite 'liberals' supported the overriding of hard-won civil and political rights in order to preserve the existing economic and social order (Brown 1999: 619).

Once the resistance was crushed, the Second Republic was officially over. Louis Napoleon took the title Emperor Napoleon III, and the Second Empire began, which lasted until 1870, when it collapsed in the wake of France's defeat in the Franco-German War.

Then, in March 1871, the workers of Paris rose up to oppose preparations by the royalist-majority National Assembly to restore the monarchy, and the provisional government's decision to disarm the National Guard, which consisted largely of workers who had fought the German forces during the siege of Paris. After municipal elections resulted in victory for representatives of the working-class resistance, they formed the Paris Commune government, which called for social measures such as the limiting of the workday to ten hours.

The Paris Commune was subjected to even more furious repression than the uprisings of 1848 and 1851–52. With active aid from German Chancellor Otto Bismarck, the aristocratic, landlord and business-dominated ruling class launched military operations against the Commune. After pitched battles, more than 20,000 Communards were killed and at least 38,000 arrested, many of whom were executed, and more than 7,000 deported (Lissagaray 2007). It was not just the fighting itself, but the firing squads, shooting of captured communards and other arbitrary executions without trial that accounted for most of the deaths. The carnage replicated the massacres committed by army officers in French colonial operations in Algeria and Mexico (Brown 1999: 620). One study concluded: 'Much of the appalling slaughter of the *semaine sanglate* [bloody week] was carried out 'systematically and coldly' because army officers were given virtual *carte blanche* when dealing with suspected rebels' (Brown 1999: 619). Again, fundamental legal and democratic norms were cast aside. Twenty-six military courts took three years to prosecute more than 13,000 communards (Brown 1999: 620).

Once capitalist rule had been stabilised, a new law on state of siege was introduced in 1878. Formally, it stipulated that a state of siege could only be declared by law and only 'in the event of imminent danger resulting from a foreign war or an armed insurrection' (Gross and Ni Aolain 2006: 28). In practice, however, this limitation was swept aside when the first test of the law came in World War I. On 2 August 1914, a state of siege covering the whole of France was imposed by a presidential decree when parliament was in recess, in order to enforce a general mobilisation for the war against Germany. Three days later, a law declared that the state of siege would remain in place 'for the duration of the war' and could be lifted, and re-imposed, by presidential decree. The declaration handed all police and security powers to the military (Gross and Ni Aolain 2006: 29).

During World I, the French cabinet also promulgated decrees that overrode previous legislation or imposed sweeping measures without any constitutional or statutory basis. In 1918, the Conseil d'Etat upheld the inherent powers of the executive government to take such actions (Bell 1992: 84).

Likewise, during the economic breakdowns, political turmoil and class battles of the 1920s and 1930s, the formal limits of 'state of siege' provisions were overturned by the adoption of enabling acts that provided for emergency powers.

First adopted by the Poincare government in 1926 (the year of the British General Strike), the use of such acts reached its epitome with the Daladier government. From 1938 until the collapse of the Third Republic and the formation of the pro-Nazi Vichy regime, Daladier's administration ruled through executive decrees facilitated by four enabling acts. The act of 8 December 1939 made executive decree a permanent emergency institution for the duration of the war (Gross and Ni Aolain 2006: 29–30). In 1940, Marshal Pétain, having been appointed premier of France by President Lebrun, signed an armistice with the Nazis, dissolved the Third Republic and established an authoritarian regime by claiming full dictatorial powers (Lackerstein 2012).

Military call-out powers

Constitutionally, French presidents today have considerable political and military power. As head of state, they command the executive apparatus, including the armed forces, and often seek to drive the national policymaking agenda with little parliamentary oversight. France's current constitutional regime, the Fifth Republic, was created in 1958 by Charles de Gaulle, a leader of the Free French resistance during World War II. He came out of retirement to be installed as president after an uprising by French colonists in Algeria threatened to stir wider unrest within France.

De Gaulle seized on the crisis to design a new constitution that would greatly expand the powers of the president and aimed to prevent the perceived parliamentary paralysis that had occurred for more than a decade. He further bolstered executive power in 1962, pushing through a referendum that replaced an electoral college system for electing presidents with direct universal suffrage.

Article 15 of the Constitution anoints the president as the head of the armed forces. It states: 'The President of the Republic shall be Commander-in-Chief of the Armed Forces. He shall preside over the higher national defence councils and committees.' The presidential powers include to appoint and dismiss senior military officers, determine the military budget and initiate military interventions in other countries.

Article 20 does potentially permit the cabinet, which must have parliament's support, to circumscribe these powers. It states:

> The Government shall determine and conduct the policy of the Nation. It shall have at its disposal the civil service and the armed forces. It shall be accountable to Parliament in accordance with the terms and procedures set out in articles 49 and 50. The Prime Minister shall direct the actions of the Government. He shall be responsible for national defence.

The defence minister oversees the military's funding, procurement and operations. In practice, however, presidents have determined the domestic use of the armed forces. Likewise, article 35 ostensibly requires parliamentary approval for a formal declaration of war, but its provisions allow the president to effectively launch military interventions and present them to parliament as a fait accompli. It states:

> A declaration of war shall be authorised by Parliament. The Government shall inform Parliament of its decision to have the armed forces intervene abroad, at the latest three days after the beginning of said intervention. It shall detail the objectives of the said intervention. This information may give rise to a debate, which shall not be followed by a vote. Where the said intervention shall exceed four months, the Government shall submit the extension to Parliament for authorisation. It may ask the National Assembly to make the final decision. If Parliament is not sitting at the end of the four-month period, it shall express its decision at the opening of the following session.

Such provisions, which can be found in legislation in some other countries, essentially make parliaments rubber stamps and legitimising institutions for military operations that are decided upon, or provoked, by the executive authorities (Head and Boehringer 2019: 34–40).

Para-military forces

In addition to the military, the French authorities can deploy significant para-military forces to deal with domestic unrest. The 100,000-strong National Gendarmerie is one of two national police forces, along with the National Police. The gendarmerie is a branch of the French Armed Forces, but placed under the jurisdiction of the interior ministry since 2009. Its area of responsibility includes smaller towns, rural and suburban areas, while the National Police, a civilian force, is in charge of cities.

The gendarmerie's relevant missions include policing public gatherings and demonstrations, crowd control and related security activities, and security of airports, civil nuclear sites and military installations. It also has military functions, such as serving as the military police for the armed forces. The 12,000 gendarmes of the *Gendarmerie Mobile* are specifically trained in crowd and riot control, although France is involved in major military missions abroad, and when French troops go overseas, gendarmes accompany them. Also, about one out of five gendarmes are permanently stationed in France's overseas departments and territories, leaving about 5,000 experienced gendarmes with training in riot control free to deploy inside mainland France (Berlinski 2018).

The 148,000-strong National Police also features 13,000 officers of the Compagnies Républicaines de Sécurité (CRS), who are specifically trained to respond to riots (Berlinski 2018). Other divisions of the National Police include the Border Police, the Judicial Police, the Central Directorate of Internal Intelligence, VIP Protection and the RAID counterterrorism unit.

8 Germany and Italy

Post-war restraints eroded

In both Germany and Italy, official challenges are being made to the restrictions on the use of the military imposed after World War II to prevent a return to the militarist and dictatorial practices witnessed under fascism. This chapter focusses on Germany but closes with a brief review of the recent developments and historical issues in Italy.

A new stage in German remilitarisation

In 2016, Germany's 'grand coalition' government of the conservative and social democratic parties embarked on a new stage in the remilitarisation of the country, both domestically and globally. That came with the federal cabinet's adoption of the 'White Paper 2016 on German Security Policy and the Future of the Bundeswehr'. The 144-page text replaced the White Paper of 2006 as Germany's official foreign policy and military doctrine, opening the way for a series of exercises to rehearse the internal deployment of the Bundeswehr (German military).

Amid deepening global geo-strategic tensions and rising political disaffection, the 2016 White Paper set far-reaching goals: an accelerated build-up of the Bundeswehr, the domestic deployment of its forces, the expansion of foreign operations independent of Germany's post-World War II allies, and a European foreign and defence policy dominated by Germany.

Brushing aside the limits imposed by the country's post-war constitution, the section 'Deployment and Role of the Bundeswehr in Germany', asserted that 'The German Constitutional Court has confirmed that, in order to assist the police in effectively managing emergency situations, the armed forces may, in certain conditions, perform sovereign tasks and exercise powers of intervention and enforcement' (White Paper 2016: 110).

The document insisted that Article 35(1) of the German constitution, which restricts the armed forces rendering technical, logistical and administrative assistance at home, does not apply 'in the event of natural disasters and serious accidents (emergency situations)' and those emergencies included 'large-scale terrorist attacks' (White Paper 2016: 110). Moreover, the White Paper declared:

> [T]he German Government can, in a state of defence or tension, employ the armed forces for facility protection and traffic control responsibilities pursuant

> to Article 87a(3) of the German constitution. According to Article 87a(4) of the constitution, the armed forces can also be deployed in the event of an internal emergency if the conditions referred to in Article 91(2) are fulfilled, in other words if there is an imminent danger to the existence or free democratic basic order of Germany or of a federal state.
>
> (White Paper 2016: 110)

In effect, the ban on military operations within Germany as well as the separation between the police and the army, embedded in the constitution after the experiences of the pre-World War I German Empire, the 1919–33 Weimar Republic and the 1933–45 Nazi dictatorship, was overturned. These principles had been softened repeatedly since the adoption of emergency laws during a previous period of anti-government protests and political instability in May 1968, but the use of the army in police operations had remained illegal in Germany.

The White Paper's list of Bundeswehr missions featured many of an internal character. They covered 'homeland security, crisis management for German nationals abroad, and subsidiary support in Germany', including

- performing national territorial tasks
- monitoring and securing German airspace and territorial waters
- monitoring critical space infrastructure
- permanently performing subsidiary tasks as part of inter-ministerial agreements
- providing assistance in the event of natural disasters, serious accidents, states of emergency, and inter-ministerial assistance
- contributing to counterterrorism operations in the framework of the constitution
- rescuing and evacuating persons isolated abroad
- contributing to evacuations from critical situations and
- contributing to hostage rescue missions abroad in order to contribute to national security and the resilience of state and society.

(White Paper 2016: 92)

Parliamentary consent for the deployment of the military, also established by the constitution, was further undermined. In chapter 8 of the White Paper, the section 'Legal Framework' stated: 'The number of deployments and missions necessitating immediate and resolute action has grown.' The 'practice of parliamentary consent has stood the test of time', the paper said, but 'in view of Germany's increased responsibility for security, we must be in a position to meet these challenges, if necessary by deploying armed German forces' (White Paper 2016: chapter 8).

The document set out a new 'whole-of-society' vision of 'national security' that foreshadowed a militarisation of foreign policy, civil and social life in preparation for war. The section 'Promoting Security and Resilience: A Whole-of-Society Endeavour' stated:

> National security is not only a task of the state, but increasingly a joint task of the state, industry, the scientific community, and society. A common understanding of potential risks is the basis on which to build whole-of-society resilience ... [the government] will render its approach to national security more comprehensive by continuously identifying and adapting areas requiring protection; further developing civil defence planning (maintenance of state and government functions, civil protection, supply, support of the armed forces) with the goal of harmonising crisis management procedures.
>
> (White Paper 2016)

Soon after the White Paper was published, Defence Minister Ursula von der Leyen stated in an interview with the newspaper *Bild* that joint exercises would start in a few weeks to prepare the Bundeswehr to be used domestically. She stated:

> In late summer, we will decide at the Conference of State Interior Ministers which scenarios we need to practice. In an emergency, the alarm chain must be ready, the responsibilities clear and sufficient staff available. Therefore, we will first undertake a command-level exercise, which will test the interaction between the federal government and the police authorities of several states.
>
> (Stern 2016)

The defence minister said that 'in an emergency', the Bundeswehr would not only handle logistics, but would also 'provide military support'. She stated: 'In acute cases, the police will decide what is needed to cope with a terrorist situation. In principle, the Supreme Court has made it clear that in extreme cases, the support of the military can be requested' (Stern 2016).

In an interview in the *Süddeutsche Zeitung*, Lieutenant General Martin Schelleis, responsible for the army domestically as chief of joint support, provided an overview of the extensive measures that were being prepared. Upon request, the Bundeswehr could provide things like 'technical capabilities such as low altitude mobile air surveillance to identify fast-flying aircraft' or advise in the event of nuclear, biological or chemical threats, 'possibly even using mobile laboratory capabilities'. In addition, the Army could assist the police with armoured vehicles (Stern 2016).

Schelleis pointed to the Bundeswehr applying the experience in controlling local populations it had obtained in military operations abroad—in places such as Kosovo, Afghanistan and Mali. 'In various missions abroad, our soldiers have also acquired considerable experience organizing checkpoints, dealing with explosive threats or guarding buildings. They bring knowledge and skills that could be used in a terrorist situation,' the general said (Stern 2016).

Both the White Paper and German politicians justified the use of the Bundeswehr by citing terrorist attacks in Europe. In reality, the 'war on terror' and its associated measures, such as the use of the army domestically, by no means prevent terrorist attacks. On the contrary, the wars conducted by the United States and its allies under the pretext of the 'war on terror' have transformed countries like Iraq, Libya and Syria into breeding grounds for terrorist networks where previously there had been none.

The White Paper advocated a European foreign and defence policy dominated by Berlin and dedicated to defending the geopolitical and economic interests of Germany worldwide. To this end, the military budget was be almost doubled from the existing level of nearly 39 billion euros. In the section 'NATO and the European Union', the White Paper stated:

> The federal government has set itself the task and will work to ensure long-term and in the context of the resources available to reach the target of two percent of GDP for defence spending and at the same time strives for an investment rate of 20 percent in the area of defence.
>
> (White Paper 2016)

As in the 1930s, the turn toward rearmament is proceeding hand in hand with authoritarian domestic measures, such as joint police–military operations, to suppress the resistance of the population. As of 2018, German soldiers have undertaken house-to-house fighting training in preparation for domestic Bundeswehr operations in what the Defence Ministry called 'the most realistic environment' in an artificial town north of Magdeburg, which forms the 'Army Combat Training Centre' (GÜZ).

The training centre contained more than 500 buildings, 300 cabins, sports facilities, bridges, an industrial area, an old town with a marketplace, a government district, a slum and a sacred building. In addition, it included an airfield, a sewage system, a two-lane highway and a 350-metre-long underground train line. According to a Bundeswehr press release, 'Schnöggersburg', as the urban environment was dubbed, presented 'typical elements of an urban conurbation in order to optimally prepare soldiers for deployments in built-up areas' (Stern 2017).

These developments were taken to a new level in 2019, when a pilot project of a Bavarian 'state regiment' commenced, effectively initiating an armed homeland security force. The Bavarian State Regiment was a joint project of the Federal Ministry of Defence, the Bundeswehr, the Reservists Association and the Bavarian state government. The project was to be extended to the whole of Germany after a trial period lasting until the end of 2021. The first state regiment included 500 reservists, as well as five active Bundeswehr soldiers. Fifty other active Bundeswehr soldiers were to take part in exercises and join the force in case of emergency (Jacobson and Schwarz 2019).

An internal analysis of the Bundeswehr in 2016 had rejected a similar proposal on the grounds that the guidelines of the Reservists Association were 'incompatible' with the German constitution. The structures of the state regiments contradicted 'the state's monopoly of force' and some of the chosen formulations placed 'the principles of our liberal and democratic constitution on its head', the Bundeswehr said (Jacobson and Schwarz 2019). Yet less than two years later, such a force was being created.

The Bavarian State Regiment relied on three reserve units: the Upper, Middle and Lower Franconia companies of the Regional Security and Support Services (RSU). There were 27 such companies nationwide. Reservists included former soldiers who had retired from active duty but remained at the disposal of the Bundeswehr and, recently, specially recruited men and women between the ages of 25 and 55, who were being trained in a crash course as soldiers.

The RSU units were trained for domestic tasks that are constitutionally forbidden for the Bundeswehr. These included 'monitoring and ensuring the safety of the German air and sea areas', 'securing domestic military installations' and deployment in a 'domestic emergency'. In addition to natural disasters and particularly serious incidents, these potential emergencies included uprisings, strikes and protests that were deemed to endanger the state order (Jacobson and Schwarz 2019).

The ban on Bundeswehr domestic missions was one of the lessons drawn from the Weimar Republic and the Nazi regime. The Reichswehr (Imperial Army), together with paramilitary combat units, the secret service and police had formed a state-within-the-state. Among other things, these forces were responsible for the assassination of the Marxist leaders Rosa Luxemburg and Karl Liebknecht and the violent suppression of the Munich Soviet Republic in 1919. Operating under the protection of the Social Democratic federal government, the Freikorps (Free Corps) murdered thousands of revolutionaries and ordinary workers. This paved the way for other far-right formations, such as the Stahlhelm (Steel Helmets) and Nazi Sturmabteilung (SA), and finally Hitler's seizure of power in 1933 (Jacobson and Schwarz 2019).

The political and military calculations behind these developments had been indicated in a 2009 document from the European Union's Institute for Security Studies, titled 'What ambitions for European Defence 2020'. It saw the task of future military operations, *inter alia*, as 'shielding the global rich from the tensions and problems of the poor':

> As the proportion of the world population living in misery and frustration will remain massive, the tensions and spillover between their world and that of the rich will continue to grow. Technology is shrinking the world into a global village, but it is a village on the verge of revolution. While we have an increasingly integrated elite community, we also face increasingly explosive tensions from the poorer strata below.
>
> (Stern 2017)

Since then, social inequality in Germany and Europe has continued to increase. In 2017, a study by the Swiss bank UBS and the consulting firm Pricewaterhouse-Coopers (PwC) revealed that 117 billionaires lived in Germany alone. Worldwide, the number of billionaires rose by 10 per cent during 2016 to 1,542 and their total assets jumped by 17 per cent to $6 trillion (Stern 2017).

Moves to overturn Germany's ban on domestic military deployment

The Constitution of the German Federal Republic, produced in the aftermath of World War II and the holocaust, was originally, like that of Japan, strictly pacifist. There was considerable opposition throughout the country to changes instituted in 1956, which allowed the Republic to have an army and conscription for military service. It was accepted that the newly created armed forces would have a purely defensive role, confined within the borders of the NATO countries. Article 35 of the Constitution (Basic Law) prohibited the German military from being deployed domestically except in cases of natural disaster. It stated:

> If the natural disaster or accident endangers the territory of more than one state, the Federal Government, insofar as is necessary to combat the danger, may instruct state governments to place police forces at the disposal of other states, and may deploy units of the Federal Border Police or the Armed Forces to support the police.

After 9/11, following the lead of the United States and the UK, leading German politicians called for increasing involvement of German troops in the war on terror, both internally and externally. A political consensus also came to support a limited peacekeeping role beyond the NATO borders. In 1998 even the formally pacifist Green Party supported German participation in military action in Kosovo. From 2001, the Chairperson of the Christian Democrats (CDU), Angela Merkel, called for constitutional amendments to allow the German military to deploy inside the country in the case of a serious terrorist threat.

With the renewed crisis over Iraq in 2002, there were major concerns inside Germany about the threat of imminent US military action. As Mary Fulbrook observed, in her *Concise History of Germany*, Chancellor Gerhard Schroeder 'in part succeeded in winning the 2002 election … because he played to the remarkable levels of pacifism among a German population which had learned only too well the historical lessons of two world wars unleashed from German soil' (Fulbrook 2006: 256–257).

For many German politicians and much of the German populace, the prospect of domestic military deployment recalled the key role of the German military in provoking and overseeing the horrors of World War I, in the rise to power of fascism and the consolidation of the Nazi police-state, built upon violent intimidation, terror and mass murder.

Nevertheless, attempts continued to break down the military/police demarcation. Following an incident in 2003 when a mentally ill man hijacked a small plane and threatened to crash it into the European Central Bank Building, Interior Minister Wolfgang Schauble and others championed a law allowing the air force to shoot down hijacked planes that posed a threat to populated areas. The changes authorised such destruction before the hijacked aircraft could be used to destroy the lives of people in addition to those on the aircraft, if force was the only way to prevent this.

In 2006, however, Germany's highest court declared the law unconstitutional (German Constitutional Court 2006). The German Constitutional Court declared that the Aviation Security Act (*Luftsicherheitsgesetz—LuftSiG*), which came into effect in 2005, was 'incompatible with the fundamental right to life' and the opening paragraph of the constitution, which obliged the state to guarantee 'human dignity to the extent that the use of armed force affects persons on board the aircraft who are not participants in the crime'. The court said: 'By the state's using their killing as a means of saving others, they are treated as mere objects, which denies them the value that is due to a human being' (German Constitutional Court 2006).

In total, the Court agreed that the Act was contrary to four provisions of the Basic Law, including the right to human dignity (in Article 1I) and the right to life (in Article 2II1). However, the Court allowed that aircraft occupied only by terrorists could be shot down without infringing the Basic Law. Hufnagel commented that 'this is consistent with other German jurisprudence establishing the legality of the "final life-saving shot"' and, in particular, with a decision allowing terrorists to be killed at any time, as a continued threat to innocent lives (Hufnagel 2008: 108).

The court also ruled that the law invalidly expanded the latitude for using the military within Germany. The judges conceded that the constitution permitted the armed forces to be deployed within Germany to support the police in extraordinary circumstances—for example, in the case of 'particularly serious accidents', natural disasters and even anticipated terrorist attacks (Hufnagel 2008: 108). However, the court said that in such cases the armed forces would not be allowed to deploy any specifically military means, that is, means that the police are not permitted to use (Hufnagel 2008: 108).

In 2007, Defence Minister Franz Josef Jung publicly stated that hijacked planes would be shot down despite the court's ruling, with such action justified by 'supra-statutory state of emergency' (Hufnagel 2008: 109–110).

Moreover, even after the court judgment, Interior Minister Schauble and other prominent politicians urged deployment of the German army during the 2006 World Cup football finals, despite the existence of a special police unit capable of dealing with terrorist attacks—the GSG9, established after 11 Israeli athletes were kidnapped during the 1972 Olympic Games in Munich. In January 2006, *United Press International* reported:

> [Interior Minister] Schauble and most conservative lawmakers are in favor of changing a nearly six decade-old law to have German soldiers boost security during the World Cup. But so far, the Bundeswehr, the German armed forces, cannot be deployed domestically. Written in 1949, the German constitution established strict separation between police and military, because the Nazis had blurred that separation leading to a ruthless police state. Conservatives have in the past called for the law to be rewritten in light of Germany's spotless democratic record since World War II. Doing that would require a two-third majority in both houses of parliament.
>
> (Nicola 2006; Leicht 2006)

As the reference to the Nazis suggests, the utilisation of an alleged terrorist threat to overturn the separation between police and military functions raises worrying historical experiences. Adolf Hitler cited the 1933 Reichstag Fire, which the Nazis falsely attributed to communists, as the reason for insisting that the parliament agree to rule by decree (Kershaw 1998: 456–460).

Despite the 2006 constitutional ruling, Chancellor Angela Merkel's coalition government continued to push for domestic military deployment, led by Interior Minister Schauble, Defence Minister Brigitte Zypries and Justice Minister Franz Josef Jung. In 2008, it looked like they might win the day, with support from leading Social Democrats, including Parliamentary leader Peter Struck, for constitutional amendments allowing military call out 'when police resources are insufficient' (Hawley 2008: 2).

However, the Social Democratic Party (SPD) subsequently withdrew its support, saying that the proposed amendment was an 'unacceptable ... qualitative shift in German security structure' (Hawley 2008: 1). In this, the SPD was supported by the Greens, the Left Party and the Free Democrats. Although this meant that the CDU could not achieve the three-quarters majority needed in both houses of the German Parliament for constitutional change, the issue was by no means dead, with the CDU continuing to affirm its commitment to such change in the future. Some argued that no such constitutional change was needed to allow for such domestic deployment (Hawley 2008: 2).

That proposition proved true when, in 2012, a rare full bench of the German Constitutional Court, consisting of both its first and second senate, essentially overturned the 2006 ruling. The court interpreted Article 35 as permitting the armed forces to intervene in any case involving 'damage of catastrophic dimensions'. The court cited the phrase 'insofar as is necessary to combat the danger' in Article 35 to say that the 'damage' need not have occurred; it need only be 'imminent' (Leicht 2012).

In an effort to limit the criticism of their ruling, the judges said army deployments should be undertaken only as a 'last resort', in 'exceptional circumstances', and limited to what is 'required'. In particular, 'danger to persons and property rising from or within a protesting crowd, any grave accident in the sense of Article 35 of the Basic Law, do not justify the use of the armed forces on the basis of this ruling' (Leicht 2012).

Despite these qualifications, the judgment helped open the way for further moves by the German government to permit the domestic deployment of the armed forces.

Germany before World War I

As well as providing historical background to this debate, and explaining the high levels of public sensitivity and hostility to increasing military involvement in civilian life in Germany, the past history of German militarism provides vivid testimony of the disastrous consequences of such increased involvement.

At the outbreak of World War I, Germany was a federal empire, or Reich, composed of a number of separate kingdoms, principalities, free states and free cities with their own local political structures and powers, unified under Prussian rule (Fulbrook 2006: 129).

The German imperial state system was not the product of any major political challenge to the landed aristocracy by the rising capitalist class. 'Revolutionary' governments and parliaments were created in the industrial and state capitals of most German principalities in the 1848 uprisings by small traders, artisans and workers, pursuing radical democratic reforms. However, the propertied middle-class citizens handed power in these assemblies were quite unwilling to organise effective opposition to defend such institutions from the old state authorities. The uprisings were crushed by 1849.

Three wars between 1864 and 1870 contributed to the unification of previously independent states under Prussian imperial domination with the proclamation of the German Empire at Versailles in January 1871. A new constitution created a tripartite structure of political power. A parliament or Reichstag, directly elected by universal male suffrage in a secret ballot, had limited veto-powers in relation to legislation initiated in a Federal Council made up of delegates from the separate states. But the Prussian leadership of emperor, chancellor and top ministers and public servants exercised effective executive authority and control of the Federal Council, with the Prussian War Minister and Prussian army leadership operating largely outside of parliamentary control (Fulbrook 2006: 128–129). This lack of effective parliamentary control of the military had profound consequences for German history 'into the First World War and well beyond' (Fulbrook 2006: 129).

At the same time, the democratic institutions of most of the local states had a restricted franchise, with the old landed aristocracy having a majority of the votes. Freedom of speech was highly restricted, with frequent attacks on the left-wing press and arrests of socialists and social democrats. In 1878 Bismarck pushed through the Reichstag a law banning socialist meetings, organisations and associations, including those of the SPD, while still allowing SPD deputies to take their seats in Parliament (Fulbrook 2006: 133). Police and troops were frequently used to attack demonstrations and strikes, 'as in 1912 when cavalry used sabres and bullets against striking miners in the Ruhr' (Harman 1982: 14).

The failed post-war revolution and the Weimar Republic

The expansion of German capitalism increasingly involved the takeover and subordination of smaller firms to giant cartels and trusts. These monopoly powers sought government support in expanding their overseas access to cheap labour and raw materials and protected markets. This inevitably brought Germany into conflict with the established imperial powers of Britain and France (Harman 1982: 22). The First World War was the logical outcome and culmination of these developments, with Germany supporting an Austrian attack on Serbia, while Russia and France backed the Serbs, and Britain joined with the French to fight in Belgium.

Despite vigorous opposition from a minority of socialists within the SPD, the majority leadership supported the war. But conditions for German workers, as well as German soldiers, progressively worsened as the war dragged on, with limited food supplies, and starvation and epidemic disease in some regions by the winter of 1916–17. Increasing numbers of workers became involved in mass street demonstrations and protest strikes against continued warfare.

For a period in November and December 1918, workers and soldiers councils 'were the only legal authority in the Reich' (Guerin 1973: 33). However, the Social Democratic leaders were implacably opposed to soviet-style revolutionary councils (Guerin 1973: 33; Fulbrook 2006: 158–160). The party leader, Ebert, moved in the Council of Peoples Representatives to enforce elections for a National Assembly to produce a constitution for a parliamentary system. Significantly, he formed an alliance with the head of the army, General Wilhelm Groener, promising not to move to reform the army command structure if the army supported him in defeating socialist revolution. 'The pair agreed to work together to restore order in the army so that the army could restore order in society as a whole' (Harman 2008: 431–432).

Ebert's use of the military to brutally suppress a Berlin army mutiny in November 1918 was condemned by left wingers. At the end of December, the Spartacist group, which had opposed the SPD-led government, formed the new Communist Party of Germany, the KPD (Fulbrook 2006: 160). In the same month, Social Democratic Minister of the Interior, Noske had agreed with the army generals to set up a special mercenary force, the Freikorps. Drawn from the officers and storm battalions of the old army, it was heavily anti-socialist, nationalist and anti-Semitic.

In January, the Social Democratic leadership 'manoeuvred with the military high command ... to provoke a rising in Berlin in order to crush it with troops from outside, blaming the bloodshed on the Communist Party leaders, Liebknecht and Luxemburg' (Harman 2008: 432). These communist leaders were murdered by army officers on the pretext that they were planning violence (Harman 1982: 86). Throughout the first half of 1919, the Freikorps moved through the country attacking organised workers and socialists. It met repeated armed resistance, culminating in the proclamation in April of a short-lived Bavarian Socialist Republic with its own Red Army of 15,000.

To escape from fighting in Berlin, the National Constituent Assembly convened in the city of Weimar. Under the Weimar Constitution, which took effect in August 1919, a president was to be elected by direct popular vote for a period of seven years, and given considerable powers. These included to appoint and dismiss Chancellors, dissolve parliament and call new elections, hold national referenda and rule by emergency decree (Article 48) (Fulbrook 2006: 162–163). The army reported directly to the president, who could thus direct military operations without reference to the parliament.

The post-World War I Versailles Treaty had limited the Reichswehr to 100,000 soldiers and 15,000 sailors. In theory it required replacement of the wartime leadership, but the old German officer class remained in control. The generals moved increasingly to expand the army's operations through the development of 'underground' units, collectively known as the 'Black Reichswehr', made up of nationalist volunteers, financed by wealthy industrialists and trained for operations against left wingers (Harman 1982: 233). These included not only the Freikorps but also the Baltikum corps, 50,000 strong, which was sent to fight the Soviet army in Lithuania in June 1919 (Campbell 2004: 132).

Between 1919, when the Weimar Republic was instituted, and 1932, on the eve of Hitler's appointment as German Chancellor, Article 48 was invoked more than

250 times, most often in the context of economic upheavals (Gross and Ni Aolain 2006: 84; Head 2016: 42–46).

Alongside the Article 42 emergency power, the Weimar Constitution also allowed the president to dismiss the chancellor, even if the chancellor retained the confidence of the Reichstag. Similarly, the president could appoint a chancellor who did not have the support of the Reichstag. In effect, the president acted as a 'replacement Kaiser', assuming powers the monarch would have wielded.

Ebert's regime faced the constant danger of a resurgence of a working-class uprising, which was to erupt again in 1921 and 1923, as well as threatened coups by the military and the Nazis. During 1923, French and Belgian troops occupied the Ruhr and re-ignited the political and social crisis in Germany. The government's counter-measures led to hyper-inflation, which devastated the lives of millions of people and triggered both an abortive coup by Hitler and a botched revolution led by the Communist Party (Trotsky 1971). Ebert's regime relied on the military generals to survive and rested on a virtual military dictatorship for months in 1923–24, legitimised by the Weimar constitution (Broué 2006).

During the final period of the republic, from 1930 to 1933, Article 48 was invoked by President von Hindenburg repeatedly. Amid the economic breakdown of the Great Depression, it was used to override the Reichstag, on behalf of German big business, at the behest of successive chancellors, Bruning, Papen, Schlicher and ultimately Hitler (Kershaw 1998: 315–423).

Throughout the Weimar period, the country's most prominent legal theorist, Carl Schmitt, justified and sought to legitimise the resort to authoritarian measures. In 1932, for example, he appeared before the Supreme Court to defend a declaration of martial law. In effect, he acted as a handmaiden to fascism, and then served the Nazi regime (Head 2016: 117–129).

Fascism and the military

In the summer of 1920, Adolf Hitler first formed a 'shock troops' unit trained to attack and disrupt the public meetings of opponents on the left. Later Hitler would boast of the extreme violence successfully employed by this group with the tacit support of local police, military and government officers. In 1922, he named his force Storm Troops, the SA. And in 1923 he formed a personal guard, the Hitler Shock Troops, known as the SS.

Hitler modelled the Nazi Party on Mussolini's Italian fascist organisation, initially recruiting war veterans, unemployed young people, peasants seeking work in the towns, desperate small businesspeople, criminals and beggars as armed gangs, attacking trade unionists and socialists. Initially small bands of armed men launched brutal surprise attacks on crowds of workers, and acted to break strikes and protect scab labour (Guerin 1973: 108).

In the third week of 1923, following the failure of Germany to pay France its full quota of reparations, the French took over two thirds of the Ruhr basin, a major centre of industrial production. These developments contributed to the rapid growth of ultra-nationalist right-wing parties, particularly recruiting from the devastated middle class, and the desperate unemployed.

It was at this time that Hitler first achieved nationwide recognition, organising right-wing terrorists, anti-Semites and former Freikorps members in a failed coup in Munich. Hitler maintained close links with the German military. 'For the Army High Command, the Nazis and kindred groups were a useful counterweight to the forces of the left', engaging in violent attacks upon any such left wingers in the streets (Harman 1982: 233). The army failed to support the coup, however, and Hitler was imprisoned for six months.

A new right-wing central government presided over the stabilisation of the mark through a tight credit squeeze, causing large-scale factory closures and higher levels of unemployment and underemployment. The chief of the Reichswehr was given powers of civil intervention. Under the protection of the military, the eight-hour day, achieved through working-class action in late 1918, was scrapped.

In 1926 and 1927, the Nazis revived successively the SS and the SA. The Hitler bands resumed their disruption of working-class public meetings, though by 1927–28 the party was only a marginal electoral force, with only a few thousand members (Guerin 1973: 37). This changed with the onset of the Great Depression. Along with the US and British economies, the German economy was beginning to turn down before the great crash of October 1929. By the end of 1930 its output was lower than it had been in previous post-World War I recessions, and things got worse with a third of the workforce jobless and major bank collapses in 1932.

The new crisis contributed to an increase in votes for the Nazi Party, reaching 6 million in 1930 and 12 million, 37 per cent of the vote, in July 1932 (Harman 2008: 483). With the established mainstream parties seemingly unable to save workers from unemployment and their own middle-class supporters from poverty and bankruptcy, increasing numbers of middle-class people, along with some workers, turned to Hitler's movement for salvation. At the same time, despite Hitler's anti-capitalist rhetoric, the Nazis were supported by significant big business leaders, who saw them as a valuable counter-force to left-wing parties, workers and unions, unrestricted by liberal 'legality' (Harman 2008: 486).

The Nazis were not simply or mainly an electoral party. At the core of their organisation were paramilitary street fighters—the SA or Stormtroopers, numbering 100,000 at the end of 1930, and 400,000 by mid-1932. These armed thugs, recruited from amongst desperate unemployed people, openly protected by the Reichswehr, were dedicated to battling against those they blamed for the social crisis—attacking supposedly Jewish finance capital on the one side and Jewish Marxist trade unionists on the other (Harman 2008: 483).

The Social Democrats did build their own paramilitary defence organisations. But they insisted on mobilising these groups for a head-on confrontation with Nazism only if Hitler 'broke the constitution' (Harman 2008: 485). This never happened. Instead, democratic 'legality' allowed President Hindenburg and von Papen to secretly negotiate with Hitler in 1932 to issue a decree overthrowing the Social Democratic government in Prussia, and ultimately to appoint Hitler as Chancellor in January 1933 (Fulbrook 2006: 177). Harman noted that:

> within a few days the paramilitary forces of the Nazis were being integrated into the state machine. The SA Stormtroopers and the police worked together to harass the working class parties. Then, on 27 February, the Nazis used a fire in the Reichstag as an excuse to ban the Communist Party, suppress its press and drag off 100,000 of its members to concentration camps.
>
> (Harman 2008: 489)

Despite mass intimidation of the electorate, the Nazis still failed to get an absolute majority in elections in March, and even with their Nationalist coalition partners they did not get the two-thirds majority required by the constitution to pass an Enabling Law (Fulbrook 2006: 179). But in March, by exploiting the infamous Reichstag fire, Hitler was able to pass the Enabling Law by preventing communists and Social Democrats from attending the parliament. After this, 'Hitler could pass any "law" he wanted, without regard for parliamentary approval' (Fulbrook 2006: 179).

The military and the post-war constitution

After World War II, the allies divided Germany into zones of occupation, agreeing to policies of denazification, demilitarisation and democratisation (Fulbrook 2006: 206). With the advent of the Cold War, Germany was split in two. In the West, the Federal Republic formally came into being in May 1949, closely followed by the German Democratic Republic in the East in October.

The Constitution of the Federal Republic, or 'Basic Law', sought to avoid the sorts of political developments associated with the Nazis' rise to power. The Basic Law has a President as formal head of state, as in the Weimar Constitution. But the president is selected by an electoral college of parliamentarians, rather than a popular vote, and has no emergency powers like those that allowed the Reichsprasident to remove Communist parliamentarians at the time of the Reichstag Fire Decree. When a new West German army, the Bundeswehr, was created in 1955, the amended Basic Law required that it answer to the Secretary of Defence during peacetime and the Chancellor during wartime, with both of them answerable to the parliament.

Following the dissolution of the Wehrmacht at the end of World War II, Germany was demilitarised, with the allied powers responsible for security issues. But, in the West, Chancellor Adenauer formed a committee to plan for future re-armament in 1950, responding, in part, to remilitarisation in the East. In 1954, following the restoration of sovereignty to the Federal Republic with the London and Paris agreements, the United States, the UK and France agreed to support West Germany's entry into NATO and rearmament, as an ally in the Cold War.

By 2008, the Bundeswehr had over 200,000 professional soldiers, with 55,000 conscripts, serving for nine months or more, and 2,500 active reservists. Yet, when the constitution was amended to allow the existence of the army, it was clearly established that its role was a purely defensive one (article 87a). Before 1990, its major active role was in disaster relief work. The peacetime commander of the

Bundeswehr was the Minister of Defence, with the Chancellor as commander in chief once a 'state of defence' was declared.

A number of Constitutional Court cases in the 1990s established that a special resolution of the Parliament is required to allow the deployment of the army outside the territory of the NATO member states. Such a resolution is required to spell out full details of the mission and the limits of its term. Recent years have seen a steady expansion of German military activity abroad, however, including in Afghanistan.

Anti-terrorism powers

A range of new anti-terrorism laws was introduced following the terrorist attacks of 9/11, with a serious impact on civil and democratic rights. 'Amendments were made to 17 existing laws and five regulations, with consequential changes to more than 100 German laws.' Contact bans with lawyers were extended to where 'there is a risk that the lawyer would conceal evidence from the investigators' (Hufnagel 2008: 102).

The issue of torture during interrogation, supposedly justified by the imminence and extent of terrorist threat, was directly addressed in the Dascher case. A senior police officer raised a defence of necessity to justify assault upon a supposed child kidnapper to try to discover the whereabouts of the victim before the child suffered harm or died. The police also appealed to the 1927 concept of 'supra-statutory emergency' (Hufnagel 2008: 102).

The German District Court held that basic values of the life of the victim as against the dignity and humanity of the prisoner could not be weighed against one another. The judges ruled that torture was never justified and found the officer liable for assault. However, they accepted that 'pressing need' could justify mitigation in sentencing.

As highlighted by Defence Minister Jung's earlier-mentioned defiant response to the similar ruling in the 2005 Constitutional Court case about shooting down hijacked aircraft, such legal judgments are by no means a guarantee against violent domestic use of the armed forces.

Italy: Thousands of troops on the streets and beaches

In the twenty-first century, no European country has seen a more protracted large-scale domestic deployment of the military to deal with civil unrest than Italy. Troops have been on the streets since 2008, when they were first mobilised by Prime Minister Silvio Berlusconi, supposedly to crack down on crime. In 2017, beachgoers were confronted by the sight of armed soldiers, part of a force of 7,000 troops deployed to stop the entry of refugees.

A resurgence of Italian military activity, both overseas and domestically, has generated concerns about the potential emergence of parallels to the 1920s and 1930s, when Mussolini's fascist regime combined an internal military-backed dictatorship with aggressive armed expansionism in Libya and Ethiopia (The Economist 2008; Arens 2008).

Domestically, the Italian government deployed 3,000 troops in 2008, supposedly to crack down on illegal immigrants and combat crime. Following a six-month trial, in 2009 the government moved to implement a second phase of 'Operation Safe Streets', involving up to 30,000 soldiers. The operation began in mid-2008, when Berlusconi proclaimed a state of emergency due to the inflow of refugees by boat across the Mediterranean Sea, and the Defence Minister signed a decree to permit the use of 3,000 troops for domestic purposes.

One thousand troops were assigned to refugee internment camps, officially called 'identification and classification centres', another 1,000 to sensitive public places (train stations, embassies, St Peter's Cathedral, etc.) and the remainder to patrol streets in Rome and other major cities, alongside police officers. Armed troops, some in body armour and with automatic weapons, appeared on the streets, including some who had previously served in Afghanistan, Iraq or Lebanon (Michaels 2008; Dinmore 2008).

There was widespread criticism, both internationally and domestically, with political commentators accusing the government of seeking to 'militarise' city centres. Others pointed out that crime rates had actually fallen in Italy and the country already had 230,000 police and carabinieri. In early 2009, the government decided to extend the operation even though crime statistics for the previous six months had not been compiled (Povoledo 2009).

While the military deployment was not unprecedented in the post-World War II period—some 20,000 troops were sent to Sicily in 1992 to combat the Mafia, and soldiers were often seen in Italian cities during the Red Brigades attacks in the 1970s and 1980s—the emergency measures revived memories of Mussolini's fascist dictatorship. Just as Jews became scapegoats for fascists in the 1930s, there were signs that gypsies and other immigrants were being targeted as economic and social conditions deteriorated in 2008 and 2009. Prime Minister Berlusconi made his announcement about expanding 'Operation Safe Streets' to 30,000 soldiers against the backdrop of a media campaign against an alleged crime wave involving an influx of Eastern European gypsies (Dinmore and Bianchi 2009).

In January 2009, military units were deployed to make arrests and break up illegally erected shacks in Rome. After allegations that units of the Folgore parachute brigade were mobilised, an army spokesman said Sardinian grenadiers had been involved in checking the identities of 70 gypsies living in an illegal camp (Dinmore and Bianchi 2009).

After the refugee crisis triggered by the US-led military interventions in the Middle East worsened further after 2015, this operation was accompanied by a 'Safe Sea' deployment patrolling the country's coastline and the Mediterranean Sea.

During the summer of 2017, the visibility of the military mobilisation increased when the government deployed 7,000 troops armed with submachine guns to patrol beaches, train stations and other locations to intercept refugees. According to one media report:

> The operation sees the rather surreal sight of uniformed, armed soldiers patrolling the Italian beaches amongst the holidaymakers … Across the

> capital, there are 158 points that have a fixed army presence, which include embassies, archaeological sites, two airports—Fiumicino and Ciampino, one port, 13 train stations and 37 metro stations.
>
> (Rogers 2017)

The Carabinieri model?

In some military-strategic circles, the Carabinieri, the military-police fourth arm of the Italian armed forces, which conducts the 'Safe Streets' operation, has been touted as a possible model for institutionalising and legitimising the greater involvement of the military in combatting civil unrest (Braw 2018).

Unlike the Polizia di Stato, one of Italy's other main policing agencies, the Carabinieri is a military force, and so is Guardia di Finanza, another law enforcement agency. There is a significant overlap between the jurisdiction of the Polizia di Stato and Carabinieri, but the latter's soldiers are heavily armed and regularly participate in military missions abroad.

The Carabinieri model has been hailed as a 'useful alternative to traditional troops', both for dealing with civil unrest at home and for performing similar tasks during external military interventions. In 2018, Elisabeth Braw, the director of the Modern Deterrence programme at Britain's Royal United Services Institute, an influential military thinktank, and an adjunct fellow at the Center for European Policy Analysis, wrote: 'With cuisine and fashion, the world has been extremely active in copying Italy. Let's do the same with the Carabinieri' (Braw 2018). She noted: 'If, say, a mass riot broke out after a Roma-Lazio game, the Carabinieri would be trusted to restore order' (Braw 2018). Braw continued:

> Crucially, the Carabinieri are also trained soldiers; they serve under both the Ministry of Defense and the Ministry of Interior … Indeed, the Carabinieri play a crucial role in international stability-projection. 'Their dual identity has allowed the Carabinieri to take part in Italian military missions abroad both as a combat unit, as a Military Police unit, as a specialized anti-riot crowd control unit, and as trainers of the indigenous police forces and security units in a crisis area,' General Claudio Graziano, Italy's Chief of Defense, told me.
>
> (Braw 2018)

Braw praised the Carabinieri's participation in the ongoing US-led operations in Afghanistan and Iraq, emphasising that some 500 Carabinieri were on foreign deployment, serving as part of 33 missions. In Afghanistan 30 Carabinieri were training and assisting the Afghan military and police forces, while in Iraq Carabinieri had trained 13,000 police officers in the previous two years. Carabinieri were also on the frontline of European governments' efforts to control and repel refugees:

> Perhaps even more significantly, some 160 Carabinieri serve as part of international Multinational Specialised Units in Bosnia and Kosovo, helping maintain public order, patrolling sensitive areas, and assisting the return of refugees and displaced persons.
>
> (Braw 2018)

Domestically, Carabinieri have policing powers that can be exercised at any time and in any part of the country, and they are always permitted to carry their assigned pistols or other weapons as personal equipment. The Carabinieri has a troubled history. In particular, it assisted in the suppression of opposition during the fascist dictatorship of Benito Mussolini during the 1920s, 1930s and early 1940s.

Recalling Italy's fascist experience

Despite this repressive history, intensive efforts have been made, as in other countries, to glorify the military and whitewash its history. In a speech on 12 November 2018 to commemorate the 100th anniversary of the end of World War I and to celebrate Italy's National Unity and Armed Forces Day, the country's president, Sergio Mattarella, declared:

> On the National Unity Day, the Italians stand by the Armed Forces with gratitude … Their history, full of heroic deeds, has continued up to our current days following the most noble traditions, yet projected into the future with the same devotion, altruism and passion … While we are celebrating this important anniversary, 5,600 Italian soldiers are deployed abroad in peacekeeping operations organized by the United Nations, the Atlantic Alliance, the European Union, with large or small contingents. Moreover, there are almost eight thousand women and men serving in the Armed Forces involved on the national territory in the operation 'Strade Sicure' ('Safe Streets') and in the Mediterranean Sea with 'Mare Sicuro' ('Safe Sea').
>
> (Mattarella 2018)

Thus, while invoking the spirit of the World War II anti-Nazi resistance, and portraying the armed forces as vehicles for advancing peace and human rights, the president urged the Italian people to support the re-emergence of the military to the centre of social and political life, as it was under Mussolini.

To assess the significance of these developments, it is necessary to briefly review the rise of Italian fascism and the essential assistance given to it by the military high command.

As in Germany, the end of World War I triggered revolutionary activity by industrial and agricultural workers and soldiers, sickened by the massive loss of life in a futile imperial conflict. Proto-fascist movements started out as aggressive 'anti-labour militia, entrusted by capitalist magnates and country landlords with the mission of harassing the organized proletariat and destroying its power of resistance' (Guerin 1973: 102).

In Italy, a succession of mass strikes and factory occupations forced major concessions, including higher wages, an eight-hour day, 'general recognition of collective contracts and a voice for the working class in the organisation of production through "factory committees"' (Guerin 1973: 37). Major industrialists and landowners, meeting in Genoa and Milan in 1919 and 1920, formed detailed plans for action against the working class, centred upon the use of armed gangs, including war veterans and unemployed people, under the control of Mussolini, to threaten, harry, attack and terrorise the organised proletariat (Guerin 1973: 38–39).

Mussolini's 'action squadrons' initially operated in the country, with support from local police and the army, launching surprise raids on workers' meetings, killing, wounding and torturing, before rapidly retreating. 'Munitions from the state arsenals came into the hands of the fascist bands, which were trained by officers on leave or even on active service' (Guerin 1973: 105).

Later, Italian capitalists assisted Mussolini to turn his organisation into a political party and increase the sales of his newspaper, the *Populo d'Italia*, campaigning for the destruction of independent labour organisations, an end to democratic rights and an increase in military spending to sustain an expansionary foreign policy.

Disappointed with the post-World War I peace settlement and fearing civilian control, the Army generals also sought an alliance with fascism, and allowed Mussolini to seize power in 1922. Over the ensuing years, the armed fascist militia, the 'Blackshirts' or National Security Volunteer Militia (Milizia Volontaria per la Sicurezza Nazionale (MVSN)), which terrorised incipient resistances in the cities and provinces, became integrated into the armed forces. By 1933, Mussolini grew powerful enough to appoint a fascist military leadership over the Army. He also created and held the supreme military rank of First Marshal of the Empire, along with the King, giving him supreme control over the military (Gooch 2008; Sullivan 1984).

Written in the aftermath of Italy's defeat in World War II, and Mussolini's overthrow, Article 11 of the post-war Italian Constitution stated that 'Italy rejects war as a means for settling international controversies and as an instrument of aggression against the freedoms of others peoples'.

Nevertheless, by the early years of the twenty-first century, Italy had the eighth highest military expenditure in the world, and the total number of military personnel was approximately 308,000. After the 2001 declaration of the 'war on terrorism', Italy sent troops to join the US-led invasion of Afghanistan and later participated in the occupation of Iraq, with troops patrolling Nasiriyah and surrounding areas in 2003 (Paoletti 2008: 205–215).

9 Japan

Creeping militarisation

Despite Japan being formally banned from maintaining a military force under its post-World War II constitution, its government has embarked on re-militarising the country since the turn of the century. A Credit Suisse survey published in 2015 ranked Japan as the world's fourth most-powerful military behind the United States, Russia and China (O'Sullivan 2015).

More specifically, deploying military troops domestically to suppress civil unrest was placed back on the political agenda in 2018 by a leading figure in the ruling Liberal Democratic Party (LDP). Shigeru Ishiba, a former LDP secretary general and defense minister, called for the party to adhere to the LDP's 2012 draft constitution, which proposed adding two new paragraphs to the country's constitution. These would establish a National Defense Force, with the prime minister as Commander in Chief, legalise its involvement in 'peacekeeping' operations abroad, and allow the military to be deployed domestically to put down public unrest (McGrath 2018a).

Proposals to revise Article 9

These proposals came as the LDP government was preparing a draft revision of Article 9 of the post-World War II constitution, which bound Japan to renouncing war. While Article 9 has not prevented Japan from building one of the world's largest military forces, Prime Minister Shinzo Abe was working to remove legal and constitutional barriers to using the so-called Self Defense Forces (SDF) to once again pursue the strategic and economic interests of the Japanese ruling class at home and abroad.

Article 9 contained two paragraphs. The first said 'the Japanese people forever renounce war as a sovereign right of the nation'. The second declared that 'war potential will never be maintained' and the 'right of belligerency of the state will not be recognised'. Aware of widespread popular opposition to rearmament, Abe proposed to leave the two paragraphs intact while adding a third paragraph that explicitly legalised the SDF. However, Ishiba and others wanted to go further, despite a Kyodo news agency poll showing that 55 per cent of voters opposed revising Article 9. The government was concerned to seek ways to overcome this opposition, because any change to the constitution must be approved by a two-thirds majority of both houses of the Diet (parliament), and a majority in a national referendum (McGrath 2018a).

At the end of 2018, Abe's cabinet approved new National Defense Program Guidelines that would accelerate Tokyo's remilitarisation, including the acquisition of offensive weaponry such as aircraft carriers, F-35 fighter jets and cruise missiles. Until then, governments had maintained the charade that the Japanese military had a purely defensive character. While admitting that the constitution prohibited aircraft carriers, the Defense Ministry said the plans to convert its Izumo-class helicopter carriers to carry and launch United States-made F-35s remained defensive in character. Over the ensuing five years, the government intended to spend approximately 27.47 trillion yen ($US248 billion) on the military, three trillion yen more than the period from 2014 to 2018 (McGrath 2018b).

In May 2017, Abe set a 2020 deadline for revising Article 9. In the meantime, in September 2015, his government had succeeded in having the National Diet enact a series of 'security' laws that allowed the SDF to undertake 'collective self-defense' of allies for the first time since World War II. This meant that the SDF could provide material support to allies engaged in combat internationally. It also allowed SDF troops to defend weapons platforms of foreign countries. The United States, which retains military bases and thousands of troops in Japan, was the most obvious of these allies, so the legislation allowed Japan to join US-led military interventions. However, this alignment could shift in the future. The legislation potentially applies to all countries designated as allies. These 2015 measures were the most significant changes to Japan's military laws since World War II (Slavin 2015).

Executive power over the military

While Japan's post-war constitution imposed constraints on the use of the SDF, the prime minister has potentially great authority to deploy the military. Under the SDF Law, or *Jieitaihō*, the prime minister is the Commander in Chief of the SDF, with the chain of command running to the Defense Minister and the Ministry of Defense (Ministry of Defense 2007: 4–5). This command structure was intended to assert civilian control over the military, as a safeguard against a reversion to the pre-war military dictatorship. One study stated:

> It makes clear that the defense affairs of the nation fall completely within the purview of the cabinet's administrative powers as part of general administrative affairs and that all matters relating to military command and administration are under the control of the cabinet. It was expected that by thus centralizing command authority over the military within the cabinet, there would be no reoccurrence of the prewar command independence.
>
> (Eldridge and Midford 2017: 234)

However, as in the United States, this concentration of control in the hands of the prime minister and cabinet also creates the conditions for political exploitation of the military power, as well as for the potential use of the armed forces to suppress political opposition. This danger was evident in 1960 when Tokyo was rocked by huge demonstrations opposing the ratification of a new US–Japan Security Treaty.

By one account, the country was plunged into a political crisis that swathed government on the brink of deploying troops against protesters:

> These massive anti-security-treaty demonstrations (*anpō tōsō* in Japanese) at one point effectively encircled the Diet building with 330,000 demonstrators, and prompted national strikes of over six million workers. As John Welfield put it, 'by June 1960 Japan had come perilously close to civil War'. In reaction, conservative Prime Minister Kishi Nobusuke called for the mobilization of the GSDF [Ground SDF] to restore order and ensure the safety of President Dwight D. Eisenhower's planned visit to Japan. In anticipation of massive anti-treaty demonstrations, Sugita Ichiji, GSDF Chief of Staff, drafted a confidential plan to mobilize the GSDF to maintain public order and shared it with high-ranking GSDF officers. However, many of these officers opposed this plan, believing it would seriously damage the GSDF's standing with the public. During the height of the crisis, Kishi himself urged Japan Defense Agency Director-General Akagi Muneyoshi to mobilize the GSDF against the demonstrators to ensure the safety and success of Eisenhower's impending visit. However Akagi refused, claiming that Eisenhower's visit did not warrant the damage mobilization would do to GSDF and SDF legitimacy. Kishi reluctantly backed down and canceled what would have been the first visit by a sitting US President to Japan.
>
> (Eldridge and Midford 2017: 302–303)

Although that extraordinary political crisis resulted in a pulling back from sending in the military to combat civilian protests, similar confrontations in the future could see troops mobilised. Article 83 of the SDF Law enables prefectural governors to request SDF deployments to protect people and property in 'natural calamities'. But in the case of such calamities or 'other disasters' that are 'pressing emergencies' the mobilisation can be ordered by the Defense Minister or designated military commanders without a prefectural governor's request (Eldridge and Midford 2017: 266).

There have been legal challenges to the expansion of the SDF's role. After the 2015 decision to allow the SDF to participate in 'collective self-defense' overseas, an active Ground SDF member brought a suit against the government demanding that it clarify whether or not he would have to go abroad if the SDF were ordered to do so. The SDF plaintiff argued that the constitution, which disavows armed aggression in any form, prohibited Japan from carrying out collective self-defence. The SDF member wanted the government to confirm that it would send him overseas if an ally requested it.

In 2017, the Tokyo District Court dismissed the suit out of hand because it found 'no specific possibility of such an order being issued'. In effect, the court said it could not rule on a theoretical scenario. In 2018, the Tokyo High Court rejected the appeal but sent the case back to the lower court, saying that the plaintiff deserved to know if he was obligated to follow such an order since he could be prosecuted if he were to disobey it. This case was one of a series of lawsuits seeking to define the role of the SDF within the scope of the constitution. All had ended in the government obfuscating that role, so that it avoided addressing the precise issues (Brasor 2018).

Disaster relief as a means of politically legitimising the SDF

Since 1960, successive governments have taken measures to rehabilitate the military's image, particularly through the heavy use of the SDF to conduct disaster relief operations and other civilian tasks at home, as well as in 'humanitarian' and 'peacekeeping' missions abroad. Through these operations, the Japanese population has been acclimatised to the sight of troop mobilisations, albeit apparently benign ones.

Japan's military has a post-war record of being heavily involved in public works, which provides a means of establishing a domestic presence and overcoming historically rooted public distrust. One study of this process concluded: 'In terms of reputation building, a large share of the GSDF's post-war operations can be classified as confidence-building measures designed to convince citizens that it poses no threat to the public or to peace, and can benefit them' (Eldridge and Midford 2017: 297). Another study noted:

> Article 83 of the Self-Defense Forces Law of 1954, required units to respond to calls for assistance from prefectural governors to aid in fire fighting, earthquake disasters, searches for missing persons, rescues, and reinforcement of embankments and levees in the event of flooding. [And] the SDF ... continued to devote much of its time and resources to disaster relief and other civic action. Between 1984 and 1988, at the request of prefectural governors, the SDF assisted in approximately 3,100 disaster relief operations, involving about 138,000 personnel, 16,000 vehicles, 5,300 aircraft, and 120 ships and small craft. In addition, the SDF participated in earthquake disaster prevention operations and disposed of a large quantity of World War II explosive ordnance, especially in Okinawa. The forces also participated in public works projects, cooperated in managing athletic events, took part in annual Antarctic expeditions, and conducted aerial surveys to report on ice conditions for fishermen and on geographic formations for construction projects. Especially sensitive to maintaining harmonious relations with communities close to defense bases, the SDF built new roads, irrigation networks, and schools in those areas. Soundproofing was installed in homes and public buildings near airfields. Despite these measures, local resistance to military installations remained strong in some areas.
>
> (Maeda 1995: 38)

Detailed studies showed that the frequency of these deployments has grown over time, with militarised operations often replacing inadequate or reduced civilian ones. From a modest beginning in 1951, the number of disaster dispatches by the Ground SDF grew to averages of more than 500 per year by 2012 (Eldridge and Midford 2017: 276). That was almost ten such operations per week.

In fiscal year 2006, said to be a typical year without any large-scale disasters, the GSDF dispatched a total of 7,000 troops 24 times for natural disaster responses, involving 1,700 vehicles and 148 aircraft. Soldiers also played a large role in the emergency transportation of medical patients and provision of other similar services. Altogether there were 579 such dispatches of 2,563 personnel, two vehicles and 599 planes in fiscal 2006. The SDF was also dispatched 117 times to assist in fire-fighting, operations that involved 3,250 personnel, 333 vehicles and 99 aircraft, and made 46 dispatches for civilian search and rescue missions, involving 3,200 personnel, 480 vehicles, and 85 aircraft (Eldridge and Midford 2017: 314–315).

Eldridge and Midford concluded: ‘It was disaster relief dispatches that enabled the GSDF to gain legitimacy in the eyes of its citizens and established its importance within Japanese society’ (Eldridge and Midford 2017: 266).

This politically driven trend reached a new height during the earthquake and tsunami disaster that devastated entire towns and triggered a nuclear reactor meltdown in eastern Japan in 2011. Prime Minister Kan Naoto ordered the mobilisation of 50,000 SDF troops on the first day of the disaster, and expanded deployment to 100,000 two days later. SDF numbers peaked at just over 106,000 a week after the quake. This constituted almost half the SDF’s troop strength, and represented the largest mobilisation in SDF history (Eldridge and Midford 2017: 331).

Media outlets, both in Japan and internationally, uncritically hailed the deployment and declared that it signalled a new relationship between the military and civil society.

> Foreign media, heavily involved in the coverage and being given unprecedented access to SDF and bilateral operations, reported that ‘it was the first time Japanese citizens acknowledged the importance of the SDF as part of the democratic nation of postwar Japan’.
>
> (Eldridge and Midford 2017: 265)

This operation corresponded to a broader official shift in the role of the SDF, from Cold War-era defence of the country against invasion to a much more active involvement domestically, as well as globally. One study explained:

> Rapid changes in the security environment after the 9/11 terrorist attacks brought drastic changes to the SDF’s policy, equipment, organization, and management. During the Cold War, the SDF was only expected to stop direct invasions, but it was now required to be a ‘functional force’ that could respond to terrorism, ballistic missiles, and other threats. As a result, in the revised 2010 National Defense Program Guidelines, the ‘Dynamic Defense Capability’ concept that emphasized the functionality of the SDF finally replaced the former ‘Basic Defense Capability’.
>
> (Eldridge and Midford 2017: 285)

The growing domestic role of the SDF was mirrored by increasing overseas deployments, also depicted as benevolent and non-threatening contributions to disaster relief, humanitarian or peacekeeping needs. For the first time since World War II, Japanese troops were sent abroad, in places as far afield as Cambodia, Mozambique, Rwanda, Syria, Honduras, Afghanistan and Iraq (Eldridge and Midford 2017: 317–330). Eldridge and Midford concluded:

> [T]oday military engagement in disaster relief operations has become an important duty globally, and militaries that contribute to disaster relief have come to be called the 'post-modern military'. In other words, disaster relief operations have come to shape the GSDF's 'main duties' and are now more than ever the basis for their legitimacy, and for overcoming the anti-military feelings of citizens.
>
> (Eldridge and Midford 2017: 289)

Because of public disquiet, such operations generally have been presented as counter-terrorist or humanitarian. As one commentator observed, even the participation of the SDF in 'peaceful overseas operations' is a 'sensitive and much debated topic' (Tharp 2008).

In 2005, Japan sent 925 SDF personnel to Indonesia after the earthquake in the Indian Ocean and the tsunami that killed more than 150,000 people. While SDF members participated in disaster relief efforts, it was the largest overseas military deployment since World War II. The following year, the Japan Coast Guard (JCG) assisted in the containment of the Guimaras oil spill in the Philippines. In 2008, Prime Minister Yasuo Fukuda announced that Japan would send SDF officials into Sudan as part of a UN peacekeeping mission.

During 2007, the inaugural cabinet-level Defense Minister, Fumio Kyuma, gave some statistical indices of the expansion of SDF activities that had already occurred since the Great Hanshin-Awaji earthquake (commonly known as the Kobe earthquake) in 1995:

> In recent years, the missions of the Self Defence Forces have been not only the defence of our nation, but its missions have expanded into response to disasters inside and outside Japan, international peace cooperation and more. And there has also been a dramatic increase in the actual activities performed. Since the Great Hanshin-Awaji Earthquake, a total of approximately 2.73 million Self Defence Forces personnel have been dispatched to engage in disaster relief missions. While overseas, roughly 30,000 Self Defence Forces personnel have been engaged in around 20 international peace cooperation activities such as PKO.
>
> (Japan Ministry of Defense 2007)

Creeping militarisation

Widespread and deep-going public hostility to military power and to military involvement in civilian life, resulting from Japan's pre-World War II history of militarisation of civil life and imperial aggression, has so far prevented the passing of specific military call-out legislation. At the same time, the continuing influence and re-assertion of militarisation can be seen in contemporary Japanese politics.

Despite being known as the pacifist clause, Article 9 of the constitution has been interpreted, since the establishment of the SDF in 1954, as permitting the SDF to exist, but only to operate strictly in terms of Japan's territorial defence. These limits have been brushed aside increasingly by Japanese governments to allow SDF deployment overseas for so-called peacekeeping, reconstruction, humanitarian and civil emergency missions in Asia and beyond.

In 2004, the Japanese government sent SDF units into an active war zone for the first time since 1945. Despite strong public opposition, 600 SDF personnel were deployed to support the US-led occupation of Iraq. Officially, they fulfilled non-combat roles, such as providing medical treatment, supplying water and reconstructing public facilities. Also in support of the US-led war, another 330 SDF personnel went to the Persian Gulf to transport vehicles and other equipment.

Since then, there has been a continual push by successive governments to expand the activities of the SDF, both at home and overseas. For the 2008 G8 summit on Hokkaido, in addition to more than 20,000 police providing ground-based security, military security included 4 fighter jets, AWACS reconnaissance planes, 12 warships and Patriot surface-to-air-missiles. According to the National Police Agency, the Japanese authorities spent about $US280 million for security at the meeting, which was more than double the $130 million that Germany spent the previous year when it hosted the meeting. Military forces were on hand, even though the police far outnumbered a few thousand anti-capitalist demonstrators. A *New York Times* report described the scene at Date, about 20 kilometres south of Lake Toya, the meeting venue: 'Groups of police officers stopped cars for inspection, and sealed off roads leading to the site. Offshore, armed cruisers were visible, a rare sight in a nation that does not even have a full-fledged military' (Fackler 2008).

Even greater measures were taken in 2019 for the G20 leaders' summit in Osaka. Heavy security restrictions went into effect, with 32,000 police officers on the streets. This was more than the 23,000 who were used for the 2016 G7 summit in Ise (Johnston 2019).

In 2005, constitutional revisions were proposed that would create a cabinet-level Defense Ministry and amend the old clauses mandating official pacifism. Under the proposed revisions, the SDF would also be formally referred to as a military force for the first time since its establishment. Nonetheless, opinion polls showed that a clear majority opposed Japan's continued military presence in Iraq. In 2006, Prime Minister Koizumi announced the withdrawal of Japanese troops from Iraq. His decision was aimed at ending what had become a major embarrassment for the government, prior to stepping down as prime minister.

Koizumi's successor Abe presided over the first ever joint naval exercise of the United States, Japan and India near the Boso Peninsula in central Japan in 2007. In the same year, the inaugural cabinet-level Defense Minister, Fumio Kyuma, outlined a vision of broadening the role of the SDF, including domestically (Japan Ministry of Defense 2007).

In 2008, Prime Minister Yasuo Fukuda invoked Article 59 of the constitution to push through legislation restarting Japan's naval refuelling assistance to the NATO-led occupation of Afghanistan, despite continuing widespread popular opposition (Article 59 allows a two-thirds majority of the lower house to override the upper house if it rejects a bill or fails to vote on it within 60 days). Opinion polls had earlier indicated that 55 per cent of voters opposed the extension of the Indian Ocean mission (Symonds 2008).

On both the domestic and international fronts, the growing use of the SDF challenges the post-war restrictions imposed on the military in the light of the pre-war army's central part in imperialist aggression throughout Asia and in the internal police-state regime. To understand the issues involved and their implications it is necessary to briefly review the relevant history.

Pre-war militarism

Before World War II, Japan remained a highly militarised, stratified and unequal society. Under the Meiji Constitution of 1889 the emperor exercised all legislative, executive and judicial powers. Theoretically his authority was supreme. In practice he delegated power to public servants. A hereditary aristocracy controlled the upper house of the national legislature, the House of Peers. And after 1900 a body of elder statesmen, the genro, played a key role in selecting prime ministers and cabinet members and advising the emperor (Allinson 2004: 19).

Article 11 of the constitution gave the emperor direct command of the army and navy, beyond the authority of the cabinet. From the 1890s, two military chiefs of staff were directly responsible to the emperor and engaged in operations increasingly divorced from ministerial control (Katzenstein 1996: 53). Only high-ranking military officers on active duty, rather than civilians, could head ministries and military cooperation was necessary to form cabinets. Military officers were appointed to more than a quarter of civilian cabinet posts between 1918 and 1945 (Katzenstein 1996: 54).

Military officers were subject to special training programmes, apart from the public educational system, where they 'learned a strategic approach that emphasized the distinctive spiritual strength of the Japanese fighting man, exemplified in massed attacks with bayonets' (Allinson 2004: 34). Such education encouraged them to reject democracy and political compromise in favour of military rule.

The militarisation of politics and of public life was carried forward by the introduction of conscription from 1873, seen as a way to build national unity around military values of bravery and self-sacrifice in combat: by the development of a military reserve by the army ministry from 1910—reaching 2.9 million people by 1936; and by the operation of military run youth training centres from 1926. These developments contributed to widespread acceptance of the military as a force for 'unselfish pursuit of national objectives' with only periodic public hostility to military organisation and operations—particularly in the period immediately following the end of World War I (Katzenstein 1996: 54).

Despite mass mobilisation of police forces, the police still relied on the military to contain popular protects, including the attacks on police stations in 1906, and large riots in 1912 and 1918 (Katzenstein 1996: 54). Though a military police force was established in 1881, the army retained a foothold on matters of internal security. Although its 1,600 members were for many years no more than a token force, the military police force was charged with planning countermeasures against popular uprisings and organising the reserves for the civilian police (Katzenstein 1996: 54).

At the beginning of the 1930s, the military exercised its influence within the government through two seats on the cabinet and through private audiences with the emperor conducted by the leaders of its general staff. Big business interests were strongly represented in and through the elected delegates of the House of Representatives (Allinson 2004: 19).

Japan was badly affected by the global Great Depression of the 1930s, which initially reduced exports and led to high unemployment. In 1931, Japanese troops moved into Manchuria, and the conquered areas became 'an adjunct to the increasingly militarised Japanese economy' undergoing 'sustained economic expansion on the basis of integrated four year plans' (Harman 1984: 68).

Following the assassination of Prime Minister Inukai in 1932, young officers in the army and navy organised a reign of terror during the 1930s. They conspired to assassinate government officials and business leaders and plotted to seize control of the government. They killed Finance Minister Takahashi Korekiyo when he tried to shift investment away from military spending. In the late 1930s the military-dominated government in Tokyo extended its invasion of China, and subsequently set out to seize pieces of Western empires in Malaya, Borneo and Singapore, along with the French colonies in Indochina and the US-run Philippines. Allison noted:

> Japan's military expansion southward into China and Southeast Asia brought insecurity and often wanton death and destruction to millions in nearby Asian nations, while costing the lives of millions of Japanese soldiers, sailors and civilians.
> (Allinson 2004: 37)

After the war

Japan emerged from the Second World War with half of the areas of its largest cities in ruins and its economy devastated. The occupying allied forces led by the Americans under General MacArthur set about reshaping the Japanese state. A new constitution went into effect in 1947. A supreme court was established, supervising the system of local courts (Allinson 2004: 60).

The drafters of the 1947 constitution sought to eliminate the political autonomy and power of the military. They dismantled the aristocratic upper chamber of the previous government, which was seen to have been an instigator and supporter of the war. However, they retained a key role for the Emperor as head of state. The emperor had been a major landholder in occupied territories overseas and Commander in Chief of the armed forces throughout the war. As Robertson argues, there was substantial evidence that Hirohito 'had personally approved all his country's barbaric military ventures and had held out against surrender' until after the bombing of Hiroshima (Robertson 2008: 257). Under US pressure he was exempted from prosecution in allied-administered War Crimes trials in Tokyo.

In the course of his own trial, Prime Minister Tojo admitted that it was 'inconceivable for a high Japanese official to take any action against the wishes of the Emperor' (Robertson 2008: 257). Yet the US stage-managed the trials in such a way as to present the Emperor as innocent of involvement in war crimes.

Public support for the pacifist constitution

There has been widespread and continuing public support for Article 9 and for the three non-nuclear principles forbidding the possession, manufacture or introduction into Japan of nuclear weapons. Remembering the horrors of pre-war militarism and imperialism, and the atrocities of the war, such as the bombing of Hiroshima and Nagasaki and the subsequent post-war poverty and chaos, large numbers of Japanese people have strongly supported the pacifist constitution. There were massive street demonstrations against the US–Japan Security Treaty in 1960, during the anti-war movement in the later 1960s, and against the renewal of the US–Japan Treaty in 1970 (Katzenstein 1996: 155).

Revision of the constitution requires a two-thirds majority in both houses of the Diet and a majority in a special referendum. Given the widespread public support for the pacifist clause, successive governments have failed to get sufficient support for any amendment. However, the government appealed to a universal 'right of self defence' to establish the SDF in 1954 as the minimum military force required to protect the peace and independence of Japan (Katzenstein 1996: 126).

During the 1950s and 1960s, lower courts declared the existence of the SDF (along with the security treaty with the United States and the presence of US forces in Japan) to be unconstitutional. But the High Court consistently upheld the SDF's legitimacy on grounds of the supremacy of the legislature in political matters and the idea that the constitution could not have intended to deny such a universal right as self-defence. The Japanese public slowly came to accept the existence of the SDF insofar as it was used only for disaster relief and never as a military force, and the political leadership continued to increase its size and its role.

During the Cold War, prime ministers agreed that it would be impossible for the SDF to function outside Japan and that the duty of the Defence Forces was purely to protect Japan from aggression. There was no conscription and a limit was placed on the defence budget of 1 per cent of GDP (McCormack 2007: 128). Governments also observed the three 'non-nuclear principles', though they turned a blind eye to nuclear-armed US warships 'docking in or passing through Japan' (McCormack 2007: 175).

Nonetheless, as Japan's industrial recovery proceeded, the SDF grew in size and in the sophistication of its weaponry. Already, by 2007, 1 per cent of the Japanese GDP amounted to $US45 billion, roughly on a par with military spending by the nuclear powers Britain and France, and supported the second largest navy in the world in tonnage terms. Its armaments included jet fighters, submarines, destroyers and aircraft carriers. It had a prototype intercontinental ballistic missile in the form of its H22A rocket capable of lifting a 5-tonne payload into space, huge stores of plutonium for nuclear warheads and high levels of scientific and technical nuclear expertise (McCormack 2007: 17).

Throughout the Cold War, Japanese policy had been to cooperate with both the United States and the Unite Nations within the general framework of international law and without any direct military support for US policy. The US bases in Japan, particularly Okinawa, played a major role in the US wars in Korea, Vietnam and the Gulf. But the SDF had no direct military role. When Prime Minister Suzuki referred publicly to a treaty relationship between Japan and the United States in 1981, there was a huge public outcry, forcing him to say that his statement had no military implications (McCormack 2007: 57).

In 1990, following Iraq's invasion of Kuwait, the Japanese government refused US requests to send minesweepers to the Gulf. Japan contributed $US13 billion to the prosecution of the first Gulf War, but played no direct military role. SDF ships arrived in the area only after the end of hostilities (Katzenstein 1996: 125). At the time, 'opposition parties, newspaper editorials and citizen protests … maintained that the Japanese government [was] constitutionally precluded from using armed force outside of its own geographic territory' (Katzenstein 1996: 125).

Shortly after 9/11, however, Japan adopted an 'Anti-Terrorism Special Measures Law' and sent 24 naval ships to the Indian Ocean to support the Afghan War (McCormack 2007: 63). These developments marked 'Japan's entry into the war against terror' (McCormack 2007: 64).

Prime Minister Koizumi cited the need for US military protection in face of the threat of attack by North Korea as grounds for Japanese support of the US-led war, including the involvement of Japanese forces to aid the Afghanistan occupation in 2004. Koizumi's later dispatch of Japanese troops to Iraq, including units from all three of Japan's Self-Defence Forces, the first to an overseas war zone since World War II, provoked widespread opposition from the public (McCormack 2007: 67).

Revival of nationalism

The mid-1990s saw the emergence of prominent neo-nationalist, revisionist and reactionary organisations, founded to resist any apologies for past Japanese aggression and colonialism. Particularly important was the Japan Conference, pushing for revision of the constitution and celebration of Japanese imperialism and the conduct of World War II (McCormack 2007: 9).

In 2006, 223 members of the Diet, including the prime minister, the foreign and finance ministers and the chief cabinet secretary, were members of the League of Shinto Politicians, looking to the establishment of a Shinto spirituality and emperor worship as the foundation of national polity, despite a constitutional ban on state support for religion (McCormack 2007: 9). In 2001, Prime Minister Koizumi started annual formal visits to the Yasukuni Shrine, honouring those who had died in the service of the emperor. McCormack explained the symbolism of the shrine visits: 'in pre-war and wartime Japan it played a central role in generating the ideology of chauvinism and militarism … After the war … the state was constitutionally proscribed from any connection with it (by Article 20)' (McCormack 2007: 15).

The addition of the spirits of 14 major war criminals to the shrine's 'deities' in 1978 had brought an end to earlier visits in defiance of the constitution by the emperor and by prime ministers. When Koizumi resumed such visits, 'neighbouring countries saw his action as an affront, and as tantamount to an attempted vindication of the war cause'. Koizumi's successor, Abe, a core member of the Japan Conference and Shinto Politics groups, was a strong supporter of such visits (McCormack 2007: 15).

Internal security

Because of the pacifist constitution, Japan's post-war internal security policy largely evolved around the police forces, including the National Police Agency (NPA) under the control of the national government, and Tokyo's Metropolitan Police Department (MPD). Until recently, the size and power of this apparatus helped subdue calls for greater SDF involvement in domestic security (Katzenstein 1996: 60–61).

The NPA retains overall control of internal security and operates in and through the MPD, with frequent interchange of personnel between the two. Attempts by the LDP from the 1950s to substantially increase police powers met with strong opposition inside and outside parliament, including, in 1958, street demonstrations and strikes involving 4 million people. In practice, however, 'informal extension of the Police Law has substantially enlarged the scope' of police activities (Katzenstein 1996: 62).

'Before major public events the police regularly search houses, with or without warrants' (Katzenstein 1996: 85). Tens of thousands of riot police are regularly mobilised on such occasions, controlling roads, buildings, stations and airports. The powers and practices of the police resemble those of the 1930s.

A Tokyo bookshop worker was held in detention and interrogated by public security police for 44 days in 2003, 'his papers and books ransacked' at the start of the US attack on Iraq, for painting 'Opposition to war' on a lavatory wall in a park in Tokyo. In 2004 a government welfare officer was arrested under the Public Service Law for distributing copies of a Communist Party newspaper. McCormack noted:

> A special taskforce of 200 men was set up to pursue his case, ransacking his files and possessions, trailing him and videotaping him with something approaching fanatical zeal. On 29 June 2006, he became the first person in 32 years to be convicted under a law that ... would certainly not have been applied to someone distributing copies of the LDP paper.
>
> (McCormack 2007: 22)

Three anti-Iraq war activists in Tokyo were held in detention for 75 days and subjected to intense interrogation in 2004 after handing out leaflets in a Defence Agency residential facility calling on SDF officers to 'think' about the leadership's decision to support the war.

Conclusion

In Japan, together with Germany and Italy, there are indications that, just as in the 1930s, when external militarism went hand in hand with internal repression, similar pressures have re-emerged, under conditions of social stress and great power conflict. Particularly since 2001, successive Japanese governments have sought to weaken, reinterpret, sidestep or remove the pacifist provisions of the post-World War II constitution, and moved to expand the role of the armed forces, both domestically and overseas.

10 Australia

Legislating and expanding military powers

In 2018, for the third time since 2000, Australia's two major parties pushed legislation through parliament that gave several government ministers and/or the armed forces chief new or extended powers to mobilise the armed forces to deal with 'domestic violence', that is, civil unrest. Little public debate occurred on why these powers needed to be expanded yet again, going beyond the call-out powers introduced in 2000 and broadened in 2006.

Successive Australian governments have thus established, and then reinforced, a statutory code authorising the domestic deployment of the armed forces. In that sense, Australia has gone further than the most comparable countries, the United States, Britain and Canada, in seeking to lay down specific military powers, rather than rely predominantly on the common law or more general legislation.

Extensive statutory provisions have been introduced, for the first time, empowering Australian government ministers, or if 'pre-authorised', the Chief of the Defence Force (CDF), to call out the Australian Defence Force (ADF) to deal with either possible 'domestic violence'—including a perceived threat to 'Commonwealth interests'—or a likely danger to 'declared infrastructure' (*Defence Act 1903* (Cth) Part IIIAAA) (*Defence Act*).

None of these terms is defined in the legislation, nor are other key phrases, effectively handing vague and potentially far-reaching powers to governments and military commanders. Once deployed, military personnel can exercise extraordinary powers over civilians, overturning basic legal and democratic rights.

Legislation was introduced in 2000, and extended in 2006 and 2018, giving federal governments and the CDF explicit peacetime powers to call out the troops if 'domestic violence is occurring or is likely to occur' that 'would be likely to affect Commonwealth interests' or require the protection of a State or Territory. Each set of legislation was justified as an urgent response to potential threats of terrorism. In the first two instances, the threat was said to relate to key sporting events, first the 2000 Sydney Olympics and then the 2006 Melbourne Commonwealth Games. No acts of terrorism occurred at those events, yet the laws have remained, and since been extended, with wording that goes far beyond counter-terrorism.

'Domestic violence' is an amorphous, anachronistic and seemingly incongruous term, which in contemporary parlance normally refers to violence in the home. Although the expression is taken from s 119 of the Australian Constitution, it is not defined there, nor in the *Defence Act* or regulations. No judicial definition exists either. Likewise, there is nothing in the law about how grave or widespread 'domestic violence' must be before the ADF is mobilised. Enormous discretion has thus been placed in the hands of the government and the ADF itself to intervene against civil unrest.

Moreover, the legislation is not simply a codification; it is an expansion of call-out powers. The *Defence Act* states that its powers are in addition to any other legal powers to deploy the armed forces domestically. Previous language to this effect, first introduced in 2000, was retained in section 51ZD of the *Defence Act*, which stated:

> [t]his Part does not affect any utilisation of the Defence Force that would be permitted or required, or any powers that the Defence Force would have, if this Part were disregarded.

Little-defined powers are said to exist, derived either from the ancient prerogatives of the British Monarchy, the common law rights of citizens, a 'nationhood' Executive power arguably implicit in the 1901 *Australian Constitution*, the powers of the Governor-General under the *Constitution*, or even martial law (Head 2009: 122–135; Moore 2017: 165–302).

No known call out has yet occurred under the legislation. Nevertheless, military forces, including elite Special Air Service (SAS) units, have been deployed for major political and sporting events, and a debate has been opened up on making domestic security a 'core business' of the ADF. These trends have largely emerged under the banner of the indefinite 'war on terror' launched by the United States and its allies following the September 2001 terrorist attacks in America. Yet, the changes underway have been broader and deeper. For example, the ADF has been used on many civilian fronts, including a Northern Territory Aboriginal intervention, the turning back of refugee boats, and the patrolling of neighbourhoods in Afghanistan, Iraq, East Timor and Solomon Islands, as well as for counter-terrorism exercises.

Reversing an historic principle

Historically, at least since the so-called 'Glorious Revolution' of 1688–89 established parliamentary sovereignty in England, there has been a political and legal tradition opposing the use of the military against society's citizens. Reflecting that history, the Australian Constitution embodies a basic division of power between domestic law enforcement and the maintenance of armed forces for external defence. At Australia's Federation in 1901, the military power was handed to the federal Commonwealth under s 51(xxxi), the colonial defence forces were transferred to the Commonwealth by s 69, and under s 114, the States were forbidden to raise military or naval forces without the consent of the Commonwealth Parliament. Residual authority over domestic law and order remained in the hands of the States and their police forces. Section 119 of the Constitution provided for the Commonwealth to protect a State against 'domestic violence'—but only on the application of 'the Executive Government of the State'.

Moreover, this historic principle has become embedded in popular consciousness. Freedom from military rule and interference in civilian affairs are seen as a hallmark of liberty. Most people regard domestic military interventions as the domains of military or fascist dictatorships. The use of troops as strike breakers in 1949 and 1953 generated intense hostility (Beddie and Moss 1982: 39–51). Deployment of soldiers against demonstrators at a military intelligence base in central Australia in 1989 caused considerable controversy (Ward 1997: 14–18).

On the only occasion since Federation that a Commonwealth government has called out the military in force in an urban situation—following a bomb blast outside a regional Commonwealth Heads of Government meeting at the Sydney Hilton Hotel in 1978—the sight of armed soldiers patrolling highways and the streets of the New South Wales town of Bowral caused public consternation (Cahill and Cahill 2005; Hocking 2004: 81–100). One local newspaper said the 'virtual siege conditions' were reminiscent of 'Franco's Spain' (Southern Highland News 1978).

However, since the terrorist attacks of September 2001, the declaration of a 'war on terror' and the wars in Afghanistan and Iraq, aspects of Australian society have been increasingly militarised. Thousands of soldiers have been mobilised, on alert, for major sporting events such as the 2000 Sydney Olympics, the 2003 Rugby World Cup and the 2006 Melbourne Commonwealth Games (Bergin and Smith 2006: 10). Naval vessels have been dispatched to repel asylum seekers, with powers to fire on boats or transport their passengers to remote islands (Head 2002a: 23–33; Laing 2005: 518–520). Frequent anti-terrorism exercises have been conducted in urban environments, involving heavily armed troops alongside police and intelligence officers (National Counter-Terrorism Committee 2003: 95). Deployments have been conducted against civilian populations in Afghanistan, Iraq, Solomon Islands and East Timor (Head 2005a: 484–492). The armed forces have been used in highly publicised shows of strength, including air force jets and helicopters flying overhead during major political events such as the 2002 Commonwealth Heads of Government Meeting at Coolum, Queensland and US President Bush's visit to Australia in 2003 (Bergin and Smith 2006: 10). 'Contingency call outs' were authorised for the 2014 G20 summit in Brisbane, the 2018 Gold Coast Commonwealth Games and the 2018 Australia-ASEAN summit in Sydney (Senate Legal and Constitutional Affairs Legislation Committee 2018: 5 [1.15]).

Already, by 2006, the frequency of such deployments had increased. A report by the Australian Strategic Policy Institute (ASPI) said a new tempo had been established in military involvement in domestic security. It calculated that between the 1956 Melbourne Olympic Games and the 2000 Sydney Olympics, there were four major special event support operations, an average of one every 11 years. The 2001–2006 period, by contrast, saw four such operations in a much shorter time span, at an average of one per 1.25 years (Bergin and Smith 2006: 10).

The 2018 expansion of military call-out powers

In late 2018, for the third time since 2000, and again with little public debate or scrutiny, Australia's Parliament gave several government ministers and/or the CDF new or extended powers to mobilise the armed forces, potentially to put down civil unrest (for details of the 2000 and 2006 debates and *Defence Act* amendments, see: Head 2009: 13–21, 100–121).

As in 2000 and 2006, the Labor Party joined a Liberal-National Coalition Government in passing the legislation, with only minor amendments. The already broad call-out powers inserted into the *Defence Act* in 2000, and significantly expanded in 2006, were widened again.

Like the measures of 2000 and 2006, the 2018 legislation was depicted in Parliament and the media largely as a means of protecting the population against terrorist attacks (e.g. Greene 2018). The measures were said to be a response to a 2014 hostage-taking incident at a Sydney café, officially described as a 'terrorist act', and the recommendations of a subsequent Coroner's Report (State Coroner 2017). Yet the legislation allowed the Prime Minister or other 'authorising' ministers to call out the military, or preauthorise deployments, on a much broader basis than combating terrorist-related activities.

The expansion of military call-out powers comes on top of numerous suites of 'counter-terrorism' and other legislation to increase the powers of the police and intelligence agencies since 2002 (Lynch, McGarrity and Williams 2015). So, in addition to boosting the legal powers and capacities of the civilian security agencies to unprecedented peacetime levels, successive governments have insisted on the necessity to be able to order the domestic deployment of the military forces.

While the latest legislation, like the 2000 and 2006 amendments, was justified in Parliament as a means of combating terrorism (Greene 2018; Head 2009: 28–31), statements by government representatives themselves pointed to the fact that the wording of the provisions permitted the use of the armed forces for other purposes.

When the bill was first tabled, Attorney-General Christian Porter told journalists the military could be used to restore order in case of 'widespread rioting' (Karp 2018). That statement was not subsequently explained. Nor was it retracted.

Former Special Air Service (SAS) officer Andrew Hastie, Chairman of the Parliamentary Joint Intelligence and Security Committee, told the House of Representatives in November 2018 he was 'very pleased' that the Bill would 'unlock' the capabilities of the country's two Special Forces units—the SAS Regiment in Perth and the 2nd Commando Regiment in Sydney. He stated:

> They benchmark against Five Eyes special operations and law enforcement units, so they have world's best practice at their fingertips. They also have significant combat experience acquired through ADF operations in Afghanistan over the past decade or so … They are surgical in the application of lethal force. Culturally—this is a key point between our police and military—they're ruthlessly mission focused, particularly when it comes to resolving these sorts of situations.
> (Commonwealth 2018)

While the committee chairman couched his remarks in terms of countering terrorism-related incidents, his references to Afghanistan, the US-led 'Five Eyes' operations and 'surgical' use of lethal force are notable. Australia's Special Forces have been under investigation, accused of war crimes against civilians during the ongoing war in Afghanistan (McKenzie and Masters 2018). The Five Eyes network—the United States, the United Kingdom, Canada, Australia and New Zealand—conducts global mass surveillance, particularly targeting people deemed a threat to any of the five governments involved (Kim et al. 2018; Head 2018a).

As detailed below, the amended *Defence Act* expands the military's powers, including to kill people, beyond situations where commanders claim it is necessary to protect a life. Lethal force could be used to protect 'declared infrastructure' or end 'threats to … public health or public safety' (e.g., *Defence Act* ss 46(5)(b), (c)). In addition, military personnel were further protected from legal liability by adding a new defence of acting in 'good faith' (*Defence Act* s 51F).

Under the new provisions, government ministers could issue call-out orders if they considered that potential 'domestic violence' could pose a 'threat' to 'Commonwealth interests', even if the relevant state or territory government did not request the call out, or even disagreed or objected (*Defence Act* s 38). Military personnel were given great powers, including to use lethal force, detain civilians, issue directives, search people and premises, question people and seize documents (e.g., *Defence Act* s 46(7)). These features of the legislation raise constitutional and legal issues, as well as those of civil rights. It will be suggested in this chapter that these provisions could facilitate the use of military force to suppress social unrest.

Wide powers

It is incontrovertible that the legislation is not confined to dealing with terrorism. In fact, the word terrorism does not appear in amended Part IIIAAA of the *Defence Act.* Rather, the government can order the military to many types of perceived potential threats, including to 'public safety' (e.g., *Defence Act* ss 46(5)(b), (c))—another undefined term. Moreover, in 'specified circumstances' the ministers can authorise a 'contingent call out', handing the call-out powers to the CDF (*Defence Act* s 34).

Supported by the Labor Party opposition, the Government refused to amend the 2018 Bill to define 'specified circumstances'. Instead, in response to two Parliamentary Committee Reports (Senate Legal and Constitutional Affairs Legislation Committee 2018; Parliamentary Joint Committee on Human Rights 2018), it changed the Bill's Explanatory Memorandum to declare: '[w]hat constitutes specified circumstances will depend on the situation in question' (Addendum to the Explanatory Memorandum 2018: 3 [205A]). Such a response undercut any claim that Parliamentary scrutiny narrowed the scope of the legislation.

The Government also rejected calls made in Parliament and Committee Inquiry submissions to define 'domestic violence'. The Explanatory Memorandum was revised to state: '[p]eaceful protests, industrial action or civil disobedience would not fall within the definition of "domestic violence"' (Addendum to the Explanatory Memorandum: 2 [165A]. However, section 39(3)(b) of the amended *Defence Act* stated that this caveat did not apply if there were a 'reasonable likelihood of: (ii) serious damage to property'. The *Defence Act* provided no definition of 'serious damage'. The likelihood of allegedly 'serious' danger to property could be cited to set troops against strikers, demonstrators or participants in civil disobedience, without any objective measure of seriousness.

'Domestic violence' is an undefined term embedded in section 119 of the Australian Constitution. Derived from the United States Constitution, it refers to serious civil unrest that endangers the existing order, but its extent remains unclear (Head 2009: 18–19).

Previously, because the Constitution left police powers in the hands of the Australian states, the ADF could be called out only if a state or territory was 'not, or is unlikely to be, able to protect' itself or Commonwealth interests 'against the domestic violence' (*Defence Act* ss 51A–51C, later amended by the 2018 legislation).

The earlier language retained a semblance of consistency with section 119 of the Constitution, which states: '[t]he Commonwealth shall protect every State against invasion and, on the application of the Executive Government of the States, against domestic violence'. Even with the old wording, constitutional doubt existed whether such a military mobilisation could proceed if a state government objected (Head 2009: 61–74, 148–61).

The constitutional limit was further eviscerated by the 2018 amendments. The Prime Minister or two 'authorising ministers'—now including the Home Affairs Minister—had the power to mobilise the ADF if they decided it 'would be likely to enhance' the state or territory's ability to protect itself or Commonwealth interests (*Defence Act* ss 33(2), 34(2), 35(2), 36(2)). This revised threshold meant it was no longer necessary for the government to assert that a state or territory was, or could be, unable to provide the required protection.

Furthermore, in the cases of 'Commonwealth interests' and 'declared infrastructure', a call out could override state and territory governments and police forces. Section 37(7) of the *Defence Act* stated that an authorising minister must notify the government of an affected state or territory 'as soon as reasonably practicable' after authorising a 'Commonwealth interests' order, but failure to do so 'does not affect the validity' of the order.

Moreover, section 38(2) provided that a 'Commonwealth interests order' could be made whether or not the relevant state or territory requested the order. In that event, an authorising minister must that government before authorising the order, but that consultation could not prevent or override the order. Plainly, consultation does not mean assent. In addition, section 38(3) stated that no such consultation was required for a call-out order if 'the authorising ministers are satisfied that, for reasons of urgency, it is impracticable to comply with' section 37(2).

Nor was an authorising minister required to consult in relation to an expedited call-out order under section 51U (*see* section 51V(6)). The same powers applied to urgent or expedited orders to protect 'declared infrastructure' (*Defence Act* ss 51H(7), (8)).

These provisions provided great latitude to pre-empt or defy state and territory objections. In effect, the state and territory governments had no say in the matter. The Explanatory Memorandum asserted: '[i]t is the Commonwealth's prerogative to make orders for the protection of its own interests, and it does not need a request from a state or territory to make or vary such an order' (Explanatory Memorandum, 49 [263]).

Expanded powers were created for ministers to order a 'contingent call out' that pre-authorises the CDF to deploy troops. It extended to cover Commonwealth and state and territory interests (*Defence Act* ss 34, 36).

Although no call-out orders have been issued since 2000, 'contingency call outs' have been ordered for numbers of political and sporting events. In a Senate Committee submission, the Attorney-General's Department stated:

> [s]uch orders have been regularly made as part of security measures to protect major Commonwealth events (for example, the G20, Commonwealth Games, and the ASEAN summit) from circumstances involving air threats.
>
> (Senate Legal and Constitutional Affairs Legislation Committee 2018: 5 [1.15])

These operations have functioned as dress rehearsals for military mobilisations, designed also to accustom the population to ADF operations, such as air force fly overs and troop deployments, in major cities (Head 2009: 77–94).

Looking beyond the terrorism pretext

In 2000 and 2006, the call-out legislation was presented to Parliament as essential to deal with potential threats to major sporting events—the 2000 Sydney Olympics and the 2006 Melbourne Commonwealth Games respectively—even though no specific terrorist dangers were cited, no plots were ever reported and no attacks occurred (Head 2009: 82–85). In 2017, the main explanation provided by both the Government and the Labor Party was that military resources should be available to respond to a terrorist attack like that which allegedly occurred in a December 2014 Sydney Lindt Café siege (InDaily 2017).

Prime Minister Malcolm Turnbull first foreshadowed the 2018 Bill in mid-2017, citing a Coroner's Report on the hostage-taking event, conducted by lone gunman Man Haron Monis (Kenny 2017). The Government and the media labelled the siege a terrorist emergency and claimed it demonstrated the need for the Special Forces regiments to intervene with lethal force. Great doubts, however, exist about Monis' actions and motivations. He was a mentally disturbed individual who had been in close contact with police and intelligence agencies for many years (State Coroner 2017: 53–72, 93–101).

As discussed in Chapter 2, great doubts also surround the entire political and geo-strategic agenda of the US-led 'war on terror', which has not only laid waste to societies throughout the Middle East and produced the worst refugee crisis since World War II, but has also provided a breeding ground for terrorism (Blum 2002: 133–134, 145–146, 155; Bacevich 2002; Tripathi 2011).

More broadly, the expansion of military call-out powers in Australia is part of the international trend explored in Chapter 2. The international character of these phenomena itself points to underlying economic and political factors, which this book suggests are related to growing social inequality, rising domestic class tensions and worsening global economic and military conflicts.

Notably, this process has been accompanied also by expansions of military spending, reassertions of executive powers to launch military conflicts without Parliamentary approval, and preparations for war between the major powers (Head and Boehringer 2019: 4–15). One expression of that trend was the 2018 US National Defense Strategy, which stated: '[i]nter-state strategic competition, not terrorism, is now the primary concern in US national security'. In particular, the document named China and Russia as such 'competitors' (Mattis 2018: 1).

This chapter assesses the 'peacetime' application of the call-out provisions. Any major war involving Australia, however, would have immense internal implications for civil rights, not least because the domestic powers of the military, as well as the police and intelligence services, would further expand, as happened in World War I and World War II (Head and Boehringer 2019: 223–229).

Expanded call-out powers in more detail

After the 2018 amendments, Division 2 of Part IIIAAA of the *Defence Act* set out four types of call-out orders:

1 call out to protect Commonwealth interests;
2 contingent call out to protect Commonwealth interests;
3 call out to protect states and territories; and
4 contingent call out to protect states and territories.

Other Divisions provided for expedited call-out orders, specified area declarations and infrastructure declarations.

These provisions, as in section 33(2), increased the power to deploy the ADF to respond to 'domestic violence' that is occurring across multiple state and territory jurisdictions. Section 34(1)(d) extended contingent call-out powers to be available in relation to land and maritime threats, in addition to aviation threats.

Before the 2018 amendments, Part IIIAAA already contained sweeping powers to call out the ADF and conferred great powers on ADF personnel once deployed (Head 2009: 100–118). According to the 2018 Bill's Explanatory Memorandum, the amendments would 'streamline the legal procedures for call out of the ADF' and 'enhance the ability of the ADF to protect states, self-governing territories, and Commonwealth interests, onshore and offshore, against domestic violence, including terrorism' (para [3]).

As stated in an Addendum to the Explanatory Memorandum—tabled to respond to questions raised in the two previously mentioned parliamentary committee reports—crucial terms remained undefined. Paragraph 163A, inserted into the Explanatory Memorandum, said:

> The term 'Commonwealth interests' is not defined in the Bill. For the purposes of Part IIIAAA, 'Commonwealth interests' would include the protection of:
>
> Commonwealth property or facilities; Commonwealth public officials; visiting foreign dignitaries or heads of state; and, major national events, including the Commonwealth Games or G20.

These words, in addition to being legally non-binding, are vague. What is 'Commonwealth property'? What is a 'major national event'?

Likewise, paragraph 165A of the memorandum stated:

> he term 'domestic violence' is not defined in the Bill but refers to conduct that is marked by great physical force and would include a terrorist attack, hostage situation, and widespread or significant violence.

What is 'great physical force'? What is 'significant violence'?

Paragraph 182A said the lower threshold regarding state or territory capacity 'is not intended to impermissibly expand the circumstances in which the ADF might be called out, or result in the ADF being called out in response to minor incidents that police routinely and appropriately deal with'. However, it provided no assurance against this or wider use of the ADF. Instead, it asserted that the authorising ministers would consider the 'same factors' as under the previous threshold. If that were true, the amendment would serve no purpose.

Paragraph 182A insisted that the new threshold in sections 33 to 36 recognised that 'calling out the ADF to respond to an incident is a significant and exceptional act, and ensures that it is not to be done in relation to incidents that are within the ordinary capability of police'. Yet, the legislation did not specify that. Rather, section 35(2) of the *Defence Act* stated that the ADF could be deployed if that 'would be likely to enhance the ability of the state or territory to protect the state or territory against the domestic violence'.

Similarly, the *Defence Act* did not define the 'specified circumstances' in the Act to issue a contingent call-out order. Paragraph 205A of the memorandum stated: '[t]here are a range of specified circumstances that could give rise to a contingent call out order'. This language is meaningless. Paragraph 205C said 'typically' the circumstances would be similar to the 2014 G20 Leaders' Summit in Brisbane, the 2018 Gold Coast Commonwealth Games and the 2018 ASEAN-Australia Summit, where contingent call-out orders were issued for aviation threats. However, the legislation contained no such limits.

A new definition of 'declared infrastructure' was inserted to replace the previous definition of 'designated critical infrastructure'. This amendment created an almost open-ended power to deploy the armed forces, because 'declared infrastructure' was defined to mean any infrastructure, or a part of infrastructure, that was declared by authorising ministers under section 51H. Section 51H(2) permitted a declaration where 'there is a threat or damage to disruption to the operation of the infrastructure or the part of the infrastructure' where the damage or disruption would 'directly or indirectly endanger the life of, or cause serious injury to, any person'.

In addition to pre-authorised contingent call outs, the legislation, via section 51U, provided for 'expedited orders and declarations' in a 'sudden and extraordinary emergency' (also undefined). The prime minister or two authorising ministers could verbally issue such orders and declarations. Such orders 'need not be in writing'. Thus, a mere phone call from the prime minister to the CDF would suffice.

This 'extraordinary' power was previously created by the 2006 amendments, but the 2018 Bill extended it to cover 'declared infrastructure' and 'specified area' declarations, and included the Home Affairs Minister and acting authorised ministers in the list of those holding the power.

Section 51U(4)(a) made clear that the making of expedited orders or declarations did not require the authorising ministers to be satisfied of the 'particular matters' in sections 33(1), 34(1), 35(1), 36(1) or 51H(2). That is, the ministers did not have to consider that there was a likely threat of 'domestic violence' or danger to 'Commonwealth interests' or 'declared infrastructure'. In effect, the alleged existence of a 'sudden and extraordinary emergency' could override these thresholds.

Greater military powers once called out

The 2018 Bill expanded the already considerable powers available to the ADF once deployed, consolidating them into four divisions of Part IIIAAA of the *Defence Act*: 'reasonable and necessary' powers ordered by the CDF (Division 2); 'special powers' generally authorised by an authorising minister (Division 3); powers exercised in 'specified areas' (Division 4); and powers to protect 'declared infrastructure' (Division 5).

Division 2 powers were subject to directions given by the Defence Minister to the CDF, and 'must not stop or restrict any protest, dissent, assembly or industrial action' except if there is a 'reasonable likelihood' of death, injury or 'serious damage to property' (section 39(3)). There was also a requirement 'as far as reasonably practicable' to utilise ADF personnel in cooperation with state and territory police forces and for tasks requested by a police officer (section 40). Both provisos left wide leeways for brushing aside these purported safeguards.

Division 3 was designed for the most heavily armed Special Forces deployments. It contained the most extensive powers. Part IIIAAA previously provided powers to prevent, put an end to, and protect persons from, acts of violence. Sections 46 (5)(b) and 46(5)(c) expanded these 'special powers' to also authorise the ADF to take action to prevent, put an end to, or protect persons from, threats to a person's life or safety, or to public health or public safety.

The terms 'safety', 'public health' and 'public safety' were vague and open to wide interpretation. According to Paragraph 56 of the Explanatory Memorandum:

> These additional limbs are intended to allow the ADF to put an end to threats which have not yet materialised into acts of violence. They are also intended to make clear that the ADF can act in relation to generalised threats which may not be directed toward any specific person but towards the community in general.

Sections 46(5)(d) and (e) extended these powers to shooting down planes and sinking vessels—which could endanger hundreds of lives—so long as an order to do so was not 'manifestly unlawful'.

In addition, section 46(7) empowered ADF members to free hostages, control movements of people or means of transport, evacuate people, search persons, locations or things, seize items, detain people, require detained people to provide identification, patrol and cordon off areas, question people and compel production of documents. Subsection 46(9) allowed an ADF member to do anything incidental to these powers.

Section 50 also removed the previous requirement for ADF personnel to wear uniforms and identification when exercising the Division 3 powers, although the requirement remained when invoking most other powers. Paragraph 332 of the Explanatory Memorandum stated:

> This is because the tasks that the ADF will be required to perform under Division 3 are higher end military actions and may involve the Special Forces. These tasks may require the ADF to operate in a covert manner where uniforms would be detrimental. ADF Special Forces soldiers have protected identity status because they are associated with sensitive capabilities.

This raised the likelihood of Special Forces troops taking 'higher end military actions' against civilians without being recognised as ADF personnel, or else not being identified and therefore not held accountable for killings or other violent acts. Special Forces soldiers could, for example, burst into a person's home, provoking an alarmed response from someone inside who did not realise they were ADF personnel, and then shoot the person in alleged self-defence.

Such a killing happened in 1989 when New South Wales Special Weapons and Operations Section ('SWOS') police officers shot and killed David Gundy, an Aboriginal man, who had reacted angrily when armed men burst into his house in a mistaken early morning raid (Royal Commission into Aboriginal Deaths in Custody 1991: 4).

Also expanded were the Division 4 powers for 'specified areas'. First, the Division abolished the previous distinction between General Security Areas and Designated Areas, allowing the full suite of powers to be exercised within a specified area (section 47).

Second, these powers were significantly broadened. Section 51A allowed ADF personnel also to search for a person who is likely to pose a threat to a person's life, health or safety or public health or public safety, as well as things and people 'connected' (another undefined term) with the domestic violence or threat specified in the call-out order. According to Paragraph 354 of the Explanatory Memorandum:

> The ability to search for persons connected with the domestic violence allows the ADF to search for people who do not pose a threat themselves, and who have not yet committed an offence, but who may be seeking to assist others in carrying out acts of violence.

Section 51A(2)(a) permitted a generic written authorisation to search all premises in the specified area. This opened up the prospect of troops conducting sweeps through entire suburbs. Paragraph 358 of the Explanatory Memorandum stated:

> These purposive powers will permit the ADF to undertake a coordinated, thorough, and systematic search of a specified area, or part of a specified area, to either find the threat, or to clear the area of a threat.

Subsections 51A(2)(c) and (d) further allowed an ADF member to search a person who was at or near premises, because the ADF member believed on reasonable grounds that the person had anything that may be seized or was a 'person who may be detained' in relation to the call-out order.

This detention power was also expanded. The phrase 'person who may be detained' was defined in section 31 as a person 'who is likely to pose a threat to any person's life, health or safety, or to public health or safety', or who has committed an offence related to the domestic violence or threat specified in the call-out order, and whom it is necessary, as a matter of urgency, to detain. This power thus covered considerable ground, well beyond the alleged commission of an offence (the previous limit), to a suspected future threat.

Also removed was a previous requirement that a search authorisation state the name, rank and service number of the member in charge of the search. Paragraph 363 of the Explanatory Memorandum simply asserted that this requirement was 'impractical'. The occupier of a premises or their representative, if present at the time of a search, was entitled to observe the search being carried out. This 'entitlement' ceased, however, if the occupier or their representative 'impedes' the search. It could be rendered meaningless anyway as a protection against abuses—such as material being planted—because two or more parts of the premises could be searched at the same time, under Section 51C(2), (3), making it difficult for the occupier to monitor the simultaneous searches.

Previously, the *Defence Act* did not permit the ADF to search for people who could pose a threat. Section 51D provided ADF members with those powers if they reasonably believed a person was 'likely to' pose a threat to, inter alia, 'public safety'. Soldiers could also establish barriers or cordons, check identities, direct people, search, question and detain people and compel the production of documents. Previous powers to search vehicles and people were extended to those leaving a 'specified area', as well as those entering it. Some of these powers also were previously available only in the offshore area.

Similar power expansions applied in Division 5, covering 'declared infrastructure'. In particular, powers to prevent, or put an end to, acts of violence were extended by section 51L to prevent or put an end to threats to a person's life, health or safety, or to public health or public safety.

As will be discussed in Chapter 11, the 2018 amendments also further weakened the accountability provisions in the Defence Act, particularly relating to the criminal and civil liability of ADF personnel for using lethal force.

Underlying legal, constitutional and political questions

The 2018 Bill has amplified many of the legal, constitutional and political issues posed by the 2000 and 2006 legislation. None have been tested yet, because no call out has occurred (except for contingency call outs) since 2000. Many questions remain from the last large-scale domestic mobilisation of soldiers, near Sydney in 1978, after the still unexplained Hilton Hotel bombing. As reviewed later in this chapter, it was not clear by what legal authority the call out occurred.

A Pandora's Box of legal questions still exists, such as the scope and effect of the 'good faith' defence, the meaning of terms like 'public safety' and the 'reasonableness' of lethal force, as well as the innate difficulties of securing judicial review of military operations conducted in the name of national security.

Likewise, it seems that a plethora of constitutional doubts was deepened, particularly by the greater capacity of the Federal Government and the ADF to deploy troops without any state or territory request and to disregard state and territory objections. Not only did the provisions arguably exceed the boundaries of section 119 of the Constitution, they may also lack a sufficient connection to the defence power or other federal heads of power (Head 2009: 63–74, 148–161).

Politically, the key question is: why have these powers been created on the pretext of combatting terrorism when the provisions are far wider? The only conclusion that can be drawn is that preparations are being made to mobilise the armed forces domestically for purposes other than counter-terrorism, such as to deal with 'rioting' or other forms of civil unrest.

A decade ago, in discussing the 2000 and 2006 legislation, this author drew attention to the underlying likelihood of these powers being employed to deal with convulsive social and political unrest under conditions of worsening social inequality, economic breakdown and rising global geo-strategic tensions (Head 2009: 2–4, 204–221). Those concerns have been amplified by the 2018 amendments.

The legislative changes, combined with a significant High Court decision, cleared the way legally and constitutionally for greater domestic use of the ADF.

In 2007, in *Thomas v Mowbray* ([2007] HCA 33), Australia's supreme court, the High Court, by a 5–2 majority, sanctioned the substantial use of the Federal defence power in peacetime and for domestic purposes. The language of the majority judgments was sweeping—both in relation to the potential breadth of the defence power and the lawful capacity of the Commonwealth government to effectively define for itself the limits of the power.

In a joint judgment, Gummow and Crennan JJ spoke of the defence power covering 'the defence of the realm against threats posed internally as well as by invasion from abroad by force of arms' (at [140]). The judges also effectively expanded the doctrine of 'judicial notice' to accept the many untested assertions about the 'war on terror' made by the Federal and State governments and their security agencies, such as the Australian Security Intelligence Organisation (ASIO). Callinan J declared it was 'blindingly obvious' that 'groups of zealots forming part of, or associated with Al Qa'ida' were 'making common cause of hatred against communities posing no threat to them' and 'planned to undertake violent, literally suicidal attacks upon even the institutions and persons of those communities' ([543–553]).

The immediate effect of the decision was to uphold the constitutionality of the 'control order' imposed on Jack Thomas, an acquitted terrorism suspect, under the provisions of the *Anti-Terrorism Act (No. 2) 2005*. By implication, the ruling constitutionally validated most, if not all, of the Federal anti-terrorism legislation introduced since 2002. Significantly, it also seemed to interpret the defence power widely enough to permit the internal deployment of troops, whether or not under the military call-out legislation, to pursue the 'war on terror' or deal with any other 'threats posed internally'.

By leaving the government and its agencies broad scope to define for themselves the nature of alleged terrorist threats, the decision eroded the 50-year-old principle adopted by the High Court in the *Communist Party Case* of 1951, that the defence power cannot be defined or expanded unilaterally by the executive for domestic political purposes (*Australian Communist Party v The Commonwealth* [1951] HCA 51; 83 CLR 1). In that case, the court rejected the attempt of the Menzies government to ban the Communist Party during the Korean War by inserting recitals in the Communist Party Dissolution Bill that the Bill's measures were required for the 'security and defence of Australia' in the face of a dire threat of violence, insurrection, treason, subversion, espionage and sabotage.

Clearly 'domestic violence' extends beyond terrorism. In discussing the term in the context of s 119 of the Constitution, Quick and Garran's *Annotated Constitution* refers to 'riots' (Quick and Garran 1901: 964). This reference was cited with approval by Dixon J in the High Court in the 1949 sedition case of *R v Sharkey* ((1949) 79 CLR 121 at 151) and in the 1951 Communist Party dissolution case, where he spoke of 'putting down of all individual or concerted attempts to obstruct or interfere with the discharge of the proper business of government' (*Australian Communist Party v The Commonwealth* (1951) 83 CLR 1 at 188). This language is wide enough to cover many traditional forms of political opposition.

The purpose of all the *Defence Act* amendments was to overcome definite legal and constitutional limits and restrictions that have, combined with political considerations, provided real constraints on the use of the armed forces in civilian settings. The amended Act goes beyond s 119 of the Constitution. In the first place, it allows a military call out where ministers are satisfied that domestic violence is occurring, 'or is likely to occur'. The latter phrase is an addition to s 119 and is therefore arguably unconstitutional.

Second, the legislation extends the call-out power to the protection of 'Commonwealth interests', regardless of whether there is a request by any state or territory government. It provides that 'the Governor-General may make the order whether or not the Government of the State or the self-governing Territory request the making of the order'. This provision, in so far as it purports to permit a military intervention without the consent of a state, may also contravene s 119, which arguably requires state assent to the use of troops on state soil. As discussed earlier in this chapter, there are provisions requiring consultation with state and territory governments, but these caveats are essentially legally meaningless.

In seeking to bypass s 119, the legislation appears to rest on a combination of other Commonwealth constitutional powers—the defence, external affairs, incidentals, executive and Governor-General's powers (see below)—yet no government has specified upon which of these powers it is relying.

Beyond the constitutional issues, the legislation is an attempt to overcome a variety of serious legal problems. Under previous legislative provisions and the common law, if military personnel kill or maim individuals, damage private property or interfere with people's liberty, they could be charged with criminal offences, including murder or manslaughter, or face civil action. Moreover, soldiers could not necessarily rely on a defence of obeying superior orders (Brett and Waller 1983: 654).

In addition, military personnel lacked legislative powers to carry out searches, seizures and arrests. That is why, when troops were called out in 1974 to guard Darwin's petrol depots from looters after the destruction of Cyclone Tracy, General Stretton, the commander of the Natural Disaster Organisation, stipulated that troops not carry arms, that they be accompanied by a police officer and that the soldier's authority would stem from a citizen's duty under common law (Stretton 1976: 82–83).

One purpose of the 2006 amendments was to give ADF members specific powers and legal immunities. Once deployed, the military could shoot down aircraft, sink ships, use deadly force, demand answers to questions and require the production of documents. Potentially lethal force could be used where an ADF member considered it necessary 'on reasonable grounds' to protect himself or herself, or another person or any infrastructure that the government designated as 'critical'. These provisions raised the possibility of soldiers—who are, after all, specifically trained to shoot to kill—killing innocent civilians.

Likewise, citizens have lost the right to refuse to answer questions or hand over material on the grounds of self-incrimination. Instead, they can be jailed for non-compliance. Similar powers have been given to the intelligence and police agencies where people are detained without trial under the counter-terrorism laws passed since 2002 (for example, *Australian Security Intelligence Organisation Act 1979* (Cth) s 34G) but their extension to the military raises even greater issues, given the lethal weaponry available to the armed forces, which may potentially be used to enforce compliance.

Since the 2018 amendments, the ADF powers have been protected by defences of 'superior orders' and 'good faith'. Furthermore, any criminal prosecutions will be handled by federal authorities under federal law, overriding state laws. The issues and problems raised by these efforts to protect military commanders and soldiers from legal liability are considered in Chapter 11.

Other call-out powers?

The amended provisions of the *Defence Act* have not been invoked since they were introduced in 2000, yet domestic military deployments have occurred with increasing frequency. It has been generally assumed that these operations have been validly conducted under executive power (for example, Moore 2005). It is therefore quite possible that future call outs could be conducted under a claim of executive power, rather than the *Defence Act*.

Three main possibilities seem to exist. One is the executive power of the Commonwealth, formally vested in the Governor-General by s 61 of the Constitution, possibly augmented by s 68, which nominates the Governor-General as the Commander in Chief of the military forces. Another is the residual prerogative power of the Crown, essentially derived from the history of the British monarchy. The third is common law power, perhaps based upon that exercised by English magistrates and ministers during the eighteenth and nineteenth centuries. Beyond that, there is another issue: does legal scope still exist to declare martial law, bypassing both the *Defence Act* and the Regulations?

Section 68 of the Constitution states: 'The command in chief of the naval and military forces of the Commonwealth is vested in the Governor-General as the Queen's representative'. On the face of it, these unambiguous words place the command of the armed forces in the personal hands of the vice-regal representative. As Governor-General Sir Ninian Stephen observed:

> [N]o mention of the Chiefs of Staff, none of the Ministers for Defence, of Cabinet or of Prime Minister. Instead all the panache of a Boulanger, a general on a white horse, at the head of his armies, with a standard unfurled.
> (Stephen 1984: 563)

(Georges Ernest Boulanger was a French general who participated in the suppression of the Paris Commune in 1871 and emerged as a potential military dictator in 1888–89, before being charged with treason and fleeing the country.)

Stephen immediately noted that constitutional and legal authorities regard it as a matter of constitutional convention, derived from the nature of representative government, that the Governor-General exercises this power on the advice of the elected government of the day. Nevertheless, unclarities persist, not the least because the drafters of the constitution decided to leave the words of s 68 untouched, despite some heated debate about amending it to specify that the Governor-General's power could be exercised only on the advice of the Executive Council.

Despite dismissing the notion that the Governor-General could call out troops without ministerial advice, Stephen concluded that a 'quite special relationship' existed between the Governor-General and the armed forces, a 'close relationship of sentiment'. He considered this an expression of a 'democratic society' with 'pride in and respect for its armed forces', on the one hand, and, on the other, 'the willing subordination of the members of those forces to the civil power' (Stephen 1984: 571).

Notwithstanding, Stephen's emphasis on its democratic content, the notion of a 'special relationship' is legally and politically problematic. The events of November 1975 demonstrate the potential for a political and constitutional crisis to arise in which a Governor-General seeks to exercise not only 'reserve' powers, but also military authority. Sir John Kerr reportedly held his own meetings, as the titular Commander in Chief, with senior defence and intelligence officials before dismissing the Whitlam government (Coxsedge, Caldicutt and Harant 1982: 35, 96). And a former Whitlam government cabinet minister alleged that Kerr secretly placed the armed forces on alert after the dismissal (Watching Brief, Workers News).

Another disturbing feature of that exercise of vice regal power to dismiss an elected government, despite its clear majority in the House of Representatives, is that, in the words of one scholar, 'constitutionally speaking, nothing prevents a repetition' (Winterton 2003: 251–252). The constitutional crisis highlighted the fact that no legal, judicial or parliamentary authority exists that can check or challenge the exercise of the reserve powers.

A final legal issue is whether the s 119 of the Constitution and the call out legislation cover the legal field, or can a government or even other official authorities invoke residual common law powers, perhaps derived from that exercised by English magistrates and ministers during the eighteenth and nineteenth centuries? In principle it would seem that the Constitution and the legislation now define and delimit the power of the Commonwealth, particularly given the critical and sensitive character of the powers involved.

However, in the *Tampa* case, the High Court effectively permitted the federal government to deploy military personnel, including SAS troops and sailors, to turn away 433 asylum seekers and forcibly transport them to Nauru, a remote Pacific island, even though the relevant legislation, the *Migration Act 1958* (Cth), required any suspected unlawful entrants to be detained in an Australian immigration facility (Head 2002a: 23–33). A panel of three justices refused to consider an appeal from a two-to-one decision of the Full Federal Court upholding the lawfulness of the detention and expulsion of the *Tampa* refugees (Vadarlis 2001). The Federal Court majority held that the government has executive or prerogative power under s 61 of the Constitution to detain and remove 'aliens' and take any other action it considers necessary to protect 'national sovereignty' (*Ruddock v Vadarlis* [2001] FCA 1329).

By analogy, similar reasoning could be applied to a troop deployment to protect 'national sovereignty'. It is doubtful, however, whether the common law power of ministers and local magistrates to use soldiers to put down riots is still intact (Greer 1983: 598). (For a more detailed exploration of these constitutional issues see Head 2007: 148–164.)

The rise of paramilitary policing

Alongside the expanding domestic role of the armed forces, militarised forms of policing have emerged and grown since the mid-1970s. Riot and counter-terrorism units have been established in the federal and state police forces, creating a network of paramilitary squads. Units such as the NSW Tactical Response Group (TRG), the Special Weapons Operations Squad (SWOS) and Victoria's Special Operations Group (SOG) have trained with the military, recruited former members of the armed forces, used a range of military weapons and equipment and engaged in high levels of force. A West Australian coroner, commenting on that state's Tactical Response Group, observed:

> [I]t is apparent that the TRG is a significant police para-military force whose tactics and weaponry are hardly less effective that [sic] those of any strictly military force … In terms of their capabilities in weapons and

> otherwise, the TRG now straddles the line between traditional police resources and the military.
>
> (Western Australia State Coroner n.d.: 65)

Although the official rationale for these paramilitary units includes combatting terrorism, they have been used in a wide and increasing range of police operations, including dealing with political and industrial unrest (McCulloch 2001). One study has documented how 'counter-terrorism' has moved beyond extreme acts of politically motivated violence into the policing of dissent and social and industrial protest and suggested that the police units herald 'an increasingly militarised approach to everyday policing' (Hocking 1993: 27, 160–179, Hocking 2004: 172–179). For instance, in 1984–85 the NSW TRG responded to 1,701 incidents and 'effected 443 arrests' and 'supported general duty and specialist police in operations' (Hocking 2004: 178).

The units are heavily armed and train with the ADF. The Victorian SOG, for example, has trained with the SAS, included former members of the SAS and other army units, and conducted regular joint exercises with the military. The SOG has had a range of military-style weapons, including Heckler and Koch 9MM submachine guns, M16 assault rifles, standard Australian Army issue Styr.223 rifles, 9mm semi-automatic pistols, Remington 870 pump action shotguns, chemical weapons, electric batons or stun guns, stun grenades, electric shields, and armoured and tactical vehicles (McCulloch 2001, 70–71). In 1982, the NSW TRG was equipped with US-made 870-type shotguns, CS and CH gas, riot and ballistic helmets, gas masks and batons, while SWOS members also received military training, including in 'tactical use of weapons' (Hocking 2004: 176).

A 1995 Victoria Police review of the SOG found that 'training is focussed on the option of last resort, that is armed confrontations' (McCulloch 2001: 71). Having been trained and equipped to use military-style levels of force, the units have been responsible for considerable numbers of civilian deaths. McCulloch has documented a pattern of fatal violence in Victorian policing. In that state, police killed 42 people between 1981 and 1998, with the SOG involved in 30 per cent of the shootings (McCulloch 2001: 118). Having been trained in how to shoot first and survive armed confrontations, rather than avoid such confrontations where possible, the SOG has been involved in a series of violent raids, ambushes and shootings (McCulloch 2001: 116–173). A coronial inquest into one of the deaths concluded:

> The policy of the Victoria Police Force and its SOG accepts … the use of force, forced entry, consequential firearms confrontation, consequential instinctive use of police firearms with legal justification, consequential personal risk to police members exposed to a person with a gun and consequentially and ultimately condones shooting by police members with legal justification.
>
> (Victoria State Coroner n.d.: 258)

The victims have included entirely innocent people, like David Gundy, a young Aboriginal man shot dead in his bed by the NSW SWOS in a mistaken early-morning raid on his home. Commissioner Wootten's Royal Commission report into the shooting found that the police officer who killed Gundy 'had not been trained to cope with an unarmed, near-naked man who reacted angrily when woken from his sleep by armed men bursting into his house' (Wootten 1991: 4). No charges were laid against any member of the police force, however.

The paramilitary units have been deployed frequently over the past two decades against political demonstrations, including anti-war marches, protests against gatherings of government leaders, demonstrations against school closures and Aboriginal rallies (McCulloch 2001: 188–213; Hocking 2004: 177, 179). The paramilitary units work closely with other specialist police squads responsible for 'protective security', 'crowd control' and 'intelligence' (McCulloch 2001: 185–188).

The interaction with the 'terrorism' legislation

The adoption of the 2000 'aid to civilian authorities' amendments to the *Defence Act* preceded the declaration of the 'war on terror'. This fact points to more underlying factors in the trend toward extending the military call-out powers. Nevertheless, the indefinite 'war' declared by the White House in September 2001 became the prime justification for the greater domestic mobilisation of the armed forces.

The expanded military call-out legislation introduced in 2006 was among the measures agreed upon by Prime Minister Howard and the state and territory Labor leaders in their joint communiqué from the 27 September 2005 Council of Australian Governments' 'counter-terrorism' summit. As a result of that bipartisan communiqué, fresh anti-terrorism laws were introduced in the Federal, State and Territory parliaments in the final months of 2005 (Head 2005b, 1–8). At the Commonwealth level, the *Anti-Terrorism Acts (Nos. 1 & 2) 2005* are among about 75 pieces of counter-terrorism legislation introduced since 2001.

The 'anti-terrorist' legislation established a special category of terrorist crimes and made them punishable by life imprisonment. It allowed secret detention and interrogation by police and Australian Security Intelligence Organisation (ASIO) officers for up to a week without charge, the ability to conduct closed-door trials and powers to ban political organisations by executive fiat (Head 2004a; Head 2004b).

The legislation introduced in late 2005 allowed the police and intelligence agencies to charge people, or alternatively, detain them without trial, without evidence of involvement in specific terrorist activity or planning. The *Anti-Terrorism Act (No. 1) (Cth)* 2005 changed the wording of many terrorist offences from 'the' terrorist act to 'a' terrorist act. In effect, it meant that people could be convicted of planning or preparing for terrorism without the police producing any evidence of a specific time, date, location or method of the supposed attack. The *Anti-Terrorism Act (No. 2) (Cth)* 2005 granted extra powers to intern 'suspects' without any charge or trial, either by way of 'preventative detention' or 'control orders'. (Lasry and Eastman 2005).

These provisions could be exploited to silence many types of political dissent. An organisation that 'advocates' a terrorist act can be outlawed. 'Advocating' includes 'praising' and could mean merely expressing sympathy for, or calling for an understanding of, the social and economic roots of terrorism (Walton 2005: 3).

The legislative proscription of anti-war and other dissenting views, especially those deemed to favour 'foreign' governments or political parties, was further extended by the packages of 'espionage and foreign interference' laws passed in 2018. (For an examination of these laws see Head 2018b.)

This author has argued elsewhere that none of these measures, including the military call-out laws, were necessary to protect ordinary people against terrorism (Head 2005b: 1–9). Every conceivable terrorist act was already a serious crime—from murder to arson and hijacking—and the criminal law amply covered planning, preparing, conspiring, financing, supporting and attempting related to such activities (Hancock 2002b). Moreover, ASIO and the state and federal police already possessed powers to infiltrate organisations, tap phones, bug premises, intercept mail, search homes and hack into computers (Head 2002b: 678–679).

By expanding the range of 'terrorist', 'espionage', 'foreign interference' and related offences, the anti-terrorism and 'foreign interference' legislative packages correspondingly enlarged the sphere of potential military deployment. Protests and demonstrations opposing Australian or allied military operations, or against police raids or arrests over information leaks that allegedly threaten 'national security' could be characterised as threats of 'domestic violence' that could endanger 'Commonwealth interests' or 'declared infrastructure'.

In 2002, the Commonwealth and the States and Territories also reached an agreement that the Commonwealth would take charge of 'national terrorist situations', with or without the consent of affected States or Territories. While the Commonwealth undertook to consult and seek agreement before declaring a national terrorist situation, the States and Territories agreed 'not to withhold unreasonably such agreement' (Laing 2005: 516). A scenario offered by the ADF to a parliamentary committee in 2003 demonstrates the potential for the military to rapidly take control of civilian areas in an alleged terrorist emergency, without prior ministerial authorisation:

> At some point the police officer may come to the view that the incident has deteriorated to such a point that, with his civil resources, he can no longer resolve the incident and will call on the Defence Commander present, who is the commanding officer of the TAG [Tactical Assault Group], to resolve the incident. If that is done in a deliberate and time-allowing way, then approval for that employment of the Defence Force will be sought through the minister to government. If, however, time does not allow—if there is a cataclysmic collapse of the situation—then the Military Commander (Forward), in conjunction with the police commander, can launch the Defence Force in an assault on his own call, but needs to satisfy a number of legal requirements, obviously, before that is done.
>
> (Joint Standing Committee 2001–2002: 13)

More generally, the 'war on terror' serves to reinforce a climate of fear and insecurity that can be exploited to justify military measures. Laing recalled the protests against the Vietnam War and President Richard Nixon's invasion of Cambodia, and the use of the Ohio National Guard to shoot down four students at Kent State University in 1970. Laing cited an address to the nation by Nixon just five days earlier, in which the United States president accused protesters of producing an 'age of anarchy' by making 'mindless attacks on all the great institutions' (Laing 2005: 507–508). Nixon's stance offers a salutary warning of how military personnel can be mobilised to quell civilian dissenters, with lethal consequences. Laing commented:

> What the world witnessed leading up to that day in Ohio is not that different to the protests we see today in Australia. Australian citizens from all backgrounds have used various city streets, parks and university campuses throughout history, including in recent years, to rally in organised demonstrations; demonstrating and voicing their concerns in relation to, amongst other things, the war on terror, globalisation, university fees and voluntary unionism.
>
> (Laing 2005: 508)

This scenario raises the spectre of troops being used against growing social and political unrest. Laing said there was concern in 2000, when the initial military call-out legislation was brought forward, that the ADF would be deployed into Australian streets to disperse such protestors if they caused a serious civil disturbance. However, he argued that this 'fear and paranoia' subsided over the following four years because: 'The current climate of terror has created an overriding and shifting attitude towards the ADF being called out' (Laing 2005: 509). Moreover, Laing concluded by asserting that calling out the ADF was not 'the end of civilisation' because 'the ADF will only ever be deployed for a legitimate purpose' and 'one must have faith in those elected representatives to undertake such a responsibility' (Laing 2005: 521).

Is such faith justified, however, in the light of the now widely acknowledged false statements made by the US, British and Australian governments to justify the invasion of Iraq as part of the 'war on terror'? As discussed in Chapter 2, the 'war on terror' itself, and its underlying political and geo-strategic purposes, have to be questioned. This suggests that whenever governments and security authorities cite 'national security' threats, especially of indefinite duration, as the reason for suspending or overturning constitutional norms and basic legal rights, the lessons of history—including the traumatic experiences of the United States in 1970–1972—demonstrate a need for distrust and vigilance.

1978—Australia's most dramatic troop call out

The only major mobilisation of troops in an urban setting in Australia's history occurred in 1978. At 12.40 am on 13 February 1978, a bomb exploded in a garbage bin outside the Hilton Hotel, the venue for the Commonwealth Heads of Government Regional Meeting (CHOGRM), a gathering of government leaders from former British colonies. The blast killed two garbage collectors, Alex Carter and William Favell, and a police officer, Paul Birmistriw. A number of other people were injured, some seriously, including another police officer, Terry Griffiths, who has continued to raise questions about the bombing and to campaign for a judicial inquiry (Hocking 2004: 82–85).

By any objective measure, the 1978 Sydney Hilton Hotel bombing remains one of Australia's most serious unresolved crimes. Not only were three people killed and several maimed, but the blast was allegedly directed against an international summit of government leaders. Moreover, the event was proclaimed the opening of a new era of terrorism, triggering a significant boosting of the powers and resources of the police and intelligence agencies. Yet, the question of who actually carried out the bombing remains unclear. Twice, the police and intelligence agencies effectively framed-up people, who were convicted and jailed in connection with the explosion, only to have those frame-ups later fall apart ignominiously. Then came a series of judicial and political reviews that failed to provide any answers, or hold anyone to account for the wrongful prosecutions. No genuine inquiry has ever been conducted into the Hilton affair, leaving open the possibility that the security agencies themselves were involved or implicated in the bombing (Head 2008).

Amid blazing media headlines, Prime Minister Fraser and New South Wales Premier Wran mobilised the military. 'Troops Placed on Anti-Terror Alert' was *The Australian's* headline (The Australian 1978: 1). 'Terrorism now "fact of life"—All Australians should morn: Wran', reported the *Sydney Morning Herald*, which editorialised: 'Australia is not immune from the international disease of terrorism and violence' (The Sydney Morning Herald 1978: 2, 6; Cahill and Cahill 2005). Without any clear legal or constitutional authorisation (Head 2001: 282–284; Blackshield 1978; Current Topics 1978), the federal Liberal government and the state Labor government deployed nearly 2,000 heavily armed troops, some with bayonets fixed, accompanied by armoured personnel carriers and helicopters. Units took up positions along a major highway on Sydney's outskirts and, for three days, patrolled the nearby Southern Highlands towns of Bowral and Mittagong, close to the site of a scheduled CHOGRM leaders' summit (Hocking 2004: 86; Cahill and Cahill 2005).

On the first morning, residents of Bowral were awoken at 6.30 am by the sound of helicopters circling overhead, while teams of soldiers scoured garbage bins, drains, hedges and shrubbery. Troops 'camped on the local football field, and patrolled the main street carrying automatic weapons and full magazines in place' (Hocking 2004: 86). It is hardly surprising that the sight of armed soldiers caused public consternation, with rumours that martial law had been imposed (Cahill and Cahill 2005). Journalists from two local newspapers recorded both fear and confusion among residents. One interviewee said: 'Now we have an idea what life in Northern Ireland is like. This is frightening.' Reflecting residents' unease, the Bowral-based *Southern Highlands News* described 'the virtual siege conditions' in Bowral (and to a lesser extent Mittagong) and commented: '[T]hose who remember Franco's Spain could see a parallel in the pairs of uniformed men, all heavily armed, steadily walking their beat, always in sight of each other' (Cahill and Cahill 2005).

The Hilton attack was not the first terrorist incident in contemporary Australia. Previous Liberal governments had largely ignored neo-fascist Croatian Ustashi bombings in the 1960s and early 1970s (Cain 1994: 206–208). Over the ensuing 18 months, however, the Fraser government, with the Labor opposition's essential support, used the Hilton bombing as the pretext to carry through a far-reaching expansion in the powers and resources of the police and security apparatus. The changes included legalised surveillance powers for the Australian Security Intelligence Organisation (ASIO), the formation of the Australian Federal Police (AFP), the establishment of the Office of National Assessments (ONA) in the Prime Minister's Department, the creation of paramilitary SWAT-style units in state police forces and domestic SAS units in the ADF (Hocking 2004: 101–119; Head 2008). The aftermath also revealed the establishment of Crisis Policy Centres with the authority to take control over parts of the country in times of alleged emergency (Hocking 2004: 180–192).

It is now known that, following the precedent established by the post-Hilton call out, the Cabinet Intelligence and Security Committee formally decided in September 1978 to adopt a policy of deploying the ADF whenever 'appropriate' in response to alleged terrorist acts. The partial release in 2009, by the National Archives of Australia, of the 1978 cabinet documents revealed that the committee agreed that:

> Australia adopt a 'hard line' policy in dealing with terrorist incidents, that is:- (i) the police and, where it is appropriate to authorize their employment, elements of the Defence Force, be instructed to take firm action against the terrorists and obtain their surrender; (ii) if tactical negotiations aimed at surrender fail and in particular if violent action by the terrorists (for example, killing or injuring hostages or major property damage) is anticipated, action be taken to subdue the terrorists by force.
>
> (Cabinet 1978: 138)

The timing, force and tactics applied were to be 'in the final balance, subject to the principle of minimising the risk of the loss of innocent life' (Cabinet 1978: 139). Who would make those critical judgments and decisions was not specified, however. It seems that intimate involvement of the Prime Minister and other ministers was intended. The cabinet minutes stated that only if the options (i) and (ii) above were considered unacceptable, 'would the possibility of concessions (other than minor concessions such as food and medical supplies) be considered by Ministers in consultation with the Prime Minister' (Cabinet 1978: 139).

Considerable secrecy surrounded this policy. It was not to be published, but statements were to be made on behalf of the government emphasising the government's intention to 'take all appropriate action' to counter terrorism (Cabinet 1978: 139). In other words, the crucial decision that the ADF would be authorised to use force on domestic soil was not communicated to the public, nor was any public debate conducted on the issue. Many of the security decisions made during 1978 remain classified to this day. The National Archives of Australia noted that material had been withheld from the released documents to 'protect Australia's defence, security or international relations' (National Archives 2009: 2). A total of 30 cabinet submissions and decisions were censored before release, and two decisions and their accompanying submissions were considered so sensitive that their titles, as well as their contents, remained secret (Solomon 2009).

Many questions remain about why, and by what legal authority, the unprecedented decision was made to call out the troops in immediate response to the Hilton blast. Official media statements were 'positively evasive' as to the legal basis for the military action (Blackshield 1978: 6). On the evening of 13 February 1978, after consultations between Prime Minister Fraser and Premier Wran, Governor-General Sir Zelman Cowan signed an Order to call out the ADF (a) 'for the purpose of safeguarding the national and international interests of the Commonwealth of Australia' and (b) 'for giving effect to the obligations of the Commonwealth of Australia in relation to the protection of internationally protected persons' because of 'terrorist activities and related violence that have occurred in the State of New South Wales' (Andrews 1995: 153). The Order was to remain 'in force until revoked' (Hocking 2004: 255). No limits were placed on the numbers of troops, the geographical area of the deployment or the powers of the ADF personnel. Subsequently, it was learned that the Rules of Engagement specifically authorised military personnel to open fire against civilians and vehicles in various circumstances, including if a person was carrying a lethal object and 'was about to use it for offensive purposes' (Beddie and Moss 1982: 81–82). The legal protection provided for soldiers by these rules of engagement, however, was unclear. One scholar accused the government of 'cavalier disregard for the legal position of army personnel' (Blackshield 1978: 10).

This official response raised significant legal questions. Two inter-related issues arose: (1) Were such interventions constitutional and, if so, what was their precise constitutional basis? (2) What were the powers of the military personnel and the rights of civilians in relation to the military? Neither question was directly addressed in the two formal documents ordering the military intervention, namely the joint statement by the Prime Minister and the New South Wales Premier, and the Order issued by the Governor-General. The wording of the Order suggested a reliance on the defence and foreign affairs powers. Presumably for the purposes of the latter, the Foreign Affairs Minister also signed a 'Requisition of the Civil Authority' requiring the call out (Hope 1979: 279). The Governor-General revoked the Order on 20 February 1978, when the last of the foreign leaders had left Australia (Moore 2005: 526).

In his statement to Parliament, Prime Minister Fraser stated that the New South Wales Premier had concurred with the call out but had not requested it. He did not specifically refer to s 119 of the Constitution, or explain the precise legal basis for the call out, instead stating:

> The mechanism for the legal approach to the call out was discussed with the Premier in two terms: In terms of a strict request from the State, and therefore in terms of aid to the civil power; or, secondly, in terms of the use of the Commonwealth's own authority and responsibility to protect people against possible acts of terrorism. For various reasons as I explained to the House I think yesterday, the second course was chosen, but the Premier had made it perfectly clear to me that if it was thought best to pursue it through the first mechanism, the Premier would certainly act in full cooperation.
>
> (Parliamentary Debates 1978: 159)

Three months later, after some speculation as to the legal basis for the Government's action, the Attorney-General Peter Durack confirmed that no recourse had been made to s 119 of the Constitution. Instead, he pointed to a 'second possible basis, namely a call out on the initiative of the Commonwealth':

> [T]he view of the government's legal advisers is that, where domestic violence is of such a character that the operations of the Commonwealth government are affected, the Commonwealth government may, without request from a State, intervene with all the force at its disposal, not to protect the State but to protect itself.
>
> (Hope 1979: 273)

For this proposition, Durack cited a passage from Quick and Garran's *Annotated Constitution of the Australian Commonwealth*, which was approved by Dixon J in the 1949 sedition case, *R v Sharkey* ((1949) 79 CLR 121 at 151). Remarkably, the Attorney-General also relied upon the authority of Regulation 415 of the *Australian Military Regulations*, which specifically recognised that the military forces could be employed by the Commonwealth on its own initiative. It goes without saying that a regulation cannot provide a constitutional foundation for federal power.

Several other possibilities were canvassed. One, asserted by Justice Hope in his 1979 *Protective Security Review*, commissioned by the Fraser Government, was that the Governor-General acted under s 68 of the Constitution, which states, without qualification, that: 'The commander-in-chief of the naval and military forces of the Commonwealth is vested in the Governor-General as the Queen's representative.' Another possibility, advanced by academic commentators, was that the Federal Government exercised its executive power, also formally exercisable by the Governor-General, under s 61 of the Constitution to ensure the 'execution and maintenance of this Constitution, and of the laws of the Commonwealth'. References were also made to the Commonwealth's defence power (s 51(vi) of the Constitution), combined with the external affairs power (s 51(xxix)) and the incidental powers (s 51(xxxix)). Other possibilities mentioned were an 'inherent self-protecting' power of the Commonwealth, 'inherent law and order powers' and the Crown's prerogative power over defence and military matters (Current Topics 1978; Lane 1974: 77).

Blackshield concluded that the call out was valid as an exercise of the Commonwealth's executive power, which 'includes an amorphous and unexplored bundle of attributes of sovereignty, "inherent in the fact of nationhood and of international personality"' (Blackshield 1978: 7). Reliance on such a vague and uncharted 'bundle' of concepts hardly seems a wise or safe manner to proceed when the issue at stake is the mobilisation of potentially lethal force by the ADF for the purposes of internal security. A 1978 note in the *Australian Law Journal* observed that the Hilton bombing call out had 'exposed gaps, inadequacies, and uncertainties in the legal and constitutional powers of Commonwealth and State enforcement agencies' (Current Topics 1978: 296).

Aware of the political sensitivity of the issue, the Fraser Government did not legislate. Instead, the only relevant legislative instruments remained the *Australian Military Regulations* and internal Defence Instructions, not all of which have been made public. Part 5 of the Regulations, 'Duties in Aid of the Civil Power During Domestic Violence', provided that a magistrate must accompany the defence forces into an area and 'read the Riot Act' before the troops moved in. 'The Defence Instructions (General) on Defence Force Aid to the Civil Power' remain a classified document (Ward 1997), a highly unsatisfactory situation when the implications for civil liberties are great. Of equal concern is the fact that under the Defence Act, the Instructions may be changed at any time without parliamentary or public scrutiny (Bayne 1991).

Two precedents were set by the 1978 call out: the open-ended use of executive power, and the utilisation of 'terrorism' as the justification for domestic military intervention (Hocking 2004: 94–97). Despite the lack of proof that the Hilton bombing was actually a terrorist act (Head 2008), the terrorism label was employed to elevate the incident into an issue of 'national security', a doctrine notorious for its vagueness and elasticity. In the words of the *Australian Law Journal*, a 'paradoxical aspect of the importance commanded by the concept is its nebulousness' (Current Topics 1984: 67). In 1984, the editors of that journal warned presciently:

> The concept of 'national security' in peacetime has in the past three decades attained a degree of significance and a measure of political and judicial recognition at the highest level that are without precedent in the past history of Australia. Already, it has had a far-reaching impact upon the law of civil liberties, and who can now say to what extent it may reach into other corners of our legal system?
> (Current Topics 1984: 67)

Two decades after the 1978 call out, and taking advantage of the 2000 Sydney Olympics, the Howard Government brought forward legislation that sought to expand the military call-out power, again in the name of 'counter-terrorism' and 'national security', without addressing the constitutional doubts or the civil liberties concerns. Just as the 1978 Hilton bombing became the occasion for claims that Australia had entered the 'age of terrorism', police and military authorities claimed that the Olympics would be a 'magnet' for terrorists. Six years later, similar unsubstantiated claims were made about the 2006 Melbourne Commonwealth Games to justify a broadening of the powers adopted in 2000. Forty years on from 1978, the dangers of terrorism were again cited as the reason for a further extension of the military deployment provisions.

For many reasons, from the collapse of its police frame-ups to the security measures adopted in its wake, the Hilton affair underscores the need to constantly challenge the claims being made by governments about the 'war on terror' and to oppose every erosion of civil liberties and basic legal rights being carried out in its name (Head 2008).

11 How can governments and military chiefs be held to account?

Many serious legal and policy issues, as well as problems and uncertainties, are raised by official measures to clothe the armed forces with immunities to protect their personnel from criminal and civil liability for their actions. These actions may lead to losses of lives, serious injuries, damage to property and other infringements of legal and civil rights.

The Australian *Defence Act*, reviewed in the previous chapter, provides called-out soldiers with explicit powers to use lethal force, combined with defences of good faith and acting in obedience to superior orders. In other countries, these powers and defences may not be specifically legislated, but may be covered by other provisions, common law, regulations or military rules of engagement. Among the issues that arise are the following:

- What degrees of violence and violation of legal rights are permissible during domestic military operations? In particular, what is the scope of terms such as 'reasonable and necessary force'?
- In the event of the unlawful killing or injuring of civilians, can members of the armed forces rely upon defences of superior orders or acting in good faith?
- What is the legal effect of any relevant manuals, rules of engagement or guidelines issued to govern the conduct of military personnel?
- Can government ministers or military officers be held liable criminally or civilly for any loss or damage?

Criminal prosecutions: the historical record

History suggests that even if soldiers are prosecuted, the prospects of conviction are not strong. As noted in Chapter 3, a test case was conducted against four members of the armed forces involved in the 1819 Peterloo Massacre, in which British soldiers killed 15 people and wounded 400–700. The case ended in acquittal, with the court ruling that the soldiers' actions had been justified to disperse an illegal gathering (Reid 1989: 203–204).

Likewise, in the Bristol riots of 1831, an officer who had fatally shot a boy was acquitted of manslaughter. Lord Tindal instructed the Grand Jury that if the shot was 'discharged in the fair and honest execution of his duty, in endeavouring to disperse the mob', the killing was justified and amounted to accidental death only (*R v Pinney* (1832) 170 ER 962, 969). By contrast, two officers who had refused to order the troops to fire without a magistrate's sanction were found guilty of neglect of duty, causing one to commit suicide. Lord Tindal insisted that soldiers had a duty, as citizens, on their own authority to do their utmost to 'put down riot and tumult'.

A similar result followed Britain's Featherstone Colliery Riots of 1893. Four people, including two bystanders, were killed when an infantry captain ordered soldiers to fire on striking coal miners and their supporters after a local magistrate had read the Riot Act proclamation. The 1893 *Report of the Select Committee on the Featherstone Riots* exonerated the captain and his troops, saying: 'The necessary prevention of such outrage on person and property justifies the guardians of the peace in the employment against a riotous crowd of even deadly weapons' (Whelan 1985: 272).

Between 1970 and 1979, the British army killed 186 people in Northern Ireland, but between 1972 and 1976, only 28 soldiers were prosecuted for offences involving shooting, of whom 13 were convicted. Only one soldier was convicted of manslaughter, and his conviction was quashed on appeal (Rowe 1985: 201). After one soldier was acquitted of murder, the House of Lords was asked to provide an advisory opinion. The Law Lords said the 'reasonableness' of force was a question of fact for a jury, although Lord Diplock stated that a jury ought to take into account that a soldier may have to make a split-second decision to open fire or not (*Reference under s 48A of the Criminal Appeal (Northern Ireland) Act 1968 (No. 1 of 1975)* [1976] 2 All ER 937). During the 1990s, as discussed below, one private was convicted of murder, after he fired a fatal shot into the back of a passing car. However, the British government released him on licence and he was ultimately acquitted of all offences after a series of re-trials.

This record indicates that in criminal cases, as in civil matters, courts are reluctant to hold members of the armed forces liable, even where they have killed civilians, at least where their actions occurred in the course of authorised military operations. Judging by history, the test of 'reasonable and necessary force' is likely to be interpreted favourably toward armed forces members acting under orders.

Two fatal shooting cases

These issues can be illustrated by two British House of Lords decisions, one from the 1970s and the other from the 1990s, arising out of fatal shootings by soldiers of unarmed men during the course of British military operations in Northern Ireland.

In *Attorney-General for Northern Ireland's Reference (No 1 of 1975)* ([1977] AC 105), a soldier on patrol in Northern Ireland shot and killed an unarmed man, who ran away when challenged. The trial judge found that the prosecution had failed to prove that the soldier intended to kill or cause serious bodily harm, and further found that the homicide was justifiable under s 3 of the *Criminal Law Act (Northern Ireland) 1967*. That section provided:

> A person may use such force as is reasonable in the circumstances in the prevention of crime, or in effecting or assisting in the lawful arrest of offenders or suspected offenders or of persons unlawfully at large.

The House of Lords decided that the judge's ruling was purely one of fact, and therefore declined to answer the question of law referred to it, as to whether the soldier had committed a crime. However, Lord Diplock made the following remarks, which point to the uncertainties and high risks associated with military mobilisations in civilian areas:

> There is little authority in English law concerning the rights and duties of a member of the armed forces of the Crown when acting in aid of the civil power; and what little authority there is relates almost entirely to the duties of soldiers when troops are called upon to assist in controlling a riotous assembly. Where used for such temporary purposes it may not be inaccurate to describe the rights and duties of a soldier as being no more than those of an ordinary citizen in uniform. But such a description is in my view misleading in the circumstances in which the army is currently employed in aid of the civil power in Northern Ireland … In theory it may be the duty of every citizen when an arrestable offence is about to be committed in his presence to take whatever reasonable measures are available to him to prevent the commission of the crime; but the duty is one of imperfect obligation and it does not place him under any obligation to do anything by which he would expose himself to risk of personal injury, nor is he under any duty to search for criminals or seek out crime. In contrast to this a soldier who is employed in aid of the civil power in Northern Ireland is under a duty, enforceable under military law, to search for criminals if so ordered by his superior officer and to risk his own life should this be necessary in preventing terrorist acts. For the performance of this duty he is armed with a firearm, a self-loading rifle, from which a bullet, if it hits the human body, is almost certain to cause serious injury if not death.
>
> ([1977] AC 136–137)

In the second case, *R v Clegg* ([1995] 1 AC 482), Lord Lloyd of Berwick cited these comments. He emphasised the last sentence in the quotation and added:

> In the case of a soldier in Northern Ireland, in the circumstances in which Private Clegg found himself, there is no scope for graduated force. The only choice lay between firing a high-velocity rifle which, if aimed accurately, was almost certain to kill or injure, and doing nothing at all.
>
> ([1995] 1 AC 497–498)

The implication, it seems, is that when a government deploys highly armed soldiers, equipped and trained to kill, in a civilian area, it is precisely because of that circumstance that the law must give the armed forces greater leeway to kill or maim than would be permitted for any other person (including, presumably, a less lethally equipped police officer).

Private Clegg was convicted by a trial judge of murder. While on a patrol to catch 'joyriders' Clegg fired three shots at the windscreen of a car as it approached at speed. He fired a fourth shot, killing a passenger, after the car had passed him and was already more than 50 feet along the road. The judge accepted that the initial three shots were fired in self-defence or in defence of a colleague, but that the fourth shot could not have been fired in self-defence because the danger to the soldiers no longer existed. The House of Lords upheld the conviction, ruling that where a person used a greater degree of force than necessary for self-defence, the charge could not be reduced to manslaughter, even if the accused was a soldier or police officer acting in the course of his duty. Yet, the court expressed regret that, under existing law, the judge had no choice but to convict Clegg of murder, and urged the parliament to change the law relating to murder and manslaughter.

In an interesting insight into the lengths that military personnel may go in conspiring together to obscure their criminal liability, Clegg argued that he had fired the fourth shot to stop the driver of the car in the belief that it had struck another member of the patrol. The judge found that bruising on the other soldier's leg had not been caused by the car but by another soldier stamping on it to give the misleading appearance that he had been struck by the car.

The House of Lords observed that an army 'yellow card' entitled 'Instructions for opening fire in Northern Ireland' could, on a literal reading, justify firing on a car where a person had been injured by it, irrespective of the seriousness of the injury. Significantly, however, the court said the card had no legal force ([1995] 1 AC 491). (This finding relates to the issue of the legal effect of any military manual or rules of engagement—see below.)

Clegg's conviction caused a considerable political backlash. The British government released him on licence, a series of re-trials ensued, evidence was found to be unreliable and he was ultimately acquitted of all offences (Guardian 2000). This outcome points to the political and legal difficulties involved in finding members of the armed forces guilty of offences committed during operations.

After reviewing the earlier cases on self-defence and excessive force, Lee drew the conclusion that 'the courts have shown a disinclination to insist on a strict standard in measuring the reasonableness of the force applied' (Lee 1984: 241). All these considerations suggest that the 'reasonable and necessary force' test is likely to be interpreted generously toward the military in circumstances where members act under lawful orders.

The Kent State shootings

The American Kent State University shootings of 1970, at the height of the movement against the Vietnam War, provide a further cautionary example of the difficulties involved in legally holding to account those responsible for shooting down protestors. On 4 May 1970, members of the Ohio National Guard killed four students and wounded nine others, one of whom suffered permanent paralysis. Ohio Governor

James A. Rhodes sent the troops to the campus, in the city of Kent, Ohio, at the request of the local mayor. The only instruments the Guardsmen had to dispel demonstrators were bayonets, CS gas grenades, and .30–06 ball ammunition (Bills 1988; Caputo 2005).

Some of the students who were shot were protesting against the American invasion of Cambodia, which President Richard Nixon had announced in a television address on 30 April. Other students who were shot were merely walking nearby or observing the protest at a distance. The shootings led to protests on college campuses throughout the United States and a student strike, causing more than 450 campuses across the country to close. Five days after the shootings, 100,000 people demonstrated in Washington against the war and the killing of unarmed student protesters.

A month after the shootings, President Nixon established the President's Commission on Campus Unrest, known as the Scranton Commission, which he charged to study the dissent, disorder, and violence breaking out on college and university campuses across the nation. The Commission issued its findings in a September 1970 report that concluded that the Ohio National Guard shootings were unjustified (President's Commission 1970). The report said:

> Even if the guardsmen faced danger, it was not a danger that called for lethal force. The 61 shots by 28 guardsmen certainly cannot be justified. Apparently, no order to fire was given, and there was inadequate fire control discipline on Blanket Hill. The Kent State tragedy must mark the last time that, as a matter of course, loaded rifles are issued to guardsmen confronting student demonstrators.

Eight of the guardsmen were indicted by a grand jury. The guardsmen claimed to have fired in self-defence. In 1974, US District Judge Frank Battisti dismissed charges against all eight on the basis that the prosecution's case was too weak to warrant a trial. Between 1970 and 1979, families of the victims filed lawsuits against the State of Ohio, in hope of placing blame on Governor Rhodes and the Ohio National Guard. Trials were held on both the federal and state levels but all ended in acquittals or were dismissed, except one.

One civil trial for wrongful death and injury against Rhodes and the National Guardsmen was originally dismissed, but eventually the dismissal was overturned due to the judge excluding evidence. The students' families were awarded approximately $63,000 per victim and the defendants agreed to state for the record that they regretted their actions.

Australia's explicit authorisation of lethal force

The Australian legislation provides a case study for considering the many legal and policy issues. As a result of the amendments passed in 2000, 2006 and 2018, Australia's *Defence Act 1903* grants Australian Defence Force (ADF) personnel extraordinary powers in various circumstances.

These include to use 'reasonable and necessary' lethal force (s 51N(3)), shoot down planes or sink ships (s 46(5)), interrogate people and command the handing over of documents (s 46(7)), search people and premises, and seize things (ss 46 (7) and 51A) and detain people (ss 46(7) and 51L(3)). ADF members also may 'do anything incidental' to these powers, 'including enter any place or premises or board an aircraft or vessel' (s 46(9)).

Many of these powers exceed those held by police officers, notwithstanding the expansion of police powers by the anti-terrorism legislation adopted by the Australian federal, state and territory parliaments. A common prerequisite for their use—that ADF personnel consider them 'reasonable and necessary in the circumstances' (s 51N(1))—provides little real safeguard against misuse or overuse.

Some of the powers require written ministerial authorisation, unless the ADF member believes on reasonable grounds that there is insufficient time to obtain authorisation because of 'a sudden and extraordinary emergency' (For example, s 46(1)(b)). But how is the existence of such an emergency to be gauged? The phrase leaves considerable leeway for unilateral military decisions.

The military's lethal force powers have been extended beyond reasonable force to protect people from death or injury, to the protection of any physical assets declared by an authorising minister as 'critical infrastructure'. The relevant parts of s 51N provide as follows:

Use of reasonable and necessary force

1 A member of the Defence Force who is being utilised under a call-out order (whether or not the member is exercising a power under this Part):

  a may use such force against persons and things as is reasonable and necessary in the circumstances (subject to subsections (2) and (3)); and
  b if using force against persons—must do so in accordance with this section.

Restrictions on use of force

1 A member of the Defence Force must not use force against persons or things in exercising a power under paragraph 46(7)(h), 51D(2)(i) or 51L(3)(g) to direct a person to answer a question put by a member of the Defence Force, or to produce to a member of the Defence Force a particular document that is readily accessible to the person.
2 In using force against a person, a member of the Defence Force must not do anything that is likely to cause the death of, or grievous bodily harm to, the person unless:

  a the member believes on reasonable grounds that doing that thing:

    i is necessary to protect the life of, or to prevent serious injury to, a person (including the member); or
    ii in relation to powers exercised under Division 5—is necessary to protect the declared infrastructure in respect of which the powers are

being exercised against the domestic violence or threat specified in the call-out order; or

iii in relation to powers exercised under paragraph 46(5)(d) or (e)—is reasonable and necessary to give effect to the order under which, or under the authority of which, the member is acting; and

b if a person against whom force is to be used is attempting to escape being detained by fleeing—the person has, if practicable, been called on to surrender and the member believes on reasonable grounds that the person cannot be apprehended in any other manner.

While, on the face it, subsections (2) and (3) limit the breadth of subsection (1), the scope that remains for the use of grievous or deadly force is substantial. Moreover, subsections (2) and (3) may have the effect of specifically authorising, or at least legitimising, such force in certain circumstances.

This opens up the possibility of military personnel justifying the infliction of fatal or serious injuries on the basis that soldiers felt threatened by the actions of their victims or others associated with them. The cases reviewed below highlight the difficulties of challenging such claims, particularly where courts are loathe to second guess judgments made in the heat of conflict or in the context of 'national security'.

Moreover, a person 'attempting to escape being detained by fleeing' may be killed or caused grievous bodily harm if they have been called on to surrender and a soldier believes on reasonable grounds that the person cannot be apprehended in any other way. This establishes the danger of killings or woundings being justified by equally difficult-to-assess allegations that the victims attempted to escape.

Subsection (3) could justify shooting people to stop a threatened disruption of any facility, without any alleged direct danger to human life. Property, no matter how 'critical', should not outweigh the right to live. In submissions on the 2006 legislation, the Australian Muslim Civil Rights Advocacy Network and the NSW Council for Civil Liberties objected that the provision deviates from the long-held legal principle that killing or causing serious injury to protect property is not permissible (Senate Report 2006: 25). In fact, intentional use of lethal or grievous force to protect property is expressly forbidden by the self-defence provisions of the Australian *Criminal Code Act 1995* (s 10.4(3)). Australia's Human Rights and Equal Opportunity Commission called for the provision to be excised from the legislation because it potentially placed Australia in breach of article 6 of the International Covenant on Civil and Political Rights (Senate Report 2006: 25). The ICCPR article 6 (1) provides: 'Every human being has the inherent right to life. This right shall be protected by law. No one shall be arbitrarily deprived of his life.'

These objections were rejected by a Senate Committee on the grounds that the power would be used only in 'the most extreme circumstances' and that an attack on any critical infrastructure has 'the potential to threaten life indirectly as well as compromise the ability of the country to defend itself' (Senate Report 2006: 26). Such vague formulations add to the concern that lethal force can now be used to protect facilities on the basis of political or military judgments about their importance to national defence.

Similar objections can be made to the power to use force against an 'aircraft (whether or not the aircraft is airborne) or vessel, up to and including destroying the aircraft or vessel' (s 46(5)). Such action requires ministerial authorisation, but a minister may issue a contingent call-out order. That is, rather than authorise the shooting down of a specific plane or vessel, the minister can issue an ongoing authorisation.

This power is similar to a superior orders requirement, but that offers little protection to passengers (see the superior orders discussion below). One caveat is that the minister must have regard to Australia's international obligations (s 45), which include the Convention on International Civil Aviation (Chicago Convention) that instructs member states not to endanger the lives of passengers on civil aircraft (Bronitt and Stephens 2007: 272–273).

Another power that raises concerns is contained in ss 46(7(h) and 51(3)(g). A called-out ADF member may 'require a person to answer a question put by the member, or to produce to the member a particular document that is readily accessible to the person'. These provisions open the prospect of interrogation of civilians by heavily armed military personnel, something normally associated with military regimes.

Significantly, the authority to use force under s 51N exceeds that given to Australian Federal Police officers, whose powers relate to arrests made for offences. None of the powers, such as to capture premises, issue directions, evacuate people or search and seize, is limited to any belief by the officer that an offence has been committed. Moreover, the risk of ADF members using lethal force in the exercise of policing functions is considerably greater, given that they are armed only with high-powered weaponry, designed to kill, and that soldiers are trained to kill, or be killed (McCulloch 2001: 17–31).

Good faith and superior orders

Introduced in 2018, section 51S of the Australian *Defence Act* added a new defence of acting in good faith. This protected ADF personnel from both criminal and civil liability, if they failed to comply with any obligation under the legislation or acted under an invalid order, provided that the powers were exercised, or purportedly exercised, in good faith:

51S Exercise of powers when certain obligations not complied with

Members who fail to comply with obligations

1 If, before, while or after exercising a power under any of Divisions 3 to 5 or this Division, a member of the Defence Force fails to comply with any obligation imposed under this Part that relates to the exercise of the power, the member is not, and is taken not to have been, entitled to exercise the power unless the member exercised the power in good faith.

Members exercising powers in relation to invalid order etc.

1 A member of the Defence Force is not liable to an action, suit or proceeding, whether civil or criminal, in relation to the exercise, or purported exercise, of powers under any of Divisions 3 to 5 or this Division in relation to a call-out order, infrastructure declaration, specified area declaration or authorisation if:

 a the order, declaration or authorisation was not validly made; and
 b if the member made the authorisation—the powers were exercised or purportedly exercised in good faith.

Before the amendments, legal doubts remained about aspects of the criminal and civil liability of military personnel in some circumstances. Despite the wide powers that the Act granted to military personnel, it was not clear that the Act covered every instance in which an officer or soldier might otherwise be exposed to criminal liability or civil actions, such as for manslaughter, assault, battery or false imprisonment. The Act did not specifically provide a blanket legal protection, nor did it follow a previous recommendation that military personnel on call out be granted the legal status of police officers.

Justifying s 51S, paragraph 79 of the Explanatory Memorandum for the 2018 Bill stated:

> [T]his proposed provision is necessary to ensure that individual ADF members have operational certainty that they will not be held responsible for procedural or other defects in the making of a call-out order, declaration or authorisation.

Potentially, however, the good faith defence could do much more than that. It could shield military personnel, including commanders, from criminal or civil prosecution for unlawful acts, as long as they could argue good faith—a defence that would be difficult to refute (Head 2009: 177–184, 187–199).

The government refused to amend the Bill to limit the scope of this defence. Instead, paragraph 446A was inserted into the Explanatory Memorandum to assert that it was ‘not intended to remove legal liability in instances where an ADF member has exceeded their legal authority in circumstances that cannot be characterised as minor or technical’. That assurance has no legal effect.

The lack of accountability was further underpinned by the Government and the Labor Party rejecting a Greens amendment. It would have made call-out orders disallowable instruments, thus able to be struck down by either House of Parliament, and require that Parliament sit within six days of any call-out order being made. A similar Greens amendment was defeated when the 2006 legislation was passed (Parliamentary Debates 2018: 8613 (Nicholas McKim)).

Under the Australian legislation, the potential for misuse of the call-out powers has been increased by overturning the common law’s rejection of a general defence of superior orders (reaffirmed in *R v Clegg*, discussed above). The traditional canons of statutory interpretation, however, provide that a court should presume that an Act is not intended to deprive members of the public of their civil liberties. The dilemma identified by Brett and Waller therefore could still arise:

> The hardship upon soldiers is, that if a soldier kills a man in obedience to his officer's orders, the question whether what was done was more than was reasonably necessary to quell civil disturbance has to be decided by a jury, probably on a trial of murder. Whereas, if he disobeys his officer's orders to fire because he regards them as unlawful, the question where they were unlawful as having commanded something not reasonably necessary would have to be decided by a court-martial upon the trial of a soldier for disobeying orders, and for obvious reasons the jury and the court-martial are likely to take different views as to the reasonable necessity and therefore as to the lawfulness of such an order.
>
> (Brett and Waller 1983: 654)

Since the Australian case of *Re Tracey; Ex parte Ryan* ((1989) 166 CLR 518) it has been reasonably clear that the defence power of the Australian Constitution cannot be used to exempt military personnel from the general criminal and civil law for conduct for which they have already been tried for a 'service offence' under military law. Five members of the High Court in that case held invalid provisions of the *Defence Force Discipline Act 1982* (Cth) (DFDA) that sought to do so, insisting that, after reviewing the history, a soldier remains a citizen and liable to the ordinary criminal law.

As a result of the 2006 and 2018 amendments, section 51Z substantially overturns that principle:

51Z Defence of superior orders in certain circumstances

1 The fact that a criminal act was done, or purported to be done, by a member of the Defence Force under this Part under an order of a superior does not (subject to subsection (2)) relieve the member of criminal responsibility.
2 It is a defence to a criminal act done, or purported to be done, by a member of the Defence Force under this Part that:
   a the criminal act was done by the member under an order of a superior; and
   b the member was under a legal obligation to obey the order; and
   c the order was not manifestly unlawful; and
   d the member had no reason to believe that circumstances had changed in a material respect since the order was given; and
   e the member had no reason to believe that the order was based on a mistake as to a material fact; and
   f the action taken was reasonable and necessary to give effect to the order.
3 Subsection (2) does not limit the defences that may be available to the person.

Section 46(6) inserted a similar superior orders defence in relation to shooting down aircraft and sinking vessels.

Superior orders defences have traditionally been confined to armed conflicts, and none currently exist for Australian police officers (Senate Report 2006: 21). Even in combat situations, the DFDA and explanatory *Australian Defence Force Discipline Act 1982 Manual* provide that only lawful commands need to be obeyed (DFDA s 27; Manual 4–33). It is a defence to any offence under the DFDA that an act or omission was performed in obedience to 'an unlawful order that the person did not know, and could not reasonably be expected to have known, was unlawful' (DFDA s 14).

The 'manifestly unlawful' proviso is arguably wider than the DFDA defence. This shift in the law opens up dangers that military personnel can kill, maim or seriously violate the rights of civilians with impunity. It may be argued that the new formulation is similar to that in Article 33 of the 1998 Rome Statute of the International Criminal Court. The adoption of the 'manifestly unlawful' test in the Rome Statute remains controversial, however, because it is arguably a retreat from the standard applied at the post-World War II Nuremburg tribunals (Garraway 1999: 785–794; Osiel 1999).

At Nuremberg, Article 8 of the Charter of the International Military Tribunal stated:

> The fact that the Defendant acted pursuant to order of his Government or of a superior shall not free him from responsibility, but may be considered in mitigation of punishment if the Tribunal determines that justice so requires.

This principle was adopted to prevent Nazi officials and officers from escaping liability for the violence and denial of basic human rights they committed against civilians, notably Jews. The experience of fascist totalitarianism was so horrific that people around the world demanded that such conduct never be permitted again.

One additional barrier to holding ADF personnel to account for abuses is the difficulty of identifying the particular officers or soldiers involved. Section 50 makes it a minor offence for ADF members to not wear uniforms bearing identification while exercising call-out powers, but s 43 removes that obligation when the powers are specially authorised by a minister, or in a 'sudden and extraordinary emergency' under Division 3 of the call-out provisions.

Restricted jurisdiction

Another provision, s 51Y, removes ADF personnel from the jurisdiction of Australian state and territory criminal law and gives the Commonwealth Director of Public Prosecutions exclusive coverage of all prosecutions arising from acts done in a military call out. Barring state and territory prosecutors from instituting proceedings against ADF members who may act illegally during a call out is a further serious abrogation of citizens' rights to be protected from criminal actions by the military.

Moreover, s 51Y applies the substantive criminal law of the Jervis Bay Territory to call out operations. The Jervis Bay law is the law of the Australian Capital Territory to the extent that it is not inconsistent with an Ordinance, and may be amended or repealed by an Ordinance. By exercising the power of the Governor-

General to make Ordinances 'for the peace, order and good government' of the Jervis Bay, and the power to make regulations under an ordinance, the federal government can readily change the applicable criminal law without parliamentary authority, subject only to possible later disallowance in the Senate.

According to the Explanatory Memorandum of the 2006 Bill, prosecutors are expected to exercise 'common sense' in prosecution decision-making, and give consideration to the applicable Rules of Engagement. This suggestion opens up many questions, given that Rules of Engagement are normally classified, and thus beyond public scrutiny. Rules of Engagement are also simply instruments of executive action, and do not strictly provide a source of legal authority, except in the sense of constituting a 'lawful general order' under the DFDA, a breach of which would be a military disciplinary offence (DFDA s 29). One submission to the Senate Legal and Constitutional Affairs Committee pointed out that

> any decision to deploy the Australian military in Australia is likely to be highly politically sensitive. This may result in pressure being brought to bear on the Commonwealth DPP not to prosecute excessive uses of force by Defence Forces personnel, and to defer to the federal government in security matters.

The submission suggested that state and territory prosecutors be empowered to investigate and prosecute where the Commonwealth Director of Public Prosecutions (DPP) was unable or unwilling to do so, under a complementarity regime similar to that applicable under the Rome Statute of the International Criminal Court. However, state or territory prosecutors would most likely come under similar political pressure not to intervene. Nor would this proposal overcome the underlying problems that Jervis Bay law would apply and that criminal acts could be protected by the good faith and superior orders defences.

Remaining uncertainties

Doubts still exist that the good faith and superior orders defences fully protects ADF personnel. As mentioned earlier, military personnel ordered to use force against civilians may face a dilemma. Under military law, if they disobey orders, they could face dire consequences, including imprisonment. However, under civilian law, if they execute orders that are subsequently ruled unlawful, they may have no defence of obeying superior orders.

While the *DFDA* and Manual provide that only lawful commands need to be obeyed, these instruments are heavily tilted toward obedience. Thus, 'a person given an order requiring the performance of a military duty may infer it to be lawful and disobeys it at peril' (Manual 4-33). Disobedience of a lawful command is punishable by up to two years' imprisonment (DFDA s 27; Manual 4-33). It is a defence to any offence under the DFDA that an act or omission was performed in obedience to 'an unlawful order that the person did not know, and could not reasonably be expected to have known, was unlawful' (DFDA s 14). For officers, the duty of obedience is reinforced by their officer's commission:

> I (name of Governor-General) … Charge and Command you faithfully to discharge your duty as an officer and observe and execute all such orders as you may receive from your superior officers.
>
> (Wheate and Wheate 2003: 21)

Under the DFDA, there is no doubt that ADF members are under a legal obligation to obey the orders of superiors. Much less clear is what is meant by 'manifestly unlawful', 'no reason to believe that circumstances had changed in a material respect', 'no reason to believe that the order was based on a mistake as to a material fact' and 'reasonable and necessary to give effect to the order'. The tests are couched in objective, not subjective, terms, so the question is not whether the ADF member believed these things to be true; the question is whether these requirements were actually met. How is a soldier to know what is 'manifestly unlawful' or what is 'reasonable and necessary'?

Two scholars, one an ADF officer, have expressed the view that the provisions, while offering some degree of legal protection to ADF members, may be 'a trap for the unwary', particularly in 'morally controversial' decisions to pre-emptively kill people in order to protect property ('critical infrastructure'). Bronitt and Stephens note:

> [U]nlike the criminal and civil immunities conferred on law enforcement officials by controlled operations legislation, there is no similar protection conferred on ADF members acting under Part IIIAAA. Indeed, the legislation states that the fact that a member of the ADF has acted in accordance with Part IIIAAA, thus attracting the superior orders defence, does not otherwise relieve that member of criminal responsibility.
>
> (Bronitt and Stephens 2007: 275)

Bronitt and Stephens describe reliance on Rules of Engagement (ROE) as another 'trap for the unwary' because ROE do not provide a source of legal authority for action, despite being a 'lawful general order' under the DFDA (Bronitt and Stephens 2007: 275).

These questions are crucial given that the common law provides no superior orders defence. In *R v Clegg*, discussed above, it was said that no general defence of superior orders was known to English law. Lord Lloyd of Berwick cited ancient authority as well as the Australian High Court in *A v Hayden (No 2)* ((1984) 156 CLR 532), followed by the Privy Council in *Yip Chiu-Cheung v The Queen* ([1995] 1 AC 111). In *Hayden*, Murphy J stated:

> In Australia it is no defence to the commission of a criminal act or omission that it was done in obedience to the orders of a superior or the government. Military and civilians have a duty to obey lawful orders, and a duty to disobey unlawful orders.
>
> ((1984) 156 CLR 532 at [5])

It must be noted, however, that the effect of this rule in *Hayden* was to permit the superior officers and other higher authorities (including the relevant minister) to disown the individual officers who had violated the criminal law. In addition, a closer examination of the case reveals that, in the end, the officers involved also escaped prosecution.

Hayden arose out of a 1983 Australian Secret Intelligence Service (ASIS) training operation at Melbourne's Sheraton Hotel, in which the masked and heavily armed participants smashed open a door, engaged in a fight in an elevator and terrified guests and staff as they ran through a lobby to a waiting car. The incident attracted media headlines and an inquiry conducted by Justice Hope concluded that the participants had possibly committed 21 serious criminal offences. However, the Minister responsible for ASIS, Foreign Minister Bill Hayden, was absolved of responsibility for the agent's misconduct. Hope concluded that Hayden had no duty to inquire into specific details of ASIS training programmes, and the Acting Director-General had no duty to inform him (Royal Commission Sheraton Hotel Report 1984: 18).

Alleged participants in the incident sought an injunction prohibiting the Commonwealth from disclosing their identities to the Victorian chief police commissioner for the purpose of investigating whether they had committed criminal offences. The plaintiffs argued that, as they worked with ASIS, their identification would endanger national security and breach confidentiality agreements in their contracts of employment with the Commonwealth.

Members of the High Court made apparently strong statements to the effect that ASIS and other security agencies must operate within the law. Mason J, for example, declared: 'For the future, the point needs to be made loudly and clearly that if counter-espionage activities involve breaches of the law they are liable to attract the consequences that ordinarily follow from breaches of the law' ((1984) 156 CLR 532, [2]). Other justices described the incapacity of the executive to dispense its servants from obedience to legislation as 'the cornerstone of parliamentary democracy' ((1984) 156 CLR 532, [6]) and essential to the 'rule of law' ((1984) 156 CLR 532, [3]).

Yet, the case was unusual because the Federal government opposed the plaintiffs, denying that national security would be threatened. (An agreement had been reached with the Victorian government and specific State legislation introduced to prevent public disclosure of the plaintiffs' identities and provide for *in camera* trials of any criminal charges). Thus, the court did not have to decide whether a government claim of national security would have protected the ASIS officers ((1984) 156 CLR 532, [18).

In addition, the judges accepted that the Commonwealth itself was immune from criminal prosecution, even though senior officials had initiated the training exercise ((1984) 156 CLR 532, [21). In other words, individual intelligence operatives might be criminally liable, but not their superior officers or members of the government. Finally, Brennan J opined that, at least during wartime, legislation could be passed exempting ASIS officers from other laws. He stated: 'The Commonwealth Parliament has made no law granting to ASIS officers exemption from any law; it is unnecessary to consider whether its constitutional powers could support such a law in times of peace' ((1984) 156 CLR 532, [8]). This suggestion could take on new meaning in the light of the 'war on terrorism'.

Finally, it must be noted that no prosecutions resulted. Public and private requests by the Commonwealth government not to proceed prevailed. Officially, the Victorian Commissioner of Police, on the advice of the State Director of Public Prosecutions, announced that matters would not proceed. It was maintained that as the suspects had worn masks, it was not possible to determine who had done precisely what, and that lack of evidence precluded the laying of specific charges. Instead, the hotel management received $259,000 in exemplary damages from the government, while employees received undisclosed payments (Grabosky 1989: ch 8).

Thus, the *Hayden* case also highlights the discretion in the hands of prosecutors not to lay charges against ADF members. This discretion, moreover, is legally unreviewable, just like an Attorney-General's decision not to intervene in a case. It is for the Commonwealth Director of Public Prosecutions to decide whether to prosecute under Part IIIAAA, and according to the Explanatory Memorandum for the 2006 amendments, prosecutors are expected to exercise 'common sense' in that decision-making, and give consideration to the applicable Rules of Engagement (ROE). That is so, even though ROE are simply instruments of executive action, not a source of legal authority.

Bronitt and Stephens opine that 'prosecutorial discretion does not provide sufficient protection for the military exercising these powers', and if innocent lives are taken there may be political and public pressure to prosecute (Bronitt and Stephens 2007: 275). This prospect can never be discounted. Nevertheless, it appears that prosecutions are unlikely to be launched, or convictions obtained, where ADF personnel rely on the superior orders defence, at least where the order was authorised by the applicable ROE. This likely result is highly problematic, not least because of the secrecy surrounding ROE. Members of the public subjected to military intervention have no means of knowing the precise orders that ADF members have been given, and hence may unknowingly conduct themselves in ways that could lead to the use of lethal force.

Rules of Engagement (ROE)

During the passage of the Australian call-out legislation in 2000, the government rejected an amendment that would have required the tabling in Parliament of the manuals and protocols that will apply to military interventions. This proposal was raised after a senator read out extracts from the then current Australian Army *Manual of Land Warfare*.

This secret manual, produced in 1983, had been leaked to the media in 1993 (McCulloch 2001: 177). It asserted an extremely wide and highly political role for the ADF, with an Introduction that stated: 'Civil disobedience, mass violence and terrorism have become common methods of dissent throughout the world in recent years' (McCulloch 2001: 178). It said the ADF may be involved in countering the threat posed by the activities of dissidents, including riots, mass demonstrations, and industrial, political and social disturbances (McCulloch 2001: 178). It referred to establishing detention centres and to opening fire on 'unlawful assemblies' (McCulloch 2001: 182–183). One section stated:

> As a last resort troops may be required to open fire on the crowd to disperse it. The principles of minimum force must be kept in mind by the commanders. Therefore, initially, only selected individuals should be nominated to fire upon selected agitators in the crowd.
>
> (McCulloch 2001: 183)

Section 543 of the manual instructed military personnel in how to then cover up the killing or wounding of 'dissidents':

> Dead and wounded dissidents, if identifiable, must be removed immediately by the police ... When being reported, dissident and own casualties are categorised merely as dead or wounded. To inhibit propaganda exploitation by the dissidents the cause of the casualties (for example, 'shot') is not reported. A follow-up operation should be carried out to maintain the momentum of the dispersing crowd.
>
> (Brown 2000: 17398)

A government minister said the Army manual was 'under revision' and would be replaced with a new version once the Act was passed. He refused, however, to give any assurance that a similar clause would not appear in the rewritten document. The rules remain withheld from the public. In 2005, the author put this question in writing to Defence Minister Robert Hill, who replied as follows:

> I am informed that there is a manual to provide guidance to ADF members for the conduct of operations under Part IIIAA of the Defence Act 1903, but this manual is not available for release to the public.
>
> If the ADF was called out under Part IIIAA of the Defence Act, the Chief of the Defence Force would issue situation-specific rules of engagement (ROE) to regulate the use of force. The Force Commander would translate these ROE into situation-specific orders for the use of force. These orders would be issued to all ADF members before they were deployed. ADF members would have those orders explained to them and would be trained in their application so they were clear as to the level of force which is authorised in a particular situation, as well as the way in which force may be used.
>
> Rules of engagement are, by necessity, highly classified. Precise knowledge by an adversary of the limitations that have been placed on the use of force by ADF members could endanger their lives. For reasons of operational security, it is not appropriate to release ROE into the public domain.
>
> (Hill 2005)

The minister's reply raised a number of questions. No reason was given for withholding the manual from public scrutiny. Presumably, the reasons given for not releasing the ROE were meant to apply. Vague and uncertain concepts, 'necessity' and 'operational security' were used to justify denying members of the public the right to know what levels of potentially lethal force have been, or could be, authorised for use against them. How such knowledge could endanger the lives of ADF members was not substantiated. The use of the term 'adversary' underscored the fact that anyone against whom the armed forces will be deployed will be regarded as an enemy, akin to a wartime target, not as a civilian member of society. Moreover, the secrecy makes more difficult the necessary task of determining the legality of any call out and the powers given to called-out ADF members.

Further questions arise about the extraordinary powers placed in the hands of military commanders—the Chief of the Defence Force and Force Commanders—to issue 'situation-specific' ROE and orders. These powers in themselves challenge the framework of civilian control over the armed forces. How can anyone be assured that the ROE and orders, presumably to be issued with great urgency in the context of a military call out to respond to imminent 'domestic violence' or threats to Commonwealth interests, will not exceed the parameters set by the legislation? The secrecy may hinder any attempt to establish whether any orders were 'manifestly unlawful'.

Finally, the minister's letter failed to explain how soldiers could be trained in the application of their orders, so they were clear about the levels of force they were authorised to use, if 'situation-specific' orders were given under conditions of urgency or emergency.

It must be noted that there is strong pressure on armed forces members to abide by ROE, regardless of any doubts they may have about their lawfulness. As Bronitt and Stephens comment, 'there is a strong culture for compliance around ROE in the military, which is underscored by the legal duty to obey lawful orders, with failure to do so constituting a disciplinary offence' (Bronitt and Stephens 2007: 275).

In sum, unclarities exist about the interplay between the superior orders defence and ROE. It is by no means guaranteed that soldiers who kill civilians while acting under orders and in line with the relevant ROE will be shielded from criminal prosecution. There is also no guarantee that a soldier who defies an unlawful order in order to refrain from causing fatalities will be protected from military disciplinary measures. Overall, it must be said, however, that wide legal scope has been created for the use of lethal force, with an apparent legislative intention to make criminal prosecutions unlikely.

How to challenge the legality of any call out?

To what extent is it possible to legally challenge decisions made under the Australian *Defence Act*, including those made by the 'authorising ministers' (or the Governor-General) to issue a call-out order, proclaim a 'specified area' or declare facilities to be 'declared infrastructure'?

There is no provision for legal review in the Part. Instead, s 51X provides for limited scrutiny, after the event, by parliament. Within seven days of a call-out order ending, the Defence Minister must present both houses with a copy of the order and a report on the utilisation of the ADF under the order. Section 51W provides that:

> If, before, during or after exercising power under Division 2 or 3 or this Division, a member of the Defence Force fails to comply with any obligation imposed

> under any of those Divisions that relates to the exercise of the power, the member is not, or is taken not to have been, entitled to exercise the power.

The effect of this section is not clear. It relates only to the legality of actions taken by individual ADF members under a call-out order, not to the lawfulness of the government's proclamations.

Australia, like Britain and Canada, has no strict US-style 'political questions' doctrine forbidding the courts from reviewing sensitive political questions. But the courts will not review the exercise of certain prerogative powers, and may decide not to intervene in controversial political or national security decisions. Decisions made under the 'prerogative powers', such as appointment and dismissals of prime ministers, and decisions relating to foreign policy, declarations of war, national security and such matters as the award of royal honours, have traditionally been regarded as 'non-justiciable', that is, lying outside the purview of the courts (Head 2017: 141–146). In Britain, the House of Lords accepted in *Council of Civil Service Unions v Minister for the Civil Service* ([1985] AC 374) that these exclusions still exist.

However, the law of 'justiciability' has become somewhat fluid, arguably reflecting popular concerns about the growth of executive power, including in the conduct of foreign affairs, involving violations of human rights. The English Court of Appeal has been prepared to consider an application for relief by an English citizen detained in the US detention camp at Guantanamo Bay (*Abbasi v Secretary of State* [2002] EWCA Civ 1598). Their Lordships said the 'forbidden area' of foreign policy identified by the House of Lords could be impinged upon where 'a clear breach of a fundamental human right' occurred (*Abbasi v Secretary of State* [2002] EWCA Civ 1598 at [66] and [107]).

This approach was followed by Tamberlin J of the Australian Federal Court when lawyers for David Hicks, an Australian citizen incarcerated at Guantanamo Bay, sought a writ of habeas corpus instructing the Australian government to ask the US authorities to release him (*Hicks v Ruddock* [2007] FCA 299). The application also sought an order that the government acted on 'irrelevant considerations' and for 'improper purposes' in refusing to request Hicks's release. Tamberlin J rejected a government application to have the case summarily dismissed on the grounds that courts should not interfere in negotiations between two countries. The judge stated: 'The concept of a "forbidden area" arguably states the position far too generally to be applied at face value' (*Hicks v Ruddock* [2007] FCA 299 [85]).

Where issues of national security are involved, Australian courts are willing to inquire into the legality of executive decisions and actions, but they have interpreted the law in ways that make it almost impossible for litigants to demonstrate that the behaviour at issue is legally flawed. One prominent example is *Church of Scientology Inc v Woodward* ((1982) 154 CLR 25). The High Court considered whether it would review decisions by the Australian Security Intelligence Organisation (ASIO) to collect information about the church as a possible security risk. While the majority insisted that no exercise of Commonwealth power could be excluded from judicial review, all the judges considered that applicants would face almost insuperable difficulties in introducing evidence and convincing a court that ASIO's judgments on national security were legally flawed.

The High Court dismissed the notion that ASIO could act lawfully beyond the limits set by the *Australian Security Intelligence Organisation Act 1979*, in purported exercise of the Commonwealth's executive power. But, in practice, the judges threw doubt on any judicial review of ASIO's security assessment decisions.

Mason J, who concurred with Gibbs CJ in ruling in favour of ASIO, forming a statutory majority, said s 17(1) of the ASIO Act contained an exclusive and comprehensive list of the activities ASIO was authorised, and *un*authorised, to engage in ((1982) 154 CLR 25, 57). Yet, in so far as those functions were required to be relevant to 'security', it would be difficult for a plaintiff to challenge ASIO's decision-making. Mason J described security as a 'fluctuating concept, relying on circumstances as they exist from time to time—not unlike the issue of defence' ((1982) 154 CLR 25, 60). The onus was on the plaintiff to establish that there was '*no* reasonable basis to conclude that the actions in question have a real connection with security' ((1982) 154 CLR 25, 61). While not, in theory, ruling out judicial review of ASIO operations, Mason J described the satisfaction of the test as a 'formidable task'. This was in part due to the severe challenges facing an applicant in satisfying a court that ASIO erred in its decisions as to national security. One such obstacle was the exclusion of material relied upon by the plaintiff by virtue of Crown privilege ((1982) 154 CLR 25, 61).

Murphy and Brennan JJ, who dissented, also maintained that, in theory, no exercise of Commonwealth power could be excluded from judicial review, at least not without clear and express words. But, in practice, they too considered that applicants would face almost insuperable difficulties in introducing evidence and convincing a court that ASIO's judgments on national security were erroneous. Brennan J, for example, asked: 'How can the gravity of a security risk be evaluated by a court?' A plaintiff would not be able to force the disclosure of ASIO documents as evidence for a challenge. 'Discovery would not be given against the Director-General save in a most exceptional case,' he stated. 'The public interest in national security will seldom yield to the public interest in the administration of civil justice' ((1982) 154 CLR 25, 76). Brennan J concluded: 'There are thus large obstacles in the path of a plaintiff who seeks to restrain an alleged activity of the Organization on the ground that it does not lie within the functions assigned to it by s. 17' ((1982) 154 CLR 25, 76).

Likewise, the majority of the court in *A v Hayden* refused to rule out the possibility that, under certain circumstances, the interests of 'national security' could override those of 'the administration of justice'. Wilson and Dawson JJ stated: 'The administration of justice, important though it is, may on occasions have to give way to an even more compelling public interest. In a proper case, national security may well satisfy that description' ((1984) 156 CLR 532 [16]). They indicated that the government's view of national security would always 'carry great weight'. 'The consequence of a decision of a court on a matter of national security which is contrary to the considered view of the government could be very serious indeed' ((1984) 156 CLR 532 [19]).

Claims of public interest immunity may be invoked to prevent access to documents said to relate to defence or national security. In *Alister v R* ((1984) 154 CLR 412), by a three-to-two majority, the High Court held that, for the purpose of an appeal by Alister, a civilian, against a conviction for conspiracy to murder, it should inspect ASIO documents subpoenaed by the defence, despite a ministerial certificate claiming public interest immunity on national security grounds. The documents concerned the activities of an ASIO agent, Richard Seary, who was involved in the alleged conspiracy. The majority said a higher standard of 'public interest' was required where the information requested related to a criminal conviction. Strong statements of principle were made. Brennan J, for example, said:

> It is of the essence of a free society that a balance is struck between the security that is desirable to protect society as a whole and the safeguards that are necessary to ensure individual liberty. But in the long run the safety of a democracy rests upon the common commitment of its citizens to the safe-guarding of each man's liberty, and the balance must tilt that way.
>
> ((1984) 154 CLR 412, 456)

Upon inspection of the documents, however, a differently constituted majority (with only Murphy J dissenting) held that, since none of the documents was relevant to the issues at the trial, the public interest in their non-production outweighed any contrary public interest. Given that the court's examination of the documents was conducted in secret, it is difficult to assess this conclusion. It remains of concern that the Attorney-General can readily claim public interest immunity and that the 'balance' to be struck with civil liberties remains substantially hidden from public scrutiny.

In another example, an applicant sought to challenge the cancellation of his passport by the Australian Foreign Affairs Minister on security grounds (*Traljesic v Attorney-General (Cth)* (2006) 150 FCR 199). In the Federal Court, Rares J dismissed an appeal against an Attorney-General's national interest certificate under ss 36, 39A and 39B of the *Administrative Appeals Act*, which barred both the applicant and his lawyer from hearing or having access to the evidence presented by ASIO, because of a 'potential but unsubstantiated risk' that the lawyer might inadvertently divulge confidential material. The judge ruled this was a relevant and not unreasonable consideration, even though the certificate effectively prevented the applicant from refuting the secret allegations made against him. Such decisions open the door to virtually unchallengeable executive power.

A similar result was achieved in another case in which two members of the High Court rejected an application for leave to appeal against a decision denying an applicant the right to even know why he had been assessed as a security risk *Leghaei v Director-General of Security & Anor* ([2007] HCATrans 655). The judges insisted that procedural fairness had to give way to 'the protection of the public interest in national security'. Their decision upheld two decisions in the Federal Court, both featuring the giving of partly confidential reasons by judges. Such decisions produce the Kafkaesque outcome that people can be deprived of passports or visas without any right to know the evidence or the legal case against them.

How these approaches might play out in the highly charged context of a military call out to put down 'domestic violence' can perhaps be seen from the House of Lords decision in *Chandler v Director of Public Prosecutions* ([1964] AC 763), which involved a prosecution for breach of the *Officials Secrets Act 1911* (UK). Lord Reid stated that he did not 'subscribe to the view that the government or a minister must always or even as a general rule have the last word' about the safety or interests of the state. But he agreed, together with the other lords, that cross-examination was not permissible to challenge the evidence of a senior Air Force officer that a proposed obstruction of an airfield was contrary to the 'safety or interests of the state', which were the relevant words of the statute. Lord Reid went on to refer to the proposition that decisions about military deployments are not justiciable:

> The defence of the State from external enemies is a matter of real concern, in time of peace as in days of war. The disposition, armament and direction of the defence forces of the State are matters decided upon by the Crown and are within its jurisdiction as the executive power of the State. So are treaties and alliances with other states for mutual defence.
>
> ([1964] AC 763, 796)

The law lords invoked a passage in *The Zamora*, where the Privy Council declared:

> Those who are responsible for the national security must be the sole judges of what the national security requires. It would be obviously undesirable that such matters should be made the subject of evidence in a court of law or otherwise discussed in public.
>
> ([1916] 2 AC 77, 107)

This statement, which amounts to placing the executive above the law when it comes to decisions made in the name of national security, cannot be dismissed as out of date. It was cited by approval by members of the House of Lords in *Council of Civil Service Unions v Minister for the Civil Service*, mentioned above, in ruling that the requirements of national security outweighed those of procedural fairness. That decision permitted the Thatcher government to ban trade union membership in the Government Communications Headquarters without consulting the unions.

Can a minister or military commander be held liable?

Can an authorising minister or senior armed forces commander be held liable for abuses or excesses that occur during a military call out? In principle, a minister or officer who issued an illegal order should be held to account. In his *Protective Security Review* report, presented to the Australian government in 1979, Justice Hope said it was undoubted that an officer 'would be liable in civil, criminal and military courts for the consequences of any illegal orders he may give' (Hope 1979: 169).

Unfortunately, the true legal picture is not so clear. In terms of civil liability, it is extremely difficult to successfully sue for damages, because plaintiffs must generally prove a specific tort, and therefore show malice, intention to cause them harm, negligence, trespass, assault or false imprisonment on the part of the decision-maker, not simply that an unlawful decision was taken.

In 1989, for example, the Australian High Court confirmed that even where South Korean businessmen had been wrongly detained, and were entitled to declaratory orders to that effect, they could not obtain damages, unless they sued separately for false imprisonment (*Park Oh Ho v Minister for Immigration and Ethnic Affairs* (1989) 167 CLR 637). An added difficulty in tort suits could be establishing that the defendants owed any duty of care to the plaintiff, rather than a duty to carry out their lawful responsibilities (*Rush v Commissioner of Police* [2006] FCA 12). In *Northern Territory v Mengel* ((1995) 185 CLR 307) the High Court rejected an attempt to establish an administrative tort based on damages simply for an 'unlawful act'.

The common law tort of misfeasance in public office offers limited prospects for obtaining damages. It applies only where a person suffered economic loss because the defendant knowingly, whether or not maliciously, committed an intentional and wrongful act amounting to an abuse of his or her public office. The plaintiff must be a member of the public to whom the defendant owed a duty not to commit the particular abuse complained, and has to show that the act was knowingly or recklessly performed without power (*Northern Territory v Mengel* (1995) 185 CLR 307).

There is authority for the proposition that officials will be liable for 'wanton or cruel acts' that were not justified by the necessities of the situation. In *Wright v Fitzgerald* ((1799) 27 St. Tr. 759), the High Sheriff of County Tipperary was held liable for a public flogging, despite an Indemnity Act (one of seven passed in Ireland between 1796 and 1800) that protected the authorities from actions brought against them as a result of their unlawful activities in suppressing rebellion.

However, unless deliberate abuses of power or malicious purposes can be proved, the overall picture is that civilians who suffer damage or loss as the result of 'military aid to the civil power' are likely to face considerable legal problems in mounting damages actions against armed forces personnel and their military and political commanders.

The culpability or responsibility might lie at a number of levels, from the authorising ministers and Chief of Defence Forces, through the military hierarchy down to individual officers and non-commissioned personnel. If the responsibility properly rests with the government that authorised the call out, political redress may be possible through parliament, except that governments will normally have parliamentary majorities to shield them. Ultimately, governments arguably can be held accountable by the population as a whole through elections, but this sanction will carry little weight if the military intervention enjoys bipartisan support.

In terms of legal redress, the prospect of government ministers or senior military officials being held culpable or liable is also dim. Not only have courts been traditionally reluctant to second-guess, or call into question, official decisions made in the realm of national security, but it is also difficult to obtain damages for a breach of exercise of a discretionary power, let alone find the decision-maker criminally liable.

If serious atrocities occurred during a domestic military intervention, some avenues of complaint or redress could be found in international law or via United Nations institutions. Government ministers could even be prosecuted before the International Criminal Court (and a brief was sent to the ICC in 2008 to request charges against former Prime Minister John Howard for deploying Australian troops to Iraq in violation of international law (Jurist 2008)), but these possibilities are beyond the scope of this book.

Both politically and legally, it is more likely that efforts will be made to blame individual members of the armed forces for any excesses and abuses that occur. In the words of Bronitt and Stephens, 'if mistakes are made and innocent lives are taken, the political and public pressure to scapegoat the military may be intense' (Bronitt and Stephens 2007: 275). Arguably, this was the case with the 1983 episode involving heavily armed ASIS operatives at Melbourne's Sheraton Hotel. As noted earlier, a subsequent inquiry found that 21 serious criminal offences had been committed but absolved the minister of responsibility (and ultimately no prosecutions resulted against the ASIS operatives either).

As another example, when revelations appeared of torture and abuse of prisoners inside Iraq's Abu Ghraib jail, mostly low-ranking soldiers were placed on trial, despite evidence of a chain of command from the White House (Hersh 2004; Mestrovic 2006; Morris and Gourevitch 2008).

Obvious conflicts of interest can arise in such circumstances. Governments and senior officers may have an interest in arguing that any excesses were the product of 'bad apples' in the ranks, rather than the result of policies or orders adopted at higher levels. Politicians and military personnel alike may seek to cover-up, obscure or minimise the extent of the abuses.

12 Wider legal, political and democratic implications

From ‘terrorism’ to ‘subversion’

The historic shifts analysed in this book have significant legal and political implications. Moves toward greater reliance on the military for domestic security indicate that serious societal threats are anticipated, not just to public safety but also to political stability. At the same time, recourse to the armed forces to deal with these threats raises serious questions about basic democratic rights, and the state of democracy itself. This is particularly so in light of the longstanding public antipathy toward internal military intervention, and the legal and constitutional traditions against such mobilisations. It can be anticipated that attempts to use the armed forces against protests, industrial action or other forms of civil unrest could be resisted, possibly triggering serious conflicts.

One example of the shift in ruling circles from ‘terrorism’ to ‘subversion’ and other perceived political threats to the existing order as the focus of the intelligence-police-military apparatus came from France. As discussed in Chapter 7, the French national intelligence and counterterrorism organisation’s five-year public strategy document, released in 2019, stated that one of the key roles of the country’s counterterrorism agencies was to fight ‘subversive movements’ and the threat of ‘insurrectional violence’ in the population (Morrow 2019).

The National Intelligence Strategy published by the National Intelligence Coordination for the Fight Against Terrorism was personally approved by President Emmanuel Macron. A comparison with the organisation’s first five-year ‘road map’ indicated a critical turn. The 2014 version had identified its five areas of operations as terrorism, espionage and economic interference, the proliferation of weapons of mass destruction, cyber attacks and organised crime. The 2019 report established a new category: ‘Anticipation of crises and the risk of major ruptures’. Under the headline ‘Violent subversion’, it stated:

> The growing strength of movements and networks of a subversive character constitutes a factor of crisis that is all the more preoccupying because they are aimed at weakening, and even destroying, the foundations of our democracy and the republican institutions through insurrectional violence.
>
> (Morrow 2019)

The document explained that by 'subversive' movements, it meant not only 'violent actions against people or goods', but 'also the collection of traditional demands that these movements employ in order to infiltrate and radicalise them'. This was a formula for the suppression of any expression of social opposition in the population. Within this framework, 'traditional demands'—such as against layoffs and welfare cuts, for higher wages, improved living standards, against war and for social equality—were not legitimate political demands. They were 'employed' by 'subversive' forces.

Under the headline 'Crises of public order', the report stated: 'The anticipation, analysis and monitoring of social movements and crises in society by the intelligence agencies constitute a double priority.' Such a preoccupation with 'social movements' again points to the expansion of police and military powers, initially conducted under the banner of the 'war on terror', being directed increasingly against social and political unrest. The report was released amid the ongoing 'yellow vest' demonstrations and the president's deployment of troops against them, as discussed in Chapter 7.

A number of underlying trends has emerged in the countries studied in this volume. They include:

- A turn from the 'war on terror' as the primary justification for military call-out provisions to wider rationales, including 'violent' demonstrations, 'street crime', political crisis (such as Brexit), 'emergencies' and 'refugee invasions'.
- Growing use of the military in civilian settings, both in overseas operations and at home, including for political unrest, as well as major political and sporting events.
- An historic pattern of governments or regimes resorting to military force when they have felt threatened by social unrest, particularly during periods of economic breakdown or intense class conflict.
- A shift in governmental and military doctrine to make 'domestic security' a core function or central mission of the armed forces, alongside the traditional role of external defence.
- The introduction of new legislation or constitutional provisions designed to break down the military/police demarcation, enhance the powers of governments to deploy the armed forces internally, and boost the powers of military personnel, notably to use lethal force against civilians.
- Expanding official claims to emergency or executive powers—often vague—to mobilise or command the defence forces, both at home and abroad.
- The maintenance or extension of measures that restrict legal and political accountability for the use of the armed forces, and provide military personnel with legal immunities.

Arguably, the expansion of the scope for domestic military intervention has been the most marked in France, where troops have been deployed in significant numbers to combat expressions of political and economic discontent, notably the 'yellow vest' protesters. This mobilisation has been one of the clearest examples of the shift from terrorism to social unrest as the reason cited by governments for calling out the armed forces. The precedents set under the banner of the 'war on terror', including the sight of heavily armed troops on the streets, have opened the way for the use of the military to suppress dissent.

Similar developments have occurred in the United States, which also spends by far the most in the world on its armed forces, and deploys the greatest number of personnel internationally. The Trump administration's dispatch of troops to the Mexican border to help halt the entry of refugees signalled a new stage in the militarisation of society, while building on previous precedents established by the George W. Bush and Obama administrations. The creation of the Northern Command, in particular, marked an historic shift. For the first time since the American Revolution, which inscribed on its banners opposition to a standing army and to any internal use of troops, a specific command has been established for the purpose of dealing with perceived security threats on home soil.

A related development, which is beyond the parameters of this book, is the development of civil–military cooperation doctrines that provide for lengthy military 'peacekeeping' and 'stabilising' interventions in civilian settings. In Europe, the NATO-related Civil-Military Co-operation Centre of Excellence was established in the light of the ongoing NATO intervention in the former Yugoslavia. Likewise, the Australian government established an Asia Pacific Centre for Civil-Military Cooperation, later named the Australian Civil-Military Centre (https://www.acmc.gov.au/). These doctrines, which envisage long-term military engagements overseas, including policing civilian populations and suppressing dissident or insurgent threats to the established order, could set precedents for domestic use, and train military personnel for similar internal purposes.

Domestic security as a 'core business'

Calls have been made within the political and military establishments for a deeper restructuring of the armed forces and a fundamental re-definition of their role to make domestic security one of their core functions. Indeed, this is the logic of the establishment of NorthCom in the United States and its cross-border partner, the Canadian Command.

One of the most explicit and public proposals for a basic shift in the function of the armed forces has come from Australia. In 2006, the government-funded Australian Strategic Policy Institute (ASPI) published a 'Strategic Insight' report suggesting that while 'impressive' progress had been made already in integrating the military into internal security, ten 'next steps' needed to be taken to establish domestic security as a 'core business' of the Australian Defence Force (ADF) (Bergin and Smith 2006: 16–22).

The ten steps included developing a 'defence domestic security strategy', strengthening 'special event security', re-orienting military education, conducting 'no-warning' exercises involving 'whole-city terrorism' and upgrading links and shared training with police and emergency services. Above all, the document called for a shift in 'defence culture', complaining that it had not yet 'embraced domestic security as core business':

> This reflects Australia's constitutional arrangements, but may not recognise the reality that, when the Australian people perceive themselves to be under attack, they will demand that governments bend every resource to their protection. Defence is a significant and highly visible government resource that will be expected to play its role in a domestic security crisis, not just trying to prevent an attack but also helping to restore some degree of normalcy after a major terrorist strike.
>
> (Bergin and Smith 2006: 21)

Hence, the report specified that the ADF's role should extend beyond a purely military function. The reference to 'restoring some degree of normalcy' envisaged a longer-term policing role, directed against any signs of political instability or popular unrest, perhaps in something akin to a martial law situation.

The ASPI report canvassed overtly political calculations in advocating a further expansion and entrenchment of the ADF's internal role. It contended that the events of September 2001 and the ensuing declaration of a 'war on terror' by the Bush administration and its allies have created a political climate in which the public will support—indeed, demand—the ADF's mobilisation for domestic purposes.

> Government is attracted to using the ADF because it projects strength. There is a high degree of public respect for the ADF. This image supports a public view that with Defence involved, security on the homefront is in capable hands. Decisions on the employment of the ADF in domestic security post-9/11 have therefore been influenced by the political necessity of demonstrating effectiveness in the face of national security threats.
>
> (Bergin and Smith 2006: 15)

Bergin and Smith dismissed concerns for civil liberties as 'an elite debate':

> Unlike in other countries ... history has provided little reason for the Australian population to develop an aversion to the use of Defence in the homeland. Although civil liberty watchdogs have at times raised concerns about the dangers of excessive involvement by the armed forces in domestic security, especially where it involves the use of force, this appears to be an elite debate that does not resonate with the general public.
>
> (Bergin and Smith 2006: 21)

Similar views have been expressed by others associated with the military. In a 2005 law journal article, Norman Laing, a barrister and former member of the parachute battalion 3 Royal Australian Regiment, depicted public concerns that troops could be deployed to disperse a serious civil disturbance as 'fear and paranoia' produced by 'scare-mongering' or 'misunderstanding'. Referring to the terrorist acts of September 2001 in the United States, and October 2002 in Bali, he asserted:

> The attacks on both the United States and Bali provided the catalyst for the government to reshape the modern ADF. Australia now has a defence force

> capability that can, and will, be utilised both inwardly on Australian soil and outwardly internationally in relation to Australia's security and defence.
>
> (Laing 2005: 515)

Referring to the military call-out legislation, Laing insisted that it would clear the way for Australians to even accept soldiers killing people who allegedly posed a threat to 'freedoms'. He wrote:

> With these crucial new provisions firmly in place, and given the current political climate, Australians should no longer fear the sight, or possibility, of Australian troops being deployed onto our streets—protecting our civil liberties is important, but protecting these liberties should not be used as an excuse to prevent soldiers from detaining, apprehending or even killing those who seek to undermine these freedoms we all take for granted.
>
> (Laing 2005: 522)

Both the ASPI report and Laing's article illustrate the use of the 'war on terrorism' as a justification for overturning long-standing limits on the internal deployment of the armed forces. They also focus on utilising fear of terrorism as a means of conditioning public opinion to accept that process. As discussed in Chapter 3, history demonstrates the readiness of governments to exploit vague and elastic phrases such as 'emergency', 'essential' and 'security', or to act without clear legal authority and, if necessary, obtain retrospective indemnity.

Civil liberties, human rights and international law

Some of the most basic civil liberties and human rights are threatened by the domestic deployment of the armed forces. Such fundamental principles as freedom of speech, association, assembly and movement, no detention without trial and freedom from arbitrary rule, can be violated, pushed aside or made difficult to exercise under conditions where troops can be called out to suppress social, political or industrial discontent, or where citizens live under the intimidating shadow of possible military intervention. Genuine democracy is impossible unless all members of society are free, and feel free, to express their views, organise against the government and even seek to overthrow the established order, without the fear of armed reprisal.

As reviewed in earlier chapters, it must be a matter of concern that essential doctrines established in centuries of struggle against absolutism in Britain and the United States, including civic freedom from military interference, the abolition of standing armies and civilian supremacy over any armed forces, have been substantially eroded. These historical principles were among the 'natural', 'self-evident' and 'inalienable' rights inscribed upon the banners of the English, American and French revolutions of the seventeenth and eighteenth centuries. ('Life, liberty and property' in the case of England—at least as defined by John Locke; 'Life, liberty and pursuit of happiness' in the 1776 American Declaration of

Independence; 'Equality, liberty, property, security and resistance to oppression' in the 1789 French Declaration of the Rights of Man and the Citizen.)

However, contemporary international human rights law provides little reliable protection against the violation of basic legal and democratic rights, including by the military. In the first place, its provisions provide numerous exemptions for alleged emergencies or dire challenges to the stability of the national state. In the Universal Declaration of Human Rights, the International Covenant on Civil and Political Rights (ICCPR), and other related instruments, such as the European Convention on Human Rights and Fundamental Freedoms and the UK *Human Rights Act 1998*, the listed civil and legal rights are mostly subject to far-reaching exemptions, including 'national security' and 'public safety'—leaving considerable leeway for draconian measures, such as the forms of detention without trial and other provisions imposed in the name of fighting the 'war on terrorism'. Thus, Article 4 of the ICCPR states:

1 In time of public emergency which threatens the life of the nation and the existence of which is officially proclaimed, the States Parties to the present Covenant may take measures derogating from their obligations under the present Covenant to the extent strictly required by the exigencies of the situation, provided that such measures are not inconsistent with their other obligations under international law and do not involve discrimination solely on the ground of race, colour, sex, language, religion or social origin.
2 No derogation from articles 6, 7, 8 (paragraphs I and 2), 11, 15, 16 and 18 may be made under this provision.

These exceptions to derogation relate to killing, torture, slavery, trial by law and freedom of religion. Neither they, nor the prohibition against discrimination, offer any guarantee of protection against the trampling over of a wide range of human rights, let alone against the mobilisation of the military itself.

Under the European Convention on Human Rights and Fundamental Freedoms, even the right to life is carefully circumscribed to permit killing by state forces in order to make arrests, prevent escapes from detention and quell riots and insurrections (Article 2). The rights of non-citizens (so-called 'aliens') are treated with particular contempt—non-citizens can be detained without trial, denied political rights and forcibly deported (Articles 5 and 16). Governments can derogate from most obligations under the European Convention 'in time of war or other public emergency threatening the life of the nation' (Article 15).

Particularly since the declaration of the 'war on terrorism', courts have tended to give executive governments considerable scope to use these provisions. In 2004, the English House of Lords, with Lord Hoffman dissenting, accepted that indefinite detention without trial of foreign national terrorist suspects, unable to be prosecuted or deported, could be permissible under the ICCPR's 'public emergency' clause in the context of the 9/11 attacks in the United States (*A and others v Secretary of State for the Home Department* [2004] UKHL 56). However, the majority ultimately declared the provisions to be discriminatory and disproportionate to the exigencies of the public emergency.

In his oft-cited dissent on the threshold issue of whether the threat of terrorism constituted a 'public emergency threatening the life of the nation,' Lord Hoffman stated: 'The real threat to the life of the nation, in the sense of a people living in accordance with its traditional laws and political values, comes not from terrorism but from laws such as these' ([2004] UKHL 56 [94–97]). Nonetheless, the eight-to-one majority view was that the courts had to defer heavily to the views of the executive government. In the words of Baroness Hale:

> Assessing the strength of a general threat to the life of the nation is, or should be, within the expertise of the Government and its advisers … If a Government were to declare a public emergency where patently there was no such thing, it would be the duty of the court to say so. But here we are considering the immediate aftermath of the unforgettable events of 11 September 2001. The attacks launched on the United States on that date were clearly intended to threaten the life of the nation.
>
> ([2004] UKHL 56 [226])

Because the nation-state system that still prevails globally, international law is not legally binding domestically unless it is incorporated into national legislation. Moreover, with some notable exceptions, such as the US Constitution's Bill of Rights, domestic human rights measures are not constitutionally entrenched, and can therefore be abridged, amended or repealed by legislatures. Generally, the provisions merely require courts to interpret all legislation, where possible, consistently with enumerated human rights, generally drawn from the ICCPR. If the legislation under consideration cannot be interpreted consistently with a human right, the court may only declare that an incompatibility exists, and report the issue to the legislature. Such a declaration does not affect the validity of the legislation in question.

Furthermore, under provisions like the UK *Human Rights Act*, the courts are instructed to permit reasonable limits to human rights if the limit is 'demonstrably justified in a free and democratic society'. This proviso, which English House of Lords judges have described as one of proportionality, leaves considerable scope for governments to brush aside or whittle down human rights. For example, in *Spinks v SSHD* [2005] EWCA Civ 275, the English Court of Appeal rejected a claim by a prisoner with a terminal cancer that his detention involved inhuman and degrading treatment. The court said the issue depended on the degree of danger posed by the prisoner.

Threats to civilian rule?

In a parliamentary democracy it is generally assumed that the final authority rests with civilian rule, secured by parliamentary control over the military budget. However, if a government calls out the military for support, the balance of power can begin to shift, particularly if the civil authorities become to any degree dependent upon, or politically indebted to, the armed forces. As noted by Jeffery:

> [W]hen the army is called in actively to support the government, both the responsibility and, perhaps more significantly, the initiative for action may shift from civilians to soldiers themselves. Between the extremes of, for example, troops assisting the police on a 'once and for all basis', meeting just one disturbance, and the full introduction of martial law and military rule, there are a number of stages during which the precise distribution of civil and military power is not at all clear.
>
> (Jeffery 1985: 57)

Even within the British-derived custom that the civilian government decides when and where military forces are to be deployed, and may give political direction to the armed forces, but has no right to issue operational directives, there is potential for disagreements and conflicts over the use of force. Jeffery pointed out that, although rare, the issue of the military disobeying civilian orders has arisen on occasions in Britain. One was the 1914 Curragh incident, when a number of officers resigned rather than accept orders that they thought sought to coerce Ulster Unionists into a united Ireland. Another was the 1918–22 breakdown in relations between Prime Minister Lloyd George and army chief, Sir Henry Wilson, who was outraged by the government's reluctance to take coercive measures against striking workers and Irish nationalists. And in 1919, the Army Council objected to cabinet plans to dismiss General Dyer after the Amritsar massacre in India (Jeffery 1985: 57–59).

Moreover, as Jeffery also observed, the use of troops to break strikes or keep order during industrial disputes 'raises the possibility that the army might be employed explicitly as an instrument of class conflict' (Jeffery 1985: 59). One could go further and suggest that, in the final analysis, the armed forces constitute the ultimate instrument of force for protecting the property and interests of the present ruling class and bolstering its power against threats posed by the industrial and political struggles that erupt in the working class. In 'normal' times, that instrument is not required, or is kept in reserve, but in periods of turmoil, such as those ignited by economic catastrophe or war, the military may be called into the frontline. In those periods, civilian and democratic forms of rule can come under acute strain, and may be dispensed with.

Furthermore, as mentioned in Chapter 4, in the United States, the pre-eminent economic power and supposed contemporary model of democracy, the 'military-industrial complex' has grown massively in size and economic influence since President Eisenhower warned of its emergence in 1961. Kohn, a military historian, and Bacevich, a former officer, have demonstrated that, while the United States may not have experienced a coup d'état, the military has grown in influence to the point of being able to impose its own perspective on many policies and decisions.

These developments have not ended with the Clinton and Bush administrations of 1993 to 2009. President Obama appointed three recently retired four-star military officers to top government positions—as national security adviser, secretary for veterans' affairs and director of national intelligence—believed to be the strongest representation of former military commanders in a Democratic Party administration (Grey 2009). The Trump administration featured, at various stages, generals and ex-generals in top-ranking posts, including retired Marine General Jim Mattis as Defense Secretary.

Retired Marine General John Kelly was named first to head the Homeland Security Department and then became White House Chief of Staff.

Canada and Australia, traditionally regarded as less militarist and more stable societies, are not exempt from these factors. In 1975, when the Governor-General dismissed the elected Whitlam government in Australia, the vice-regal representative conducted his own meetings with defence officials and may have been prepared to invoke his formal constitutional authority as Commander-in-Chief of the armed forces to deal with resistance by the ousted government or large-scale protests and strikes against the dismissal. And during 2008 there was a reminder of the 'reserve powers' of the vice-regal post in Canada when the Governor-General granted Prime Minster Stephen Harper his request to suspend parliament for more than a month to avoid almost certain defeat in a parliamentary vote of no-confidence over the government's reaction to the economic crisis (Gillies 2008).

Finally, the lessons of what happened in France, Italy, Germany and Japan in the inter-war years must be recalled. In all four countries, albeit in somewhat different forms, a combination of economic tensions and acute political conflicts produced a turn by the old establishment and authorities to rely upon military and para-military methods of rule. The integration of the armed forces and their generals into the civilian government apparatuses was central to the establishment of dictatorial forms of rule.

Social, economic and political tensions

Today's utilisation of alleged terrorist threats or potential political upheaval to erode traditional civil liberties, and argue for greater domestic use of the military, raises disturbing historical experiences. Adolf Hitler cited the 1933 Reichstag Fire, which the Nazis falsely attributed to communists, as the reason for insisting that the parliament agree to rule by decree (Kershaw 1998: 456–460). The morning after the fire, Hitler's cabinet adopted the emergency decree, 'For the Protection of the People and State'. In the words of historian Ian Kershaw:

> With one brief paragraph, the personal liberties enshrined in the Weimar Constitution—including freedom of speech, of association and of the press, and privacy of postal and telephone communications—were suspended indefinitely … The hastily constructed emergency decree amounted to the charter of the Third Reich.
>
> (Kershaw 1998: 459)

A month later, on 23 March 1933, the Nazi-controlled Reichstag passed 'enabling' legislation declaring that the executive had the power to make laws. 'The Act to Relieve the Distress of the People and the Reich' cemented dictatorial power in Germany under Hitler. It essentially transformed into legislation legal opinions previously prepared by the leading Nazi jurist Carl Schmitt. These authorised executive rule because of the 'state of exception' in Germany, namely its economic and political crisis and the alleged threat of revolution. Schmitt set out a 'legal defence' of the enabling legislation in the *Deutsche Juristen Zeitung*, in which he opined that the executive prerogative was unlimited at a time of national crisis (Neumann 1942; Meier 1988; Muller 2003). Significantly, during the previous Weimar Republic, Schmitt had acted as a theoretical handmaiden for the installation of a fascist regime (Head 2016: 117–179).

This is not to say that contemporary Western societies face the imminent danger of fascist dictatorship. There is no mass base of support for such totalitarian tendencies. Nevertheless, there is a resurgence of fascistic and far-right parties, whipping up scare campaigns against immigrants and refugees, and often enjoying considerable support within the military, police and intelligence forces (Vandreier 2019).

The very fact that governments and security authorities are citing 'national security' threats, especially of indefinite duration, as the justification for suspending or overturning constitutional norms and basic legal rights, and that calls are being made for the military to embrace a 'core' function of domestic security, are causes for grave concern. Any attempt to explain this trend as a temporary aberration in order to defeat 'terrorism' also fails to address the issue as to why terrorism has become such an allegedly all-pervasive threat. Exploring the roots of disaffected movements engaged in violent attacks is beyond the scope of this book. However, it is suggested that they lie, ultimately, in deepening global inequality and the increasingly aggressive military activities of the major powers themselves, notably the United States (Zinn 2002).

Moreover, the potential for widespread social unrest in the years ahead has been demonstrated by the meltdown of the global financial and share markets that began with the sub-prime crisis in the United States in mid-2007. The fallout quickly triggered the collapse of some of the world's largest banks and financial institutions, and then spread to the 'real' economy, causing rising unemployment, house repossessions and cuts to living standards in many countries. As a result, by the end of 2008, substantial political turmoil had already erupted in a number of countries, including Iceland and Greece.

Over the ensuing decade, as social inequality grew, strikes and demonstrations began to break out, including walkouts by teachers across the United States and the mass 'yellow vest' protests in France. The post-2007 crash also undermined faith in the market, raising political and ideological issues. Politicians, businessmen, professional economists and media commentators who had insisted that all economic problems were best left to the market, pleaded, amid the backdrop of failing banks, for gargantuan government bailouts to prop up their institutions. It was widely noted in the media that the United States and other governments offered 'socialism for the rich', while insisting on capitalism for everyone else. In reality, government policy had nothing to do with socialism. All of the measures taken were aimed at securing the interests of the financial and corporate elites. But the massive state intervention in the economy dealt blows to the intellectual legitimacy and prestige of the private profit system.

The economic breakdown came on top of several decades in which, around the world, the jobs, wages, conditions and welfare entitlements of working people were driven down in order to satisfy the demands of global corporations and wealthy investors for lower tax rates, cheaper labour and greater profits. Through downsizing, outsourcing and privatisation, full-time, permanent jobs were replaced increasingly by insecure, temporary and part-time employment. Driven by global competition for markets and profits, transnational corporations had demanded, as the price for their investment, continual cutbacks to working-class wages and basic rights (United Nations 2005).

Among the results was a wide gulf between the rich and the poor. The 2019 Oxfam world inequality report, noted in Chapter 1, calculated that just 1 per cent of the $112 billion fortune accumulated by Amazon owner Jeff Bezos, then the world's richest man, was equivalent to the entire health budget for Ethiopia, a nation of 105 million people. The report found that the top tax rate for the rich in the developed countries plunged from 62 per cent in 1970 to 38 per cent by 2013, while in developing countries, the top personal tax rate was just 28 per cent. It added that between 1980 and 2016, the poorest 50 per cent of the world's population received only 12 cents in every dollar of global income growth, while the top 1 per cent captured 27 cents of every dollar (Oxfam 2019: 8–26).

In 2019 also, *Bloomberg* magazine reported that the wealth of the 12 richest attendees at the annual Davos World Economic Forum soared in the previous ten years by a combined $175 billion, and the overall wealth of the world's billionaires grew, in the same period, from $3.4 trillion to $8.9 trillion. Mark Zuckerberg, the CEO of Facebook, increased his wealth from $3 billion to $55.6 billion, a rise of 1,853 per cent. Stephen Schwarzman, the head of the hedge fund Blackstone, saw his personal wealth shoot up from $2.1 billion to $10.1 billion, an increase of 486 per cent. The media baron Rupert Murdoch increased his wealth from $3.2 billion to $15.1 billion, a rise of 472 per cent, while Jamie Dimon, the head of JP Morgan, enjoyed a 276 per cent wealth increase, from $0.4 billion to $1.1 billion (Metcalf and Kennedy 2019).

The Oxfam (2019) report called for a 'human economy' that would instead provide health care, education and gender equality, and create the best conditions for shared wealth. It said just a 0.5 per cent increase in taxes on the richest individuals would raise enough money to educate the 262 million children who did not receive an education, and provide health care that would save 3.3 million people from preventable deaths. Oxfam, however, had been making such proposals for the previous eight years, to no avail. Every year since it began its reports in 2011, the situation had worsened, as Oxfam itself acknowledged.

The scourge of social inequality cannot be ended through futile appeals, made to the very powers that preside over the current system, to change course.

These inequalities, exacerbated by the post-2007 global economic meltdown, are highly likely to generate deep disaffection and unrest, which could see resort to armed force by the political establishment. As noted in the Introduction and earlier in this chapter, police and intelligence officials have identified economic and political instability as a primary threat to 'national security'.

Marxist insights

As I have argued elsewhere, these developments confirm the Marxist view of the state (Head 2007). Karl Marx and Frederick Engels famously characterised the capitalist state as a 'committee for managing the common affairs of the whole bourgeoisie' (Marx and Engels 1973: 110–111; Engels 1977: 167). Engels (1977) described the emergence, at the heart of the state, of bodies of 'armed men' alongside 'material adjuncts, prisons and institutions of coercion'. He warned that this apparatus of force grew stronger as class antagonisms within the state became more acute and as tensions grew between rival international powers.

Another Marxist, Vladimir Lenin, the foremost leader of the October 1917 revolution in Russia, observed that behind the democratic façade of modern capitalist states, with their formal undertakings to uphold freedom of assembly, freedom of the press and 'equality of all citizens before the law', there existed provisions allowing for all these guarantees to be swept aside to suppress threats from below during periods of crisis:

> There is not a single state, however democratic, which has no loopholes or reservations in its constitution guaranteeing the bourgeois the possibility of dispatching troops against the workers, of proclaiming martial law, and so forth, in case of a 'violation of public order,' and actually in case the exploited class 'violates' its position of slavery and tries to behave in a non-slavish manner.
>
> (Tucker 1975: 468)

Marxist theory also offers crucial insights into the processes and tendencies at work in periods of economic, social and international crisis. Leon Trotsky, the co-leader of the 1917 revolution, warned in 1933, after the Nazis took power in Germany:

> The old view about the backwardness of countries seized by dictatorships can no longer be maintained. Though it was possible to apply it to Italy, with some exaggeration, it cannot possibly be applied to Germany, which is a highly developed capitalist country in the very heart of Europe.
>
> (Trotsky 1933)

Under conditions of acute international antagonisms between the major powers and domestic social tensions, Trotsky analysed, 'capitalism in its agony can only preserve its existence by using the most brutal anti-cultural methods, the extreme expression of which is Fascism. That historic fact appears in Hitler's victory'. Trotsky recalled what he had written in 1929:

> On the analogy of the electrical industry democracy may be defined as a system of switches and fuses directed against the violent shocks of national or social struggle. No epoch in the history of man has been so filled with antagonisms as our own. The switches of democracy are fusing or breaking under the violent pressure of class and international antagonisms. That is the kernel which explains the rapid rise of dictatorship.
>
> (Trotsky 1933)

Perhaps the best-known early Soviet jurist, Evgeny Pashukanis, contended that the capitalist state was bound up with the principle of commodity exchange, and hence the protection of dominant private interests. These interests required, as far as possible, limits on the power of the state, and an avoidance of dictatorial methods that could threaten personal and property rights (Pashukanis 1978: 149). However, in times of crisis, particularly when capitalist interests as a whole were threatened from below, the ideal of the constitutional state would be dispensed with:

> For the bourgeoisie has never, in favour of purity of theory, lost sight of the fact that class society is not only a market where autonomous owners of commodities meet, but is at the same time the battlefield of a bitter class war, where the machinery of state represents a very powerful weapon … The more the hegemony of the bourgeoisie was shattered, the more compromising these corrections became, the more quickly the 'constitutional state' was transformed into a disembodied shadow, until finally the extraordinary sharpening of the class struggle forced the bourgeoisie to discard the mask of the constitutional state altogether, revealing the nature of state power as the organised power of one class over the other.
>
> (Pashukanis 1978: 149–150)

Pashukanis noted that in the face of exceptional revolutionary upheaval, the impersonal nature of public power could give way to the private or semi-private wielding of power, via the mobilisation of fascist and other violent militias.

> In our times of heightened revolutionary struggle, we can observe how the official machinery of the bourgeois state retires into the background as compared with the volunteer corps of the fascists and others. This further substantiates the fact that, when the balance of society is upset, it seeks salvation not in the creation of a power standing above society, but in the maximal harnessing of all forces of the classes in conflict.
>
> (Pashukanis 1978: 139, fn 10)

These observations, like those of Trotsky, were highly pertinent in the 1920s and 1930s, when fascist thugs, and later storm troopers, were let loose in Italy and Germany, and totalitarian forms of rule emerged in other major countries, such as Spain and Japan. But the analysis remains relevant today (Head 2007: 231–252). A new period of economic breakdown, soaring social inequality and great power conflict has commenced, once more generating 'violent shocks' that are producing military and other authoritarian responses in capitalist ruling circles.

Conclusion

There are many reasons to be concerned about the expansion of military powers. In most cases, the legislative provisions or other instruments have a wide, ill-defined scope, leaving broad discretions in the hands of government ministers and military officers. Soldiers have already been seen on the streets of France, Britain and Italy, and at the US–Mexico border.

In Australia, where the most complete codification of domestic military powers has been attempted, the enlarged scope of the military call-out power, covering 'designated infrastructure' and 'acts of violence', could allow domestic military deployments to become much more common. Once called out, military personnel have unprecedented powers, such as to shoot down passenger aircraft, use lethal force, interrogate civilians and seize documents. The exercise of these powers are protected by legal immunities. Secrecy surrounds the Rules of Engagement that will apply. At the same time, vague common law or prerogative powers remain in the hands of the executive.

Moreover, in most jurisdictions, these measures are in addition to the growth of paramilitary policing. They are part of a more general challenge to civil liberties and human rights in the context of the 'war on terror'. The historical record demonstrates that such anti-terrorism powers can be misused for political and industrial purposes. Finally, the provisions have been advanced amid a broader, creeping militarisation of official policy, designed to accustom ordinary people to the sight of troops on the streets. The global dimensions of this trend further suggest that preparations are being made to deal with domestic unrest as social and international tensions rise. Hopefully, this book will contribute to the development of an informed and vigilant response to these dangers.

Bibliography

ACLU. 2008. 'ACLU Demands Information on Military Deployment within U.S. Borders'. Media Release. 21 October 2008, https://www.aclu.org/press-releases/aclu-demands-information-military-deployment-within-us-borders

Addendum to the Explanatory Memorandum. 2018. Defence Amendment (Call Out of the Australian Defence Force) Bill 2018 (Cth)

Adelaide, D. 2002. 'G-8 Security Operation—The Stifling and Criminalizing of Dissent', World Socialist Web Site 27 June 2002

Allinson, G. 2004. *Japan's Postwar History*, Cornell University Press

Amnesty International. 2002. 'Amnesty International's Concerns Regarding Post September 11 Detentions in the USA', Amnesty International, March 2002

Andrews, E. 1995. 'Civil Power, Aid to the (ACP)' in Dennis *et al. The Oxford Companion to Australian Military History*, Oxford University Press

Arens, M. 2008. 'Italian Government Imposes National State of Emergency', World Socialist Web Site, 6 August 2008, http://www.wsws.org/articles/2008/aug2008/ital-a06.shtml

Associated Press. 2018. 'Equating Rocks with Rifles, Trump Proposes Radical New Rules of Engagement for Troops along Border' *Military Times*, 1 November 2018, https://www.militarytimes.com/news/your-military/2018/11/01/equating-rocks-with-rifles-trump-proposes-radical-new-rules-of-engagement-for-troops-along-border/

Babington, A. 1990. *Military Intervention in Britain, From the Gordon Riots to the Gibraltar Incident*, Routledge

Bacevich, A. 2002. *American Empire: The Realities and Consequences of US Diplomacy*, Harvard University Press

Banks, W. 2005. 'Mold, Mildew and the Military Role in Disaster Response' *Jurist*, 17 October 2005

Barnes, J. 2008. 'Military to Be on High Alert for Inauguration' *Los Angeles Times*, 18 December 2008

Basic Law of the Federal Republic of Germany. 1949. 'Basic Law of the Federal Republic of Germany', http://www.iuscomp.org/gla/statutes/GG.htm

Bassiouni, M. (ed) 1971. *The Law of Dissent and Riots*, Charles C. Thomas

Bayne, P. 1991. 'Policy Guidelines and The Law: Some Intersections', 65*Australian Law Journal* 607

BBC. 2019. BBC News. 'Brexit: MoD Prepares for No-deal in Whitehall Bunker', BBC, 21 March 2019, https://www.bbc.com/news/uk-47658403

Beddie, B. and Moss, S. 1982. 'Some Aspects of Aid to the Civil Power in Australia', *Occasional Monograph* 2, University of New South Wales Department of Government

Bell, J. 1992. *French Constitutional Law*, Oxford University Press

Bell, J. B. 1993. *The Irish Troubles. A Generation of Violence 1967–1992*, St. Martin's Press

Bergin, A. and Smith, A. 2006. *Australian Domestic Security: The Role of Defence*, Australian Strategic Policy Institute

Berlinski, C. 2019. 'France Doesn't Have Enough Cops', *The American Interest*, 13 December 2018, https://www.the-american-interest.com/2018/12/13/france-doesnt-have-enough-cops/

Bills, S. 1988. *Kent State/May 4: Echoes through a Decade*, Kent State University Press

Blackshield, A. 1978. 'The Siege of Bowral—the Legal Issues', *Pacific Defence Reporter* 4

Blackstone, W. 2001. *Commentaries on the Laws of England* (Morrison, W., ed.), Routledge-Cavendish

Bloody Sunday Inquiry, http://www.bloody-sunday-inquiry.org.uk/

Blum, W. 2002. *Rogue State: A Guide to the World's Only Superpower*, Zed Books

Bonnet, F. 2019. 'Sending in the Troops', *Jacobin*, 28 March 2019, https://jacobinmag.com/2019/03/macron-yellow-vests-army-france

Bramall, E. 1985. 'The Place of the British Army in Public Order' in Rowe, P. and Whelan, C. (eds). *Military Intervention in Democratic Societies*, Croom Helm

Brasor, P. 2018. 'Japan's Courts Are Being Asked to Define the Role of the SDF', *The Japan Times*, 19 May 2018, https://www.japantimes.co.jp/news/2018/05/19/national/media-national/japans-courts-asked-define-role-sdf/#.XRLWD-szaUk

Braw, E. 2018. 'For Not-Quite-Wars, Italy Has a Useful Alternative to Traditional Troops', *Defense One*, 16 April 2018, https://www.defenseone.com/ideas/2018/04/todays-not-quite-wars-italy-has-alternative-traditional-troops/147457/

Brett, P. and Waller, P. 1983. *Brett and Waller's Criminal Law: Text and Cases*, Butterworths

Brinkerhoff, J. 2002. 'The Posse Comitatus Act and Homeland Security', *Journal of Homeland Security*, February 2002

Britton, B. 2018. 'British Troops on Standby as Government Ramps Up No-Deal Brexit Preparations', CNN, 18 December 2018, https://edition.cnn.com/2018/12/18/uk/no-deal-brexit-plans-intl-gbr/index.html

Bronitt, S. and Stephens, D. 2007. '"Flying Under the Radar"—The Use of Lethal Force Against Hijacked Aircraft: Recent Australian Developments', *Oxford University Commonwealth Law Journal* 7, 265

Brooke-Holland, L. 2017. 'Military Aid to the Civil Authorities', House of Commons Library Briefing Paper Number 08074, 18 August 2017

Broué, P. 2006. *The German Revolution 1917–1923*, Haymarket Books

Brown, B. 2000. Commonwealth of Australia. Parliamentary Debates, Senate, 6 September 2000

Brown, H. 1999. 'Domestic State Violence: Repression from the Croquants to the Commune', *The Historical Journal* 42, 3, 597–622

Burghardt, T. (ed). 2002. *Police State America: US Military 'Civil Disturbance' Planning*, Arm The Spirit

Cabinet. 1978. '1978 Cabinet Records—Selected Documents', National Archives of Australia, http://www.naa.gov.au/Images/1978_Cabinet_Records_Selected_Documents_Security_tcm2-16435.pdf

Cahill, D. and Cahill, R. 2005. 'Civilian Responses to Peace-Time Military Occupation: The 1978 Bowral Call-Out and Its Implications for the "War On Terrorism"', Australian Society for the Study of Labour History Conference Proceedings, Australian Society for the Study of Labour History, http://www.historycooperative.org/proceedings/asslh/cahill.html

Cain, F. 1994. *ASIO: An Unofficial History*, Spectrum

CAIN Web Service. 'Background Information on Northern Ireland Society—Security', http://cain.ulst.ac.uk/ni/security.htm#06

Calder, G. 2008. 'Routing a Rebellion or Crushing a Crime Wave? Proclaiming Martial Law and a Call-to-Arms in Van Diemen's Land, 1828–1830', *Legal History*, 12, 127

Campbell, B. 2004. *The SA Generals and the Rise of Nazism*, University of Kentucky Press

Campbell, C. 1994. *Emergency Law in Ireland, 1918–1925*, Clarendon Press

Campbell, C. 2008. 'Law, Terror and Social Movements: The Repression-Mobilisation Nexus' in *Emergencies and the Limits of Legality* (Ramraj, V. ed.), Cambridge University Press

Canada. 1997. 'Dishonoured Legacy—The Lessons of the Somalia Affair: Report of the Commission of Inquiry into the Deployment of Canadian Forces to Somalia', Public Works and Government Services

Canada. 2017. 'Strong, Secure, Engaged, Canada's Defence Policy', Minister of National Defence, http://dgpaapp.forces.gc.ca/en/canada-defence-policy/docs/canada-defence-policy-report.pdf

Canada Defence Policy Statement. 2006. http://www.forces.gc.ca/site/reports/dps/index_e.asp

Canada First. 2008. 'Canada First Defence Strategy 2008', Department of National Defence

Canadian Forces. 2008. 'Joint Task Force Two', http://www.jtf2.forces.gc.ca/index-eng.asp

Capua, J. V. 1977. 'The Early History of Martial Law in England from the Fourteenth Century to the Petition of Right', *Cambridge Law Journal* 36, 1, 152–173

Caputo, P. 2005. *13 Seconds: A Look Back at the Kent State Shootings*, Chamberlain Bros

Cavallaro, G. 2008. 'Brigade Homeland Tours Start Oct. 1', *Army Times*, 8 September 2008

Chalmers, J. 2004. *The Sorrows of Empire: Militarism, Secrecy, and the End of the Republic*, Metropolitan Books

Chrisafis, A. 2016. 'Thousands of Troops on Paris Streets But Are They France's New Maginot Line?', *The Guardian*, 16 April 2016, https://www.theguardian.com/world/2016/apr/15/paris-attacks-operation-sentinelle-soldiers-patrolling-streets-france-safer

Clark, D. 2007. *Principles of Australian Public Law*, 2nd ed., LexisNexis, Butterworths

Coates, S. 2019. 'Troops Must Be Ready for Brexit Chaos, Says Defence Minister Tobias Ellwood', *The Times*, 5 January 2019, https://www.thetimes.co.uk/article/troops-must-be-ready-for-brexit-chaos-says-defence-minister-tobias-ellwood-s8sppbrsr

Commonwealth. 2018. 'Parliamentary Debates, House of Representatives', 18 October 2018, 10436–10439 (Andrew Hastie)

Congressional Research Service. 2001. 'National Emergency Powers', http://fpc.state.gov/documents/organization/6216.pdf

Connor, S. 2017. 'Media Remains Silent on Appearance of Military Officers at Trump's Inauguration', World Socialist Web Site, 28 January 2017, https://www.wsws.org/en/articles/2017/01/28/mili-j27.html

Copp, T. 2018. 'Here Are the Rules of Engagement for Troops Deploying to The Mexican Border', *Military Times*, 2 November 2018, https://www.militarytimes.com/news/your-military/2018/11/02/here-are-the-rules-of-engagement-for-troops-deploying-to-the-mexican-border/?utm_source=clavis

Coxsedge, J., Caldicutt, K. and Harant, G. 1982. *Rooted in Secrecy: the Clandestine Involvement in Australian Politics*, Committee for the Abolition of Political Police

Current Topics. 1978. 'Current Topics: Legal and Constitutional Problems of Protective Security Arrangements in Australia', *Australian Law Journal* 52, 296

Current Topics. 1984. 'Current Topics: Scope and Content of Concept of "National Security"', *Australian Law Journal* 58, 67
Daly, M. 1988. *The British Occupation, 1882–1922*, Cambridge University Press
De Smith, S. A. 1981. *Constitutional and Administrative Law* (4th ed), Penguin/ Longmans
Defence Planning and Management. 2004. 'Scenario 7—Aid of the Civil Power', http:// www.vcds.forces.gc.ca/dgsp/pubs/rep-pub/dda/scen/scen-7_e.asp
Dennis, P. 1981. 'The Territorial Army in Aid of the Civil Power in Britain, 1919–1926', *Journal of Contemporary History* 16, 705–724
Dennis, P., Grey, J., Morris, E. and Prior, R. 1995. *The Oxford Companion to Australian Military History*, Oxford University Press
Department of Defence. 2004. 'Aid to the Civil Power', http://www.defence.gov.au/arm y/AHU/HISTORY/aid_to_the_civil_power.htm
Dewar, M. 1997. *The British Army in Northern Ireland*, Arms and Armour Press
Dicey, A. 2005. *Introduction to the Study of the Law of the Constitution*, Adamant Media Corporation
Doyle, C. 2000. 'The Posse Comitatus Act and Related Matters: The Use of the Military to Execute Civilian Law', CRS Report for Congress, 1 June 2000, Congressional Research Service
Dinmore, G. 2008. 'Italy Deploys Troops to Fight Urban Crime', *Financial Times*, 4 August 2008, http://www.ft.com/cms/s/0/4141be22-6238-11dd-9ff9-000077b07658.html
Dinmore, G. and Bianchi, B. 2009. 'Tensions Rise Over Italy's Gypsy Migrants', *Financial Times*, 27 January 2009
Ehling, M. 2008. 'U.S. Military will Have Role in RNC Security', *Twin Cities Daily Planet*, 29 June 2008
Eisenhower, D. 1961. 'Farewell Radio and Television Address to the American People', *Public Papers* 1035 (17 January 1961)
Eldridge, R. and Midford, P. (eds) 2017. *The Japanese Ground Self-Defense Force: Search for Legitimacy*, Palgrave Macmillan US
Engdahl, D. 1971. 'Soldiers, Riots and Revolution: The La and History of Military Troops in Civil Disorders', *Iowa Law Review* 57, 1
Engdahl, D. 1985. 'Foundations for Military Intervention in the United States' in Rowe, P. and Whelan, C. (eds), *Military Intervention in Democratic Societies*, Croom Helm
Engels, F. 1977. *The Origin of the Family, Private Property and the State*, Progress Publishers
Euler, M. 2017. 'Young French Soldier from Operation Sentinelle Commits Suicide', *RFI*, 27 August 2017, http://en.rfi.fr/france/20170827-young-soldier-operation-sentinelle-commits-suicide
Explanatory Memorandum. 2018. 'Defence Amendment (Call Out of the Australian Defence Force) Bill 2018 (Cth)'
Fackler, M. 2008. 'A Lockdown on Hokkaido as Police Outnumber Summit Protesters', *New York Times*, 9 July 2008
Farmer, B. 2017. '1,000 Troops on the Streets after Manchester Bombing Attack', *The Telegraph*, 24 May 2017, https://www.telegraph.co.uk/news/2017/05/24/1000-troop s-streets-manchester-bombing-attack/
Forcese, C. 2008. *National Security Law, Canadian Practice in International Perspective*, Irwin Law
France 24. 2017. 'Opération Sentinelle: Is France's Fight against Terrorism Working?', France 24, 8 October 2017, https://www.france24.com/en/20170810-operation-sen tinelle-france-fight-counter-terrorism-working

France 24. 2018. 'France's Domestic Security Operation "Sentinelle" to Undergo Revamp', France 24, 28 August 2017, https://www.france24.com/en/20170822-frances-domestic-security-operation-sentinelle-become-more-mobile

Fudge, J. and Tucker, E. 2004. *Labour Before the Law: The Regulation of Workers' Collective Action in Canada, 1900–1948*, University of Toronto Press

Fulbrook, M. 2006. *A Concise History of Germany*, Cambridge University Press

Gardina, J. 2008. 'Toward Military Rule? A Critique of Executive Discretion to Use the Military in Domestic Emergencies', *Marquette Law Review*, 91

Garraway, C. 1999. 'Superior Orders And The International Criminal Court: Justice Delivered Or Justice Denied', *International Review of the Red Cross* 836, 785–794

Geraghty, T. 1998. *The Irish War*, HarperCollins

German Constitutional Court. 2006. 'Aviation Security Act Case', BVerfG, 1 BvR 357/05 of 15 February 2006 (Germany); Bundesverfassungsgericht, Press release No. 11/2006 of 15 February 2006

Gillies, R. 2008. 'Analysis: Quiet Canada Mired in Unexpected Chaos', Associated Press, 8 December 2008

Gillmor, D. 2002. *Canada: A People's History. Volume 2.* McClelland & Stewart

Gillmor, D. and Turgeon, P. 2001. *Canada: A People's History, Volume 1*, McClelland & Stewart

Girard, L. 2018. 'Canadian Authorities Prepare Mass Repression of Anti-G7 Protests' World Socialist Web Site, 6 June 2018, https://www.wsws.org/en/articles/2018/06/06/malb-j06.html

Gooch, J. 2008. *Mussolini and his Generals, The Armed Forces and Fascist Foreign Policy 1922–1940*, Cambridge University Press

Goodale, R. 2019. 'Statement from Minister Goodale Regarding Situation in Gillam, MB', https://www.canada.ca/en/public-safety-canada/news/2019/07/statement-from-minister-goodale-regarding-situation-in-gillam-mb.html

Goodman, A. 2008. 'Invasion of the Sea-Smurfs', *Democracy Now!*, 2 October 2008

Gosden, E. 2015. 'Secret Plan to Deploy 5,000 Soldiers on UK Streets in Wake of Major Terror Attacks', *Daily Telegraph*, 26 July 2015, https://www.telegraph.co.uk/news/uknews/defence/11764301/Secret-plan-to-deploy-5000-soldiers-on-UK-streets-in-wake-of-major-terror-attacks.html

Grabosky, P. 1989. *Wayward Governance: Illegality and its Control in the Public Sector*, Australian Institute of Criminology

Graham, B. 2005. 'War Plans Drafted to Counter Terror Attacks in U.S.—Domestic Effort is Big Shift for Military', *Washington Post*, 8 August 2005

Greene, A. 2018. 'Shakeup of Defence "Call-Out" Powers Will Make it Easier for Police to Request Military Backup During Terror Attacks', ABC News, 28 June 2018, https://www.abc.net.au/news/2018-06-28/military-call-out-powers-up-for-debate-legislation-in-parliament/9916636

Greer, S. 1983. 'Military Intervention in Civil Disturbances: The Legal Basis Reconsidered', *Public Law* 573

Grey, B. 2001. 'New York Times Documents Military Role in Theft of 2000 Election', World Socialist Web Site, 19 July 2001

Grey, B. 2009. 'Obama Names Third Republican to Cabinet: A Further Bow to The Right', World Socialist Web Site, 4 February 2009, http://www.wsws.org/articles/2009/feb2009/obam-f04.shtml

Gross, O. and Ni Aolain, F. 2006. *Law in Times of Crisis: Emergency Powers in Theory and Practice*, Cambridge University Press

Guardian. 1980. 5 March 1980

Guardian. 2000. 'Paratrooper Lee Clegg Cleared of Last Charge over Death of Teenagers', *Guardian*, 1 February 2000, http://www.guardian.co.uk/uk/2000/feb/01/northernireland.nicholaswatt3

Guerin, D. 1973. *Fascism and Big Business*, Monad Press

Hague, W. 2007. 'The Seal of Approval', *Guardian*, 15 May 2007, http://www.guardian.co.uk/commentisfree/2007/may/15/thesealofapproval

Hailsham, Lord (ed). 1973. *Halsbury's Laws of England* (4th ed), LexisNexis, Butterworths

Hale, M. 2000. *The History and Analysis of the Common Law of England*, The Law Book Exchange

Hall, T. 2019. 'Trump Unleashes Torrent of Militarism in Fourth of July Speech', World Socialist Web Site, 5 July 2019, https://www.wsws.org/en/articles/2019/07/05/trum-j05.html

Hamill, D. 1986. *Pig in the Middle. The Army in Northern Ireland 1969–1985*, Methuen

Hammond, M. 1997. 'The Posse Comitatus Act: A Principle in Need of Renewal', *Washington University Law Quarterly* 75, 953

Hancock, N. 2002a. 'Terrorism and the Law in Australia: Supporting Materials', Department of Parliamentary Library, Research Paper No 13, 2001–2002

Hancock, N. 2002b. 'Terrorism and the Law in Australia: Legislation, Commentary and Constraints', Department of Parliamentary Library, Research Paper No 12, 2001–2002

Harman, C. 1982. *The Lost Revolution; Germany 1918 to 1923*, Bookmarks

Harman, C. 1984. *Explaining The Crisis*, Bookmarks

Harman, C. 2008. *A People's History of the World*, Verso

Haslip, S. 2002. 'A Critical Consideration of the Use of the Aid to Civil Power Provision Against Aboriginal Peoples in the Light of the Promises of Protection Made to Aboriginal Peoples in Canada', CDA-CDAI Symposium, 2002, http://www.cda-cdai.ca/symposia/2002/haslip.htm at 15 August 2008.

Hawley, C. 2008. Spiegel OnLine, 20 October 2008, http://www.spiegel.de/international/germany/0,1518,druck-585276,00.html

Head, M. 2001. 'The Military Call-out Legislation—Some Legal and Constitutional Questions', *Federal Law Review* 29, 273–294

Head, M. 2002a. 'The High Court and the Tampa Refugees', *Griffith Law Review* 11, 23–33

Head, M. 2002b. 'Counter-terrorism Laws: A Threat to Political Freedom, Civil Liberties and Constitutional Rights', *Melbourne University Law Review*, 26666–689

Head, M. 2004a. 'Another Threat to Democratic Rights: Asio Detentions Cloaked in Secrecy', *Alternative Law Journal* 29, 127

Head, M. 2004b. 'ASIO, Secrecy and Lack of Accountability', *Murdoch University Electronic Journal of Law* 11

Head, M. 2005a. 'Calling Out the Troops—Disturbing Trends and Unanswered Questions', *University of NSW Law Journal* 28, 484–492

Head, M. 2005b. 'Editorial: Detention and the Anti-Terrorism Legislation', *University of Western Sydney Law Review* 9, 1

Head, M. 2007. *Evgeny Pashukanis: A Critical Reappraisal*, Routledge-Cavendish

Head, M. 2008. 'Thirty Years since Sydney's Hilton Hotel Bombing—Unanswered Questions', *Legal History* 12, 241–258

Head, M. 2009. *Calling Out the Troops: The Australian Military and Civil Unrest: The Legal and Constitutional Issues*, Federation Press

Head, M. 2016. *Emergency Powers in Theory and Practice: The Long Shadow of Carl Schmitt*, Ashgate

Head, M. 2017. *Administrative Law: Context and Critique* (4th ed), Federation Press

Head, M. 2018a. 'Leaked Documents Expose Plans for Internal Surveillance by Australia's Electronic Spy Agency', World Socialist Web Site, 2 May 2018, https://www.wsws.org/en/articles/2018/05/02/asdem02.html

Head, M. 2018b. 'Australia's Anti-democratic "Foreign Interference" Bills', *Alternative Law Journal* 43, 3, 160–165

Head, M. and Boehringer, K. 2019. *The Legal Power to Launch War: Who Decides?*, Routledge

Head, M. and Mann, S. 2009. *Domestic Deployment of the Armed Forces: Military Powers, Law and Human Rights*, Ashgate

Hennessy, P. 1985. 'Whitehall Contingency Planning for Industrial Disputes' in Rowe, P. and Whelan, C. (eds), *Military Intervention in Democratic Societies*, Croom Helm

Hermann, P. 2017. 'Security Grid for Inauguration Means Thousands of Police, Many Street Closures', *Washington Post*, 15 January 2017, https://www.washingtonpost.com/.../a33a444c-d821-11e6-9a36-1d296534b31e_story

Heron, C. 1998. *The Workers' Revolt in Canada, 1917–1925*, University of Toronto Press

Hersh, S. 2004. *Chain of Command: The Road from 9/11 to Abu Ghraib*, HarperCollins

Heuston, R. 1964. *Essays in Constitutional Law* (2nd ed), Stevens

Hickley, M. 2008. 'Military Told to Wear Uniform in Public as Often as Possible to Improve National Recognition of The Armed Forces', *Daily Mail*, 29 October 2008, http://www.dailymail.co.uk/news/article-1081608/Military-told-wear-uniform-public-possible-improve-national-recognition-armed-forces.html

Hill, R. 2005. Minister of Defence, letter, 4 August 2005, on author's personal file

Hocking, J. 1993. *Beyond Terrorism: The Development of the Australian Security State*, Allen & Unwin

Hocking, J. 2004. *Terror Laws: ASIO, Counter-Terrorism and the Threat to Democracy*, UNSW Press

Holdsworth, W. S. 1902. 'Martial Law Historically Considered', *Law Quarterly Review* 18, 117

Hope, R. 1977. *The Royal Commission on Intelligence and Security*, Reports I, II, III, IV, Australian Government Publishing Service

Hope, R. 1979. *Protective Security Review Report*, Australian Government Publishing Service

House of Commons Defence Committee 2001–2. 'Defence and Security in the UK, 2001–2002', HC 518

Hufnagel, S. 2008. 'German Perspectives on the Right to Life and Human Dignity in the "War On Terror"', *Criminal LJ* 32, 100

Ignatieff, M. 2004. *The Lesser Evil: Political Ethics in an Age of Terror*, Penguin Canada

InDaily. 2017. 'Military to Gain New Terror Powers', *InDaily*, 17 July 2017, https://indaily.com.au/news/2017/07/17/military-gain-new-terror-powers/

International Labour Office. 2019. 'The Global Labour Income Share and Distribution', https://www.ilo.org/ilostat-files/Documents/Labour%20income%20share%20and%20distribution.pdf

International Labour Organization. 2009. 'Global Employment Trends 2009', ILO, https://www.ilo.org/global/publications/WCMS_101461/lang–en/index.htm

Jacobs, J. 1985. 'The Role of Military Forces in Public Sector Labor Relations', in Rowe, P. and Whelan, C. (eds), *Military Intervention in Democratic Societies*, Croom Helm

Jacobson, T. and Schwarz, P. 2019. 'German Government Prepares Troops for Domestic Missions', World Socialist Web Site, 18 May 2019, https://www.wsws.org/en/articles/2019/05/18/bava-m18.html

Jankowski, J. 2000. *Egypt: A Short History.* Oxford: Oneworld Publications

Japan Ministry of Defense. 2007. Speech by Defense Minister Fumio Kyuma, 9 January 2007, http://www.mod.go.jp/e/publ/lastest/press01.html

Jeffery, K. 1985. 'Military Aid to the Civil Power in the United Kingdom – An Historical Perspective' in Rowe, P. and Whelan, C. (eds), *Military Intervention in Democratic Societies*, Croom Helm

Jeffery, K. 1996. 'The British Army and Ireland since 1922' in Bartlett, T. and Jeffery, K. (eds), *A Military History of Ireland*, Cambridge University Press

Johnston, E. 2019. 'Osaka Braces for Unprecedented Security Measures ahead of G20 Summit', *Japan Times*, 23 June 2019, https://www.japantimes.co.jp/news/2019/06/23/national/osaka-braces-unprecedented-security-measures-ahead-g20-summit/#.XRLS7eszaUk

Joint Standing Committee. 2001–2002. 'Review of the Defence Annual Report 2001–2002', Joint Standing Committee on Foreign Affairs, Defence and Trade, http://www.aph.gov.au/House/committee/jfadt/defence_report2001-2002/d_annualreport/chapter2.pdf

Jordan, R. 2017. 'Canada to Hike Military Spending by 70 Percent Over Next Decade', World Socialist Web Site, 10 June 2017, https://www.wsws.org/en/articles/2017/06/10/cawa-j10.html

Jurist. 2008. 'Australian Group Seeks ICC War Crimes Charges against Ex-Pm For Iraq Deployment', 2 June 2008, http://jurist.law.pitt.edu/paperchase/2008/06/australia-group-seeks-icc-war-crimes.php

Karp, P. 2018. 'Military Could Be On Call for Sieges and Riots, Attorney General Says', *The Guardian*, 28 June 2018, https://www.theguardian.com/australia-news/2018/jun/28/military-could-be-on-call-for-sieges-and-riots-attorney-general-says

Katzenstein, P. 1996. *Cultural Norms and National Security; Police and Military in Post-war Japan*, Cornell University Press

Kenny, M. 2017. 'Lindt Siege Findings: Malcolm Turnbull Flags Changes to Make Defence Force Intervention Easier', *The Sydney Morning Herald*, 25 May 2017, https://www.smh.com.au/politics/federal/lindt-siege-findings-malcolm-turnbull-flags-changes-to-make-defence-force-interventioneasier-20170524-gwc705.html

Kershaw, I. 1998. *Hitler, 1889–1936: Hubris*, Allen Lane

Kim, S. *et al.* 2018. 'Newly Disclosed Documents on the Five Eyes Alliance and What They Tell Us about Intelligence-Sharing Agreements', *Lawfare*, 23 April 2018, https://www.lawfareblog.com/newly-disclosed-documents-five-eyes-alliance-and-what-they-tell-us-about-intelligence-sharing

Kishore, J. 2019. 'Trump's Fourth of July: The Militarist Bombast of a Crisis-ridden System', World Socialist Web Site, 6 July 2019, https://www.wsws.org/en/articles/2019/07/06/pers-j06.html

Kitson, F. 1971. *Low Intensity Operations: Subversion, Insurgency, Peacekeeping*, Faber & Faber

Kohn, R. 2002. 'The Erosion of Civilian Control of the Military in the United States Today', *Naval War College Review*, Summer 2002

Kostal, R. 2005. *A Jurisprudence of Power: Victorian Empire and the Rule of Law*, Oxford University Press

Lackerstein, D. 2012. *National Regeneration in Vichy France: Ideas and Policies, 1930–1944*, Ashgate

Laing, N. 2005. 'Call-Out the Guards—Why Australia Should no Longer Fear the Deployment of Australian Troops on Home Soil', *University of NSW Law Journal* 28, 507

Lane, P. 1974. *An Introduction to the Australian Constitution*, Law Book Company

Lantier, A. 2019a. 'Macron Sends the French Army against Anti-Austerity Protests', World Socialist Web Site, 22 March 2019, https://www.wsws.org/en/articles/2019/03/22/pers-m22.html

Lantier, A. 2019b. 'French Army Receives Authorization To Shoot "Yellow Vest" Protesters', World Socialist Web Site, 23 March 2019, https://www.wsws.org/en/articles/2019/03/23/fren-m23.html

Lantier, A. and Ira, K. 2017. 'French State Of Emergency Expires in Name, But Police State Remains', World Socialist Web Site, 4 November 2017, https://www.wsws.org/en/articles/2017/11/04/fran-n04.html

Lasry L. and Eastman, K. 2005. 'Memorandum of Advice: Anti-Terrorism Bill 2005 (Cth) and the Human Rights Act 2004 (ACT)', *University of Western Sydney Law Review* 9, 111

Laybourn, K. 1993. *The General Strike of 1926*, Manchester University Press

Leahy, P. 2008. 'Bush Signs Bill Enacting Leahy's National Guard Empowerment Reforms, and Leahy's Repeal of the "Insurrection Act Rider"', Office of Senator Leahy, Press Release, 30 January 2008, http://leahy.senate.gov/press/200801/013008b.html

Lee, H. 1984. *Emergency Powers*, Law Book Company

Legras, F. 1998. 'Quebec's Winter Storm: The Social Issues', World Socialist Web Site, 24 February 1998,

Legras, F. 2001. 'Rubber Bullets, Tear Gas and Mass Arrests at the Summit of the Americas in Quebec City', World Socialist Web Site, 2 May 2001

Leicht, J. 2006. 'Germany: Politicians Urge Army's Deployment for World Cup', World Socialist Web Site, 11 January 2006, http://www.wsws.org/articles/2006/jan2006/wcup-j11.shtml

Leicht, J. 2012. 'German Constitutional Court Legalizes Use of Army Inside Germany', World Socialist Web Site, 22 August 2012, https://www.wsws.org/en/articles/2012/08/germ-a22.html

Lendrum, S. 1977. 'The "Corrong Massacre": Martial Law and the Aborigines at First Settlement', *Adelaide Law Review* 6, 26

Lerhe, E. 2004. 'Civil Military Relations and Aid to the Civil Power in Canada: Implications for the War on Terror', CDAI-CDFAI 7th Annual Graduate Students Symposium, RMC, 29–30 October 2004, http://www.cda-cdai.ca/symposia/2004/Lerhe,%20Eric-%20Paper.pdf

Liberty. 2004. 'Liberty's Second Reading Briefing on the Civil Contingencies Bill in the House of Lords', June 2004

Lissagaray, P. 2007. *History of the Paris Commune of 1871*, Red and Black Publishers

Longley, R. 2019. 'Posse Comitatus Act and the US Military on the Border', ThoughtCo., 25 January 2019, https://www.thoughtco.com/posse-comitatus-act-military-on-border-3321286

Louis, L. 1992. '"Operation Alien" and the Cold War in Australia, 1950–1953', *Labour History* 62, 1–18

Lynch, A., McGarrity, N. and Williams, G. (eds) 2015. *Inside Australia's Anti-Terrorism Laws and Trials*, NewSouth

McClusky, S. 2004. 'USNORTHCOM and Canadian Domestic Operations: An Opportunity for Positive Change', School of Advanced Military Studies, United States Army Command and General Staff College, Fort Leavenworth, Kansas

McCormack, G. 2007. *Client State: Japan in the American Embrace*, Verso

McCulloch, J. 2001. *Blue Army, Paramilitary Policing in Australia*, Melbourne University Press

McGrath, B. 2018a. 'Japan's Ruling Party Pushing to End Constraints on Military', World Socialist Web Site, 14 February 2018, https://www.wsws.org/en/articles/2018/02/14/japa-f14.html

McGrath, B. 2018b. 'Japan Plans for Massive Military Build-Up Aimed at China', World Socialist Web Site, 29 December 2018, https://www.wsws.org/en/articles/2018/12/29/japa-d29.html

McKenzie, N. and Masters, C. 2018. 'Police Investigate Ben Roberts-Smith over Alleged War Crimes', *The Sydney Morning Herald*, 29 November 2018, https://www.smh.com.au/national/policeinvestigate-ben-roberts-smith-over-alleged-war-crimes-20181126-p50ihb.html

McKinlay, B. 1979. *A Documentary History of the Australian Labor Movement, 1850–1975*, Drummond

MacAskill, E. 2015. 'British Army Reluctant to Post Troops on UK Streets after Terror Attacks', *The Guardian*, 26 July 2015, https://www.theguardian.com/uk-news/2015/jul/26/british-army-reluctant-post-troops-uk-terror-attack

Madsen, C. 2011. 'Military Responses and Capabilities in Canada's Domestic Context Post 9/11', *Journal of Military and Strategic Studies* 13, 3

Maeda, T. 1995. *The Hidden Army: The Untold Story of Japan's Military Forces*, Edition Q

Mallett, V. 2019. 'Macron's Plan to Use Troops in Paris Protests Sparks Anger', *Financial Times*, 22 March 2019, https://www.ft.com/content/fee7281c-4c9d-11e9-bbc9-6917dce3dc62

Maloney, S. 1997. 'Domestic Operations: The Canadian Approach', *Parameters* (US Army War College Quarterly), Autumn 1997, 135–152

Mark, R. 1978. 'Report to The Minister for Administrative Services on The Organisation of Police Resources in The Commonwealth Area and Other Related Matters', Australian Government Publishing Service

Marx, K. 1969a. *The 18th Brumaire of Louis Napoleon*, International Publishers

Marx, K. 1969b. Preface to *A Contribution to the Critique of Political Economy* in Marx K. and Engels F., *Selected Works, Vol 1*, Progress Publishers

Marx, K. and Engels, F. 1973. *The Communist Manifesto* in *Selected Works, Vol 1*, Progress Publishers

Mattarella, S. 2018. 'Speech by the President of the Republic, Sergio Mattarella, at the Ceremony Held to Commemorate The 100th Anniversary of The End of The Great War and to Celebrate Italy's National Unity and Armed Forces Day', https://ambsarajevo.esteri.it/ambasciata_sarajevo/bs/ambasciata/news/dall-ambasciata/2018/11/intervento-del-presidente-della.html

Mattis, J. 2018. *Summary of the 2018 National Defense Strategy of the United States of America*, US Department of Defense

Mazoue, A. 2019. 'Yellow Vest Protests: Macron's "Risky" Plan to Put Army on Streets', France 24, 23 March 2019, https://www.france24.com/en/20190322-france-macron-risky-plan-army-streets-yellow-vests-protests-sentinelle

Meier, H. 1988. *The Lesson of Carl Schmitt*, University of Chicago

Merrick, J. 2008. 'Security Bill for London's 2012 Olympics to Hit £1.5 bn—Triple the Original Estimate', *The Independent*, 28 September 2008, http://www.independent.co.uk/news/uk/politics/security-bill-for-2012-olympics-to-hit-16315bn–triple-the-original-estimate-944766.html

Mestrovic, S. 2006. *The Trials of Abu Ghraib: An Expert Witness Account of Shame and Honor*, Paradigm Publishers

Metcalf, T. and Kennedy, S. 2019. 'Davos Billionaires Keep Getting Richer: The World's Elite Have Prospered since the Financial Crash', Bloomberg, 20 January 2019, https://www.bloomberg.com/news/articles/2019-01-20/dimon-schwarzman-and-other-davos-a-listers-add-175-billion-in-10-years

Michaels, A. 2008. 'Silvio Berlusconi Calls in the Troops to Reassure his Countrymen', *Telegraph*, 6 August 2008, http://www.telegraph.co.uk/opinion/main.jhtml?xml=/opinion/2008/08/06/do0603.xml

Ministry of Defence. 2005. *Operations in the UK, The Defence Contribution to Resilience*, https://assets.publishing.service.gov.uk/government/uploads/system/uploads/attachment_data/file/61965/defenceconrtibution1.pdf

Ministry of Defence. 2018. *Mobilising, Modernising & Transforming Defence A report on the Modernising Defence Programme*, Ministry of Defence, https://assets.publishing.service.gov.uk/government/uploads/system/uploads/attachment_data/file/765879/ModernisingDefenceProgramme_report_2018_FINAL.pdf

Ministry of Defense. 2007. *The Ministry of Defense Reorganized: For the Support of Peace and Security*, Japan Ministry of Defense, http://www.mod.go.jp/e/about/organization/reorganized/p4-5.pdf

Ministry of Justice. 2007. *The Governance of Britain—Constitutional Renewal*, HMSO

Moore, C. 2005. '"To Execute and Maintain the Laws of the Commonwealth" the ADF and Internal Security—Some Old Issues with New Relevance', *UNSW Law Review* 28, 523

Moore, C. 2017. *Crown and Sword: Executive Power and the Use of Force by the Australian Defence Force*, ANU Press

Morgan, M. 2008. 'London Olympics Terror Threat Used to Vastly Increase Surveillance Powers', World Socialist Web Site, 3 May 2008,

Morris, E. and Gourevitch, P. 2008. *Standard Operating Procedure*, Penguin

Morrow, W. 2019. 'French Intelligence Strategy Document Warns of "Insurrectional Violence"', World Socialist Web Site, 19 July 2019, https://www.wsws.org/en/articles/2019/07/19/fran-j19.html

Muller, J. 2003. *A Dangerous Mind; Carl Schmitt in Post War European Thought*, Yale University Press

National Archives. 2009. 'The 1978 Cabinet Records', http://www.naa.gov.au/collection/explore/cabinet/by-year/cabinet-records-1978.aspx

National Counter-Terrorism Committee. 2003. 'National Counter-Terrorism Plan', National Security Australia

National Security Australia. 2005. National Security Australia web site, http://www.nationalsecurity.gov.au/agd/www/nationalsecurityHome.nsf/headingpagesdisplay/9F291545F46DC7B9CA256E43000565D4?OpenDocument

Neumann, F. 1942. *Behemoth, The Structure and Practice of National Socialism*, Victor Gollanz

Nicola, S. 2006. 'Germany Debates World Cup Security', United Press International, 5 January 2006, http://www.upi.com/InternationalIntelligence/view.php?StoryID=20060105-122459-5392r

NorthCom News. 2007. 'Exercise Vigilant Shield '08 slated for October', 30 August 2007, http://www.northcom.mil/News/2007/083007.html

NorthCom News. 2008a. 'U.S. Northern Command, Canada Command establish new bilateral Civil Assistance Plan', 14 February 2008, http://www.northcom.mil/News/2008/021408.html

NorthCom News. 2008b. 'Top Army Leader Visits Newly Assigned Consequence Management Force', 15 September 2008, http://www.northcom.mil/news/2008/091508.html

Osiel, M. 1999, *Obeying Orders: Atrocity, Military Discipline and the Laws of War*, Transaction Publishers

O'Sullivan, M. 2015. *The End of Globalization or a more Multipolar World?*, Credit Suisse, 17 October 2015, http://publications.credit-suisse.com/tasks/render/file/index.cfm?fileid=EE7A6A5D-D9D5-6204-E9E6BB426B47D054

Oxfam. 2019. *Public Good or Private Wealth?*, Oxfam Briefing Paper, January 2019, https://oxfamilibrary.openrepository.com/bitstream/handle/10546/620599/bp-public-good-or-private-wealth-210119-en.pdf

Paoletti, C. 2008. *A Military History of Italy*, Greenwood Publishing Group

Parliamentary Debates. 1978. Commonwealth, 'Parliamentary Debates', House of Representatives, 23 February 1978,

Parliamentary Debates. 2000. Commonwealth, 'Parliamentary Debates', House of Representatives, 7 September 2000,

Parliamentary Debates. 2018. Commonwealth, 'Parliamentary Debates', Senate, 26 November 2018,

Parliamentary Joint Committee on Human Rights. 2018. 'Human Rights Scrutiny Report Report 12', November 2018,

Pashukanis, E. 1978. *Law and Marxism, A General Theory*, Ink Links

Plesset, E. 2018. '5 Times U.S. Presidents Deployed the Military Domestically', PBS, 4 April 2018, https://www.pbs.org/weta/washingtonweek/blog-post/5-times-us-presidents-deployed-military-domestically

Povoledo, E. 2009. 'Italy Tones down Berlusconi's Vow to Increase Military Presence in Cities', *International Herald Tribune*, 26 January 2009

President's Commission. 1970. 'Report of the President's Commission on Campus Unrest', US Government Printing Office

Privacy Commissioner. 2002. 'News Release, Office of the Privacy Commissioner, Amendments to Bill C-55', June 18 2002

Pugliese, D. 2002. *Canada's Secret Commandos: The Unauthorized Story of Joint Task Force Two*, Esprit de Corps Books

Quick, J. and Garran, R. 1901. *The Annotated Constitution of the Australian Commonwealth*, Angus and Robertson

Rasmussen, M. 1999. 'The Military Role in Internal Defense and Security: Some Problems', Occasional Paper #6, The Centre for Civil-Military Relations Naval Postgraduate School, Monterey, California, http://www.ccmr.org/public/images/download/defense.pdf

Rayner, G. 2017. 'What is Operation Temperer: Theresa May Becomes First PM to Deploy up to 5,000 Soldiers on Streets', *The Telegraph*, 24 May 2017, https://www.telegraph.co.uk/news/2017/05/23/operation-temperer-theresa-may-becomes-first-pm-deploy-5000/

Reid, R. 1989. *The Peterloo Massacre*, William Heinemann

Reza, S. 2007. 'Endless Emergency: The Case of Egypt', *New Criminal Law Review* 10, 532–553

Robertson, G. 2005. *The Tyrannicide Brief: The Story of the Man who sent Charles I to the Scaffold*, Chatto & Windus

Robertson, G. 2008. *Crimes Against Humanity*, Penguin Books

Rogers, J. 2017. 'Italy Deploys 7,000 Soldiers Armed with MACHINE GUNS Along Coastline', *The Express*, 4 August 2017, https://www.express.co.uk/news/world/837172/Italy-armed-soldiers-troops-safe-streets-Rome-Serena-Natolini

Rowe, P. 1985. 'Keeping the Peace: Lethal Weapons, the Soldier and the Law' in Rowe, P. and Whelan, C. (eds), *Military Intervention in Democratic Societies*, Croom Helm

Rowe, P. 2006. *The Impact of Human Rights Law on Armed Forces*, Cambridge University Press

Rowe, P. and Whelan, C. (eds). 1985. *Military Intervention in Democratic Societies*, Croom Helm

Royal Commission into Aboriginal Deaths in Custody. 1991. 'Report of the Inquiry into the Death of David John Gundy'

Royal Commission Sheraton Hotel Report. 1984. 'Royal Commission on Australia's Security and Intelligence Agencies: Report on the Sheraton Hotel Incident', Mr Justice Hope, Royal Commissioner, Australian Government Publishing Service

Ruddock, P. 2004. 'A New Framework: Counter Terrorism and the Rule of Law', Address to the Sydney Institute, 20 April 2004, https://search.informit.com.au/documentSummary;dn=841376910101659;res=IELHSS;type=pdf

Rudé, G. 2005. *The Crowd in History*, Serif

Scripps, T. 2018. 'UK Military Step Up Marches and Parades On Streets of Britain', World Socialist Web Site, 26 September 2018, https://www.wsws.org/en/articles/2018/09/26/brit-s26.html

Séguin, P. 1990. *Louis Napoléon Le Grand*, Bernard Grasset

Seligman, L. 2019. 'Pentagon Eyes Windfall as Trump Seeks $750 Billion Defense Budget', Foreign Policy, 10 March 2019, https://foreignpolicy.com/2019/03/10/pentagon-eyes-windfall-as-trump-seeks-750-billion-defense-budget-military/

Senate Legal and Constitutional Affairs Legislation Committee. 2018. Parliament of Australia, 'Defence Amendment (Call Out of the Australian Defence Force) Bill 2018 [Provisions] Report', September 2018,

Senate Report. 2006. 'Senate Legal and Constitutional Affairs Committee, Defence Legislation Amendment (Aid to Civilian Authorities) Bill 2005 Department of the Senate', Parliament House

Shalom, S. 1993. *Imperial Alibis: Rationalizing US Intervention After the Cold War*, South End Press

Singer, P. 2003. *Corporate Warriors: The Rise of the Privatized Military Industry*, Cornell University Press

Slavin, E. 2015. 'Japan Enacts Changes to Its Self-defense Laws', Stars and Stripes, 18 September 2015, https://www.stripes.com/news/pacific/japan-enacts-major-changes-to-its-self-defense-laws-1.368783

Solomon, D. 2009. 'Some Secrets Too Sensitive to Release', *The Courier-Mail*, 1 January 2009, 26

Southern Highland News. 1978. *Southern Highland News*, 15 February 1978, 1

State Coroner. 2017. State Coroner of New South Wales, 'Inquest into the Deaths Arising from the Lindt Café Siege: Findings and Recommendations', (Report, May 2017)

Stephen, N. 1984. 'The Governor-General as Commander-in-Chief', *Melbourne University Law Review*, 14, 563

Stern, J. 2016. 'German Defence Minister Announces Domestic Use of Armed Forces', World Socialist Web Site, 6 August 2016, https://www.wsws.org/en/articles/2016/08/06/bund-a06.html

Stern, J. 2017. 'German Military Builds Training Ground for Civil War', World Socialist Web Site, 30 October 2017, https://www.wsws.org/en/articles/2017/10/30/bund-o30.html

Stevens, S. 2019. 'European Union leaders grant May extra time to pass Brexit deal in UK Parliament', World Socialist Web Site, 22 March 2019, https://www.wsws.org/en/articles/2019/03/22/brex-m22.html

Stretton, A. 1976. *The Furious Days: The Relief of Darwin*, Collins

Sullivan, B. 1984. 'A Thirst for Glory: Mussolini, the Italian Military and the Fascist Regime, 1922–1936', PhD thesis, Columbia University, New York

Superville, D. 2019. 'Trump May Get Parade After All, But Don't Call It a Parade', *Military Times*, 12 February 2019, https://www.militarytimes.com/news/pentagon-con

gress/2019/02/12/trump-says-planning-underway-for-july-4-parade-or-gathering-a fter-cost-scuttled-proposed-military-parade/

Sutton, M. 1994. *Bear in Mind these Dead. An Index of Deaths from the Conflict in Ireland 1969–1993*, Beyond the Pale Publications

Symonds, P. 2008. 'Japanese Government Pushes through Law to Allow Naval Support for Afghan Occupation', World Socialist Web Site, 18 January 2008, http://www.wsws.org/articles/2008/jan2008/japa-j18.shtml

Taylor, M. 2019. 'Pentagon Extends Troop Deployment at Mexican Border until September', World Socialist Web Site, 17 January 2019, https://www.wsws.org/en/articles/2019/01/17/bord-j17.html

Tharp, D. 2008. 'To Send Or Not To Send—Japanese Military Disaster Relief Assistance', The Nippon Foundation, 4 February 2008, http://www.nippon-foundation.or.jp/eng/current/20080204APIMilDisasterRelief.html

The Australian. 1978. *The Australian*, 14 February 1978

The Economist. 2008. 'The Thin Green Line', *The Economist*, 7 August 2008, http://www.economist.com/world/europe/displaystory.cfm?story_id=11893683

The Guardian. 2005. 'Pentagon prepares for homeland security role', *The Guardian*, 8 August 2005, http://www.guardian.co.uk/usa/story/0,12271,1545109,00.html

The Herald. 2008. 'RAF Drones to Be Used for 2012 Olympics Security', *The Herald*, 9 January 2008

The Strategic Review: A New Chapter. 2002. House of Commons Defence Committee Cm 5566

The Sydney Morning Herald. 1978. *Sydney Morning Herald*, 14 February 1978

The Times. 1974. Walker, C., June 1974

Thronson, P. 2013. 'Toward Comprehensive Reform of America's Emergency Law Regime', *University of Michigan Journal of Law Reform*, 46, 737–778

Toledo Blade. 2008. 'Mayor to Marines, Leave Downtown', 9 February 2008, https://www.toledoblade.com/local/2008/02/09/Mayor-to-Marines-Leave-downtown/stories/200802090034

Torres, A. 2018. 'France Sends Military against Protesters on Réunion Island', World Socialist Web Site, 23 November 2018, https://www.wsws.org/en/articles/2018/11/23/reun-n23.html

Torres, A. 2019. 'Macron to Deploy French Army against "Yellow Vest" Protests', World Socialist Web Site, 21 March 2019, https://www.wsws.org/en/articles/2019/03/21/macr-m21.html

Trebilcock, C. 2000. 'The Myth of Posse Comitatus', *Journal of Homeland Security*, October 2000, http://www.homelandsecurity.org/journal/articles/Trebilcock.htm

Tripathi, D. 2011. *Breeding Ground: Afghanistan and the Origins of Islamist Terrorism*, Potomac

Trotsky, L. 1933 'From the Archive, 22 March 1933: Trotsky on the New Germany, Originally Published in the Manchester Guardian on 22 March 1933', *The Guardian*, 23 March 2011, https://www.theguardian.com/theguardian/2011/mar/22/archive-trotsky-on-the-new-germany-1933

Trotsky, L. 1971. *The Lessons of October*, New Park

Trump, D. 2019. 'Presidential Proclamation on Declaring a National Emergency Concerning the Southern Border of the United States', 15 February 2019, https://www.whitehouse.gov/presidential-actions/presidential-proclamation-declaring-national-emergency-concerning-southern-border-united-states/

Tucker, R. 1975. *The Lenin Anthology*, Norton

UK government 2015. 'National Security Strategy and Strategic Defence and Security Review 2015', Cm 9161

United Nations. 2005. 'Report on the World Social Situation 2005: The Inequality Predicament', United Nations, http://www.un.org/esa/socdev/rwss/media%2005/cd-docs/media.htm

Van Auken, B. 2007. 'New York Times Public Editor Repudiates MoveOn.org Ad on General Petraeus', World Socialist Web Site, 25 September 2007

Van Auken, B. 2018a. 'Trump's Parade and the Threat of Military Dictatorship', World Socialist Web Site, 8 February 2018, https://www.wsws.org/en/articles/2018/02/08/pers-f08.html

Van Auken, B. 2018b. 'Central American Migrants Facing Horror on US Border', World Socialist Web Site, 1 December 2018, https://www.wsws.org/en/articles/2018/12/01/migr-d01.html

Vandreier, C. 2019. *Why Are They Back? Historical Falsification, Political Conspiracy, and the Return of Fascism in Germany*, Mehring Books

Vadarlis, E. 2001. Vadarlis v MIMA & Ors M93/2001 [2001] HCATrans 625

Vatikiotis, P. 1992. *The History of Modern Egypt* (4th ed), Johns Hopkins University Press

Victoria State Coroner n.d. 'Investigation into the Death of Jedd Malcolm Houghton'

Wade, E. and Phillips, G. 1970. *Constitutional Law* (8th ed), Longmans

Walker, C. and Broderick, J. 2006. *The Civil Contingencies Act 2004: Risk, Resilience and the Law in the United Kingdom*, Oxford University Press

Walton, M. 2005. 'The Anti-Terrorism Bill (No. 2) 2005: An Overview', *Human Rights Defender* 3

Ward, E. 1997. 'Call out the Troops: An Examination of the Legal Basis for Australian Defence Force Involvement in 'Non-Defence' Matters', *Australian Parliamentary Research Paper* 8, Parliament of Australia

Warfare.Today. 2017. 'First Troops Deployed in Operation Temperer', Warfare.Today, 24 May 2017, http://www.warfare.today/2017/05/24/first-troops-deployed-in-operation-temperer/

Washington Post. 2008. 'Pentagon to Detail Troops to Bolster Domestic Security', *Washington Post*, 1 December 2008, http://www.washingtonpost.com/wp-dyn/content/article/2008/11/30/AR2008113002217_pf.html at 5 December 2008

Watching Brief. 1986. 'Interview with Clyde Cameron, for "The CIA in Australia" Part 2', Public Radio News Service, October 1986

Watts, J. 2018. 'No-deal Brexit: Troops Put on Alert as Cabinet Splits Over "Car Crash" Departure from EU', *The Independent*, 18 December 2018, https://www.independent.co.uk/news/uk/politics/no-deal-brexit-army-troops-eu-uk-leave-remain-date-vote-tory-party-theresa-may-a8689771.html

Western Australia State Coroner. n.d. 'Investigation into the Death of Daniel Mark English'

Wheate, R. and Wheate, N. 2003. 'Lawful Dissent and the Modern Australian Defence Force', *Australian Defence Force Journal* 160, 20

Whelan, C. 1985. 'Military Intervention in Democratic Societies: The Role of Law' in Rowe, P. and Whelan, C. (eds), *Military Intervention in Democratic Societies*, Croom Helm

White, M. 2005. 'The Executive and the Military', *UNSW Law Journal* 28, 438

White Paper 2016. *White Paper 2016 on German Security Policy and the Future of the Bundeswehr*, German government, http://www.gmfus.org/publications/white-paper-german-security-policy-and-future-bundeswehr

Wikipedia. 2019. 'Japan's Self Defense Forces', https://en.wikipedia.org/wiki/Japan_Self-Defense_Forces

Willsher, K. 2019. 'France Drafts in Troops to Prevent Further Gilets Jaunes Violence', *The Guardian*, 22 March 2019, https://www.theguardian.com/world/2019/mar/22/france-drafts-in-troops-to-prevent-further-gilets-jaunes-violence

Windeyer, V. 1979. 'Certain Questions Concerning the Position of Members of the Defence Force When Called Out to Aid the Civil Power', in Hope, R. *Protective Security Review Report*, Australian Government Publishing Service, Appendix 9

Winterton, G. 1992. 'Dissolving the Communists: The Communist Party Case and its Significance', in *Seeing Red: The Communist Party Dissolution Act and Referendum 1951: Lessons for Constitutional Reform*, Evatt Foundation

Winterton, G. 2003. '1975: The Dismissal of the Whitlam Government', in Lee, H. P. and Winterton, G. (eds), *Australian Constitutional Landmarks*, Cambridge University Press

Wootten H. 1991. *Report of the Inquiry into the Death of David John Gundy*, Australian Government Publishing Service

Workers News. 1976. *The Canberra Coup*, Labour Publications

World Socialist Web Site. 2019. 'Trump's State of Emergency: A Step Towards Presidential Dictatorship', World Socialist Web Site, 16 February 2019, https://www.wsws.org/en/articles/2019/02/16/pers-f16.html

Zinn, H. 2002. *Terrorism and War*, Seven Stories Press

Index

Afghanistan, intervention in 7, 10, 39, 44, 59, 61–2, 86–7, 123–5, 134, 143–5
aid to the civil power see Military aid to civil power
aid to the civil community see Military aid to the civil community
aircraft, power to shoot down 2, 94, 97, 115–6, 155, 174
American Declaration of Independence 28, 42, 46
American Revolution 8, 27–8, 59
Amritsar massacre 21–2, 197
asylum seekers see refugees
Australia: anti-terrorism legislation 154–5; Communist Party case 154; Constitution 141–6, 176; constitutional crisis (1975) 36, 156–7; 'domestic violence' 2, 7, 33, 160, 165–6, 173, 183, 187; Eureka Stockade 32; executive powers 148; historical experiences 31–7; Melbourne 2006 Commonwealth Games 37, 141, 143, 147, 166; military callout legislation 2, 10, 144–7, 159–66, 194, 202; military callouts, requests for 33–5; paramilitary policing 157–9; Sydney Hilton Hotel bombing (1978) 36, 143, 153, 161–4; Sydney 2000 Olympic Games 37, 141, 143, 147, 166; 'war on terrorism' 143, 147–8, 180

Belgium 1, 102
Berlusconi, Silvio 123–4
'Bloody Sunday' 24, 88
Brexit crisis 5, 80–2
Britain: Brexit crisis 5, 80–2; Civil Contingencies Act 82–95; colonial massacres 20–2; common law powers 93–6; emergency powers 80–1, 84, 86–97; English Civil War 11, 13–14; General Strike (1926) 19–20, 25, 35, 87, 108; 'Glorious Revolution' (1688–9) 11, 14, 142; Heathrow airport, troops at 22, 26, 83–4, 87; historical experiences 13–27; London 2012 Olympic Games 97; Mansfield doctrine 14–16; military call-out laws 82–95; Northern Ireland operations 8, 22–5, 84, 87–8, 94–6, 168–70; Operation Temperer 82–3; Operation Yellowhammer 80–2; Peterloo Massacre 15, 167; secret preparations 96–7
Bush, George W: assertion of executive powers 9, 39, 41, 47, 51–2

Cambodia, invasion of 10, 160, 171
Canada: Bill of Rights 66–7, 71–2, 79; Canada Command 7, 60–5; Charter of Rights and Freedoms 66, 73, 79; Constitution 61, 65–7, 79; Emergencies Act 67–8, 70–2, 74, 76; G8/G7 summits 78; historical experiences 74–78; Joint Task Force Two 62; military call-out laws 67–73; Montreal Olympics 76; National Counter-Terrorism Plan 68, 72–3; National Defence Act 64, 67–8, 69–70; Oka Standoff 76–7; Quebec crisis (1963-70) 75–6; Red River Flood 77; Somalia Affair 77; Vancouver 2010 Winter Olympics 62, 64; Winnipeg general strike 74
Chartist movement 16–17
Chile, 1972–73 coup 6
Churchill, Winston 18–19
civil liberties 194–6
civilian supremacy, principle of 42–7, 52–5, 61, 65–6, 94, 196–8

deadly force see lethal force
democracy 11–12, 28, 72, 180, 186, 190–203
democratic rights 190–203
dictatorships 1, 6, 11, 26–7, 93, 108, 111, 120–22, 126–7, 129, 135–6, 198–9, 201–2
domestic security 2, 8–9, 63, 139, 190–4
'domestic violence' 2, 7, 28–30, 33, 46, 49–52, 56, 141–2, 145–54, 160, 165–6

economic instability 198–203
Engels, Frederick 200

fascism 3–4, 201–2
France: 1848 Revolution 8, 105–6, 118; history of military repression 104–8; Macron, Emmanuel 99–104; military call-out powers 108–9; Operation Sentinelle 99–104; Para-military forces 109; Paris Commune 8, 107, 156; Réunion, troops to 101; 'state of siege' 105–8; 'subversion' 101–2, 190–1; 'yellow vests' 1, 5, 99–102, 104, 191, 199

Germany: anti-terrorism powers 123; constitutional issues 115–7, 122–3; fascism 3–4, 201–2; increased military powers 115–17; post-WWI revolutions 118–19; Reichstag Fire (1933) 117, 122, 198–9; remilitarisation 110–14; Weimar Republic 118–20
global financial crisis 198–200
Great Depression (1930s) 3, 29, 61, 87, 120–1, 136
Guantanamo Bay 11, 42, 47, 184

Heathrow airport, troops at 22, 26, 83–4, 87
Hitler, Adolf 6, 114, 117, 119–22, 198, 201
human rights 194–6
human rights legislation 194–6

indemnities from legal liability 20–1, 25–6, 27, 188
Indonesia, 1965-66 coup 5
inequality See social inequality
International Covenant on Civil and Political Rights 9, 71, 173, 195
Iraq, intervention in 7, 10, 39, 44, 46, 54–5, 59, 62, 81, 85–7, 103, 113, 115, 125, 127, 134, 138, 142–3, 161, 189
Italy: armed forces 123–5; Carbinieri 125–6; domestic troop deployment 1, 5, 7, 123–5; fascism 126–7; Operation Safe Streets 123–5

Japan: military disaster relief 131–3; executive power over military 129–30; historical background 135–7; increased military powers in 128–30; internal security 139; National Police Agency 139; nationalism 138–9; 'pacifist clause' 128–9, 137–8; post-war occupation 136–7; pre-war military-backed regime 135–6; re-militarisation 128–9, 133–5; Self-Defence Forces 128–35, 137–8
Jefferson, Thomas 4

Kent State University shootings 10, 29, 161, 170–1

legal immunities 8, 155, 167, 179, 191, 203
Lenin, Vladimir 201
lethal force, against civilians 2, 5, 40–1, 56–7, 70, 84, 95–6, 144–5, 152–5, 167, 171–7, 181–3, 191, 203; see also reasonable and necessary force
liability: civil 187–9; criminal 174–89

Macron, Emmanuel 99–104
Magna Carta 8, 11–12, 13, 47, 80, 89
Mansfield doctrine 14–16
martial law 9, 13, 15, 18, 20–2, 26–7, 28, 31–2, 40, 51, 57, 68, 82, 120, 142, 156, 162, 193, 197, 201
Marxist theory 200–2
militarisation of society 2, 5, 7, 8–9, 80, 110, 111–12, 133–5, 143, 157–9, 192–4
'Military aid to civil power' 87, 98
'Military aid to the civil community' 84, 94
'military-industrial complex' 2, 44–6
Mussolini, Benito 6, 120, 123–4, 126–7

National Guard (US) 29, 41–3, 45, 50–2, 57, 58–9, 170–1
'national security' 38, 43, 45, 51, 56, 62, 67, 72, 81–7, 111–12, 148, 153, 160–1, 166, 173, 180, 184–7, 193, 195, 199, 200
Nixon, Richard 10, 29, 30, 42, 160–1, 171

Northern Command (US) 42–3, 51, 54–6, 62–3, 192
Northern Ireland, military operations in 8, 22–5, 84, 87–8, 94–6, 168–70

Obama Administration 41–2, 46, 192, 197

Papua New Guinea secessionist agitation 35–6
para-military forces 5, 8, 20, 23, 109, 125–6, 157–9
Pashukanis, Evgeny 201–2
Peterloo Massacre 15, 167
political instability 198–200
posse comitatus doctrine 14–16
Posse Comitatus Act (US) 28–31, 39–43, 48, 52–4
prerogative powers 66–7, 87, 93–5, 156–7, 165, 184, 203; see also reserve powers

reasonable and necessary force 167–70, 172–7; see also lethal force
refugees 1, 5, 38–41, 64, 123–5, 142, 147, 157, 191–2, 199
Reichstag Fire 97, 179–80
reserve powers 157, 198
Réunion, troops to 101
Riot Act 14–15, 19, 166
riots 14–18, 24, 29, 74–5, 82, 105, 135, 144, 154, 169, 181–3, 195; Bristol riots (1832) 16–17, 93–4, 96, 167–8; Featherstone riots (1893) 17, 94, 96, 168; Gordon riots (1781) 15; Los Angeles riots (1992) 30–31, 55, 57; Peterloo Massacre 15, 167
Royal prerogative powers see prerogative powers
Rules of Engagement 24, 41, 55–7, 63–5, 76–7, 95–6, 99–100, 164, 167, 178–9, 181–2
Russian Revolution 18, 19

security see national security and domestic security
September 11, 2001 attacks 9–10, 39, 45, 56, 59, 63–4, 93, 115, 123, 132, 138, 142–3, 159, 193, 195–6
social inequality 1, 3–4, 198–200
state of exception doctrine 198–9
superior orders defence 70, 155, 167, 174–83
Sydney Hilton Hotel bombing (1978) 36, 143, 153, 161–4

Trotsky, Leon 201–2
Trudeau, Justin 61, 78
Trudeau, Pierre 75–76
Trump, Donald 3, 5–6, 38–43, 46, 192, 197

United Kingdom see Britain
United States: American Revolution 27–8, 192; Bush, George W. 9, 39, 41, 46, 47–8, 51–2, 193; Constitution 28–9, 39–40, 42, 45, 46–52, 59; Declaration of Independence 4, 28; Guaranty Clause 28, 46–52; historical experiences 27–31; Kent State University shootings 10, 29, 161, 170–1; Mexican border, troop to 5, 31, 36–41, 192; National Guard 29, 41–3, 45, 50–2, 57, 58–9, 170–1; Northern Command 42–3, 51, 54–6, 62–3, 192; Obama Administration 41–2, 46, 192, 197; Posse Comitatus Act 28–31, 39–43, 48, 52–4; Presidential powers 49–54, 58–9; Trump administration 3, 5–6, 38–43, 46, 192, 197; Wounded Knee, 1973 confrontation 30, 53

Vietnam War 10, 29, 37, 59, 138, 160, 170

'war on drugs' 53
'war on terrorism' 2, 5, 7, 8–9, 11, 41, 48, 59, 61, 72, 86, 94, 100, 112, 115, 127, 142–3, 147, 153–4, 160–1, 180, 191–5
Wounded Knee, 1973 confrontation 30, 53

'yellow vests' 1, 5, 99–102, 104, 191, 199

For Product Safety Concerns and Information please contact our EU representative GPSR@taylorandfrancis.com
Taylor & Francis Verlag GmbH, Kaufingerstraße 24, 80331 München, Germany

www.ingramcontent.com/pod-product-compliance
Ingram Content Group UK Ltd.
Pitfield, Milton Keynes, MK11 3LW, UK
UKHW011006180926
475701UK00004B/592

* 9 7 8 1 0 3 2 0 8 3 2 1 6 *